Read Callivios 'Against Postmodernism' for
critiqu... ...tics.

Ideas to touch...
Jameson's di...
    " ... op

overly reductive analysis of development
of art forms coinciding with changes
of 'base' of capitalism?
eg. 'post-industrial'/'multi-national'
    capitalism = Postmodernism.

good = Jamesons approach to history &
    opposition to New Historcism from
        Marxist position.

# Jameson on Jameson

POST-CONTEMPORARY

INTERVENTIONS

*Series Editors:*

Stanley Fish and Fredric Jameson

# Jameson

# on Jameson

CONVERSATIONS ON CULTURAL MARXISM

*Edited by* IAN BUCHANAN

DUKE UNIVERSITY PRESS
*Durham & London*
2007

© 2007 DUKE UNIVERSITY PRESS
All rights reserved
Printed in the United States of America
on acid-free paper ∞
Designed by Amy Ruth Buchanan
Typeset in Minion by G&S Typesetters.
Library of Congress Cataloging-in-Publica-
tion Data appear on the last printed page of
this book.

*Every effort has been made to trace copyright
holders and to obtain their permission for the
use of copyright material. The editors would be
pleased to be notified of corrections that should
be incorporated in future editions of this book.
Finally, the editors would like to give thanks
to Tanya Buchanan who did an enormous
amount of behind-the-scenes work to help
realize this project.*

FOR MY STUDENTS

# CONTENTS

## FOREWORD

You have to take the work as a whole, to try and follow rather than judge it, see where it branches out in different directions, where it gets bogged down, moves forward, makes a breakthrough; you have to accept it, welcome it, as a whole. Otherwise you just won't understand it at all.

—GILLES DELEUZE, *Negotiations*

Terry Eagleton's quip that Fredric Jameson appears to have read every significant work of literature is only a partial acknowledgment of his accomplishments as a comparativist: one needs to add that he appears to have watched every significant movie, listened to every significant piece of music, visited all the major cities and viewed all the major buildings as well.[1] Probably the only adequate compliment is Colin MacCabe's admiring remark that nothing "cultural is alien to" Jameson.[2]

But to call Jameson a comparativist only makes sense to the extent that it is understood that he is foremost a historical materialist and that comparative studies in art, film, and literature are his means of mapping historical change. His means of tracking down change, though, is not, as it might sometimes appear, the relentless cataloguing of all the new things that are constantly being thrown up by this enormously productive global culture we know today. Yet having said that, there is no one more aware of or more sensitive to the breadth of cultural production operative in the world today. Piling example upon example of what has been said and done does not give rise to an understanding of history; it simply gives us an accumulatively produced description that has no way of discerning in any analytically useful way what should or should not be subsumed under its categories. If every new thing is postmodern or a sign of postmodernism, say, then that particular periodizing category is effectively voided. Its result is that "heap of fragments" Jameson warns us about that is no more legible to us than a pile of shoes. What Jameson tries to do instead is triangulate

*'always historicos' from Political Unconscious.*

what is missing, or, more specifically, that which could not be said, written, painted, sculpted, or filmed in our time because somehow and for reasons not disclosed it was out of step with history. He does not so much *read* texts as *diagnose* them.

I would claim that it is the development of (dialectical criticism) that stands as Jameson's supreme achievement.[3] The "dialectic is not a thing of the past," he insists, "but rather a speculative account of some thinking of the future which has not yet been realised: an unfinished project, as Habermas might put it; a way of grasping situations and events that does not yet exist as a collective habit because the concrete form of social life to which it corresponds has not yet come into being."[4] Dialectical criticism's twofold purpose, as Jameson defines it, is to uncover the ways in which a now more or less fully global culture disguises its strategic interests while simultaneously keeping alive thoughts of the future. This task can be specified, in practical terms, as the urgent need to track down and diagnose two different kinds of failure of the imagination: the first is the failure to develop a usable representation of the present, one that enables us to see its limitations as well as it strengths, but more importantly enables us to perceive its deep systemic nature; the second is a failure to imagine a form of the future that is neither a prolongation of the present nor its apocalyptic demise.

There is no one—or final—form of dialectical criticism. "Dialectical terminology is therefore never stable in some older analytical or Cartesian sense: it builds on its own uses in the process of development of the dialectical text, using its initial provisory formulations as a ladder that can either be kicked away or drawn up behind you in later 'moments' of the text."[5] Marxism "is a critical rather than a systematic philosophy," Jameson argues; its appearance always comes in the form of "a correction of other positions" or "a rectification in dialectical fashion of some pre-existing phenomenon," so that we should not expect it to (also) take the form of self-contained or scholastic doctrine. "This is to say that we cannot really understand Marx's materialism until we understand that which it is directed *against*, that which it is designed to *correct*; and it is worth pointing out that the materialist dialectic has not one basic philosophical enemy but two"—namely, idealism (history as prediction) and realism (common sense), understood in their classical or philosophical senses.[6] These two enemies are as adaptable to circumstances and as resilient to attack as viruses: "The question becomes one of deciding which of these two philosophical attitudes is to be understood as the principal ideological instrument of the middle classes, which of them is the source of the mystification which then becomes the object of the

Reach for Utopianism.

Does Jameson see culture as a monolith or a space of contested ideas?

Jameson: Postmodernism as all glittering surface.

☆ ??

specifically Marxist critique" (366). Jameson concludes that "the dominant ideology of the Western countries is clearly that Anglo-American empirical realism for which all dialectical thinking represents a threat, and whose mission is essentially to serve as a check on social consciousness: allowing legal and ethical answers to be given to economic questions, substituting the language of political equality for that of economic inequality and considerations about freedom for doubts about capitalism" (367). One does not even have to squint one's eyes to see that these remarks from thirty years ago describe with uncanny accuracy the political situation we are faced with today. In such a situation, Jameson's conviction, expressed in the same place, that it falls to literary and cultural criticism "to continue to compare the inside and the outside, existence and history, to continue to pass judgement on the abstract quality of life in the present, and to keep alive the idea of a concrete future" (416), has the same fresh urgency today as it did then. This is why Jameson's work proves so important. Ours still seems to be an age "when people no longer understand what dialectical thinking is or why the dialectic came into being in the first place, when they have abandoned the dialectic for less rewarding Nietzschean positions."[7]

In a late aperçu on the fate of the dialectic in contemporary theory, Jameson writes: "I have found it useful to characterise the dialectic in three different ways, which surely do not exhaust the possibilities, but may at least clarify the discussion and also alert us to possible confusions or category mistakes, to interferences between them."[8] The three ways of characterizing the dialectic are: (1) in terms of reflexivity, as a necessary second-guessing or reconsideration of the very terms and concepts of one's analytic apparatus; (2) in terms of a problematization of causality and historical narrative; and (3) in terms of the production of contradiction. The third form is the most developed in Jameson's work and finds its most refined expression in his account of what he calls "metacommentary," which is as near as he comes to offering a method (but it is a method that is adapted and altered according to the demands of the specific case at hand). Needless to say, these three ways of conceiving the dialectic should not be seen as in any way mutually exclusive of one another. It would be more accurate to see them as the three sides of a triangle.

The nearest Jameson comes to offering a template for dialectical criticism is his essay entitled "Metacommentary," first presented at the 1971 convention of the Modern Language Association, where, as it happens, it was awarded the association's William Riley Parker Prize. In typical fashion, he approaches the general theoretical problem that concerns him via a confrontation with a contemporary false problem, in this case the alleged end of interpretation, or more specifically the end of content, the former being conditional on the latter, which we associate with Susan Sontag's influential 1965 essay "Against Interpretation." As Jameson points out, Sontag's piece was only the latest permutation of this critical turn. All the great schools of thought that shaped twentieth-century literary and philosophical thinking, from logical positivism and pragmatism through existentialism, Russian formalism and structuralism "share a renunciation of *content*" and "find their fulfillment in formalism, in the refusal of all presuppositions about substance and human nature, and in the substitution of method for metaphysical system."[9]

Jameson's response to these debates was to stage a threefold reversal:

1. At the local level, that of the highly routinized practice of interpreting texts, Jameson argues that there is no need to interpret texts (not that it is impossible to do so) because they come to us as already interpreted.

2. At the wider level of how one should go about interpreting texts, and indeed concerning the question of whether it is even possible to do so, Jameson argues that this question is always decided in advance in the logic of the mode of criticism itself. The important question is therefore not how one should interpret a text but why one would want to do so in the first place.

3. At the level of discourse, or of the social itself, he argues that both these questions need to be reexamined from the perspective of their historical necessity—why is it, in other words, that one kind of critical practice is able to triumph at another's expense?

Taken together, these three propositions constitute the basic architecture of the method Jameson provisionally termed metacommentary.

The first proposition, that texts do not need to be interpreted because they are already interpreted, is argued for in the following way: the raw material of texts, what is usually called content, is "never initially formless, never, like the unshaped substances of the other arts, initially contingent, but rather is itself already meaningful from the outset, being nothing more nor less than the very components of our concrete social life: words, thoughts, objects, desires, people, places, activities."[10] The work of art does not make these things meaningful—they are already meaningful—but rather transforms their meaning, or else rearranges them in such a way as to heighten and intensify their meaningfulness. This process is not arbitrary, however, but follows an inner logic that can be abstracted, which is to say thought about and considered independently of the text itself. Jameson's hypothesis is that this logic takes the form of a censorship, the internally consistent and inwardly felt need to not say some things and to try to say other things in their place.

In this respect, as Jameson readily acknowledges, metacommentary "implies a model not unlike the Freudian hermeneutic (divested, to be sure, of its own specific content, of the topology of the unconscious, the nature of the libido, and so forth), one based on the distinction between symptom and repressed idea, between manifest and latent content, between the message and the message disguised."[11] This image can stand as shorthand for what it is the metacommentary does, provided it is understood that the object of the game is not to redeem or restore the suppressed content, but to uncover the logic of that suppression. As Slavoj Žižek helpfully reminds us, the structure of Freud's interpretative model is in fact triple, not double as is commonly assumed: its three operative elements are (1) the manifest content; (2) the latent content; and (3) unconscious desire:

> This desire attaches itself to the dream, it intercalates itself in the interspace between the latent thought and the manifest content; it is therefore not "more concealed, deeper" in relation to the latent thought, it is decidedly more "on the surface," consisting entirely of the signifier's mechanisms, of the treatment to which the latent thought is submitted. In other words, its only place is in the *form* of the "dream": the real subject matter of the dream (the unconscious desire) articulates itself in the dream-work, in the elaboration of its "latent content."[12]

Not only is the manifest content already meaningful but so is the latent content as well—indeed, if this were not the case, the entire Freudian hermeneutic would be disabled.

It follows, then, that the essential dialectical question is not what has been repressed in the course of the writing process, although that is important, nor why it is repressed, though that is important too, but rather how does that repression work. The cognate concepts of the "political unconscious," "*pensée sauvage*," as well as the later notion of "cultural logic," all refer essentially to this process and not, it must be added, to some secret reservoir of meanings buried deep in the text. In answer to the "why" question, Jameson finds a great deal to interest him in Freud's short paper of 1908, "Creative Writers and Day-Dreaming."[13] Freud's basic argument is that other people's fantasies—including fetishes and obsessions—when communicated in their raw form are actually kind of boring and even

*[handwritten margin note: explore this comparison between 'dialectical criticism' & Freudian dream analysis?]*

a little repellent (this is true even for the psychoanalyst whose job often consists in nothing more than listening to precisely such boring and repellent stories). If the writer does not want to put us off—if, in other words, he or she is to take proper notice of their audience—then he or she has to find a way of disguising their fetishes and giving them another form. This, Freud suggests, is the basic task of aesthetics, and our pleasure in reading derives from our appreciation of the skill the writer exercises in keeping their text free from embarrassingly personal elements, all the while giving us access to the full power of their imagination.

We cannot complete this task in any satisfactory way, however, without also determining the nature of the repressed message itself, which for Jameson is not a matter of private fantasies and fetishes, but rather the public—that is to say, collective—anxiety of the nature and quality of lived experience itself for which the shorthand *history* serves duty to refer to throughout Jameson's work. Private fantasies and fetishes are simply symptomal responses to the deeper realities of what has been described above as the mode of production and need to be interpreted in terms of the privations of history rather than the psychopathologies of sexual dysfunction. More pointedly, they express in their own perverse way a longing for an altered form of life, one in which certain satisfactions are readily supplied and do not suffer the proscriptions of our own moralizing universe, and can in this sense be seen as utopian:

> Yet the content of such experience can never be determined in advance, and varies from the most grandiose forms of action to the most minute and limited feelings and perceptions in which consciousness can be specialised. It is easier to express the properties of this phenomenon negatively, by saying that the idea of Experience always presupposes its opposite, that is, a kind of life that is mere vegetation, that is routine, emptiness, passage of time.[14]

The work of art juxtaposes the representation of a lived experience as its basic content with an implied question as to the very possibility of a meaningful "Experience" as its form:

> It thereby obeys a double impulse. On the one hand, it preserves the subject's fitful contact with genuine life and serves as the repository for that mutilated fragment of Experience which is her treasure, or his. Meanwhile, its mechanisms function as a censorship, which secures the subject against awareness of the resulting impoverishment, while pre-

venting him/her from identifying connections between that impoverishment and mutilation and the social system itself.[15]

The ultimate obscenity, and that which we must try to find the means of coming to terms with, is history itself, but not the dry and inert catalogue of "facts" and spurious narratives we encounter in textbooks. History, for Jameson, is a living thing, and it is the task of critics to show how its beating heart animates *all* forms of cultural production. Here we have to be careful not to lapse into the backward idea that history is simply the context against which cultural texts should be read.

Jameson's slogan "Always historicize," with which *The Political Unconscious* famously opens, means something rather more than simply reading texts in their historical context, yet this is very often how it is understood. His purpose is not, for instance, either comparable or compatible with the New Historicist project initiated by Stephen Greenblatt and Walter Benn Michaels, among others, even though at first glance there might appear to be some obvious affinities.[16] The difference, and it is a large one, is that their relative conceptions of history are utterly at odds. New Historicism is committed to a subject-centered view of history. It is concerned with the intriguing texture of specific lives. It exhumes the objects and documents, public records and private memoirs, of a distant past to fashion a "montage" (Jameson's word) of details creating the illusion of interiority, very much in the manner of cinema, thereby giving us a vivid sense of what it must have felt like to be that person. But it is a hallucination. By assembling the everyday items some historical figure or other, Shakespeare or Marlowe say, must have been surrounded by, must have routinely used, or thought about, the historian's eye begins to seem as though it is mimicking the subject's I, and the illusion is formed. We feel as though we are seeing "their" world in the same way they did, and as a consequence, they always seem more modern than we expected them to be.

By contrast, Jameson is committed to an object-centered view of history in which private lives are lived in confrontation with the deeper drama of what Marxism terms the mode of production, which refers to the manner and means of generating and distributing wealth on a social scale. He rejects those histories which continue to believe (as New Historicism plainly does) that social and cultural change can be grasped phenomenologically, from the perspective of a single individual, and argues in favor of a philosophy of history which can come to grips with what he calls the "scandal" of social and cultural change, which always comes from the outside and in a form that is beyond sense.[17] The only philosophy of history capable of satisfying that demand, Jameson argues, is Marxism.

> To imagine that, sheltered from the omnipresence of history and the implacable influence of the social, there already exists a realm of freedom—whether it be that of the microscopic experience of words in a text or the ecstasies and intensities of the various private religions—is only to strengthen the grip of Necessity over all such blind zones in which the individual seeks refuge, in pursuit of a purely individual, a merely psychological, project of salvation. The only effective liberation from such constraint begins with the recognition that there is nothing that is not social and historical—indeed, that everything is "in the last analysis" political. (20)

"Only Marxism," he writes, "can give us an adequate account of the essential *mystery* of the cultural past, which, like Tiresias drinking the blood, is momentarily returned to life and warmth and allowed once more to speak, and to deliver its long forgotten message in surroundings utterly alien to it" (19).[18] Only Marxism situates the individual life "within the unity of a single great collective story," namely, the "collective struggle to wrest a realm of Freedom from a realm of Necessity" (19). The principal polemical purpose of his work, then, is to "argue the priority of a Marxian interpretive framework" (10), but not as one might expect by arguing against other interpretative frameworks in a combative spirit and knocking them out of contention (which is not to say, however, that he does not do precisely that, namely, argue against other interpretative frameworks, only that this is not his principal aim, nor indeed his principal strategy). His strategy is rather bolder, and indeed rather more combative, than that. Jameson proposes to subsume all the other interpretative frameworks by subsuming them under one single, "untranscendable horizon," that of Marxism itself (10). His point, as *Marxism and Form* instructed, is that "Marxism is not just one more theory of history, but on the contrary the 'end' or abolition of theories of history as such."[19]

—Ian Buchanan

*how is this possible? An eg. of Jameson being unwilling to make value judgements?*

**NOTES**

1. Terry Eagleton, "Making a Break," *London Review of Books*, 9 March 2006, 25–26. Jameson's capacity to watch movies is indeed a kind of perceptual athleticism, as the editors of the "Sport" issue of the *South Atlantic Quarterly* 95:2 (1996)

comically imply in their picture gallery of the volume's authors doing something sporty, in which Jameson is depicted as a "movie marathoner."

2. Colin MacCabe, preface to *The Geopolitical Aesthetic: Cinema and Space in the World System*, by Fredric Jameson (London: British Film Institute, 1992), ix.

3. See my *Fredric Jameson: Live Theory* (New York: Continuum, 2006).

4. Fredric Jameson, "Persistencies of the Dialectic: Three Sites," *Science and Society* 62:3 (1998): 359.

5. Fredric Jameson, interview with Green, et al., this volume, 24.

6. Fredric Jameson, *Marxism and Form: Twentieth-Century Dialectical Theories of Literature* (Princeton: Princeton University Press, 1971), 366.

7. Fredric Jameson, "Interview with Fredric Jameson," in Eve Corredor, *Lukács After Communism: Interviews with Contemporary Intellectuals* (Durham, NC: Duke University Press, 1997), 93.

8. Jameson, "Persistencies of the Dialectic," 360.

9. Fredric Jameson, *The Ideologies of Theory: Essays, 1971–1986*, vol. 1, *Situations of Theory* (Minneapolis: University of Minnesota Press, 1988), 3.

10. Ibid., 14.

11. Ibid., 13.

12. Slavoj Žižek, *The Sublime Object of Ideology* (London: Verso, 1989), 13.

13. Fredric Jameson, *The Political Unconscious: Narrative as a Socially Symbolic Act* (London: Routledge, 1981), 175; Jameson, *Ideologies of Theory*, 76–77; Fredric Jameson, *Archaeologies of the Future: The Desire Called Utopia and Other Science Fictions* (London: Verso, 2005), 45–47.

14. *Ideologies of Theory*, 16.

15. Ibid.

16. Jameson gives a long account of his response to New Historicism in his *Postmodernism; or, The Cultural Logic of Late Capitalism* (Durham, NC: Duke University Press, 1991), 181–217.

17. Jameson, *Political Unconscious*, 26.

18. The same image is used in Jameson, *Ideologies of Theory*, 158.

19. Jameson, *Marxism and Form*, 321.

# INTRODUCTION: On Not Giving Interviews

The mixed feelings I have about these interviews has little enough to do with their quality. Sometimes, indeed, having not only forgotten what I said but even the occasion and the question that was asked in the first place, I am able to indulge myself in admiring my answers. Most often, however, it is the skill of the interviewer that is to be admired, in a subtle and demanding form that has its own strategy and tactics, so that its practitioners have a chance to shine as much as their subjects: a work in two voices, then, which at its best can offer a counterpoint of curiosity and avowal, the enthusiasm of occasional agreement, the peremptory taking of positions on both sides, along with tactful modulations, the reprise of second thoughts, the satisfaction of formulations, and in general a lively variation in the tempo of the exchange.

The gratification an interviewee can take from these situations is to find confirmation of the interrelationship of his work within itself, and of the connections of one kind of thought or interest with another, connections which are not often remembered or evident. To discover the kinship between earlier positions or interests and much later ones is, to be sure, not quite so satisfying: as though you never really moved from the spot after all, or kept returning to it. My initial formation in Jean-Paul Sartre's philosophy, for example, is often today more insistent in the return of its habits; and it ought perhaps to be an embarrassment in a historical period in which, for all kinds of reasons—humanism, feminism, Marxism, elitism, totalization—this figure is still under a massive cloud. I can, to be sure, tell myself—and demonstrate for others—the degree to which much remains productive in existential philosophy, not least in emphases which contemporary thought has neglected or forgotten.

But I feel it is best to come at such matters from a different way, and to grasp one's relationship to such a system as one of learning a code or a language. Influence, to be sure, is one of the stupider ways of talking about it, which should rather be turned inside out and described in terms of need, and indeed, the need for a new language. A philosophy grips us because it suddenly has answers for our questions and solutions to our problems: but that is the least of it, and the answers and solutions are what become most quickly dated. What electrifies us is not so much those, but rather the new language in which the need—the questions and problems— suddenly become visible in the first place. Now suddenly the syntax of this new language makes it possible to think new thoughts and to perceive the landscape of a whole new situation, as though the mist of older common-places had begun to burn away. My point is that the conceptual language we first learned with such a passion is not really to be replaced by the newer languages we add to it, any more than our exciting new German causes the primal French to disappear—at best, you end up speaking the former with a French accent, and even returning to English itself as though it were the idiom of an unfamiliar tribe.

It is a position which is probably not calculated to comfort the philos-ophers in their vocation: for it presupposes a situation in which some immense preverbal *In-der-Welt-sein* (being-in-the-world) exists, which can be modeled now this way, now that, by the philosophical terminology of what is essentially a representational rather than a conceptual system. Like those lenses the opticians alternate across the vision of the individual eye, these constellations of philosophical nomenclature bring into focus and then lose again whole zones of what lies out there to be seen, and which they can be said to construct; just as one language can say things which another cannot (however subtly it registers its own syntactical world).

Is this to say that all conceptuality is figurative, or that philosophy is just another form of literature? Only if you complete the seemingly trivializing and reductive thought by insisting on the conceptuality inherent in figura-tion itself, and on the way in which "literature" is itself an operation we perform on reality, which brings it into being just as surely as the terms and concepts of the philosophers, or as we might prefer to call them, the theore-ticians. Yes, in that case, literature is just as surely theory as the philosophi-cal text: but we have to work hard at each of these kinds of printed materials in order to grasp them as machines for constructing the world at the same time that they register it.

But this is a position of mine which leaves me fairly indifferent to the kinds of differences philosophers generally fight about. It is certainly al-ways helpful to have some really sharp and tough thinker and writer make an inventory—with the polemical passion of the disciple or the withering coolness of the expert—of the incompatibilities, say, between the idealism of the one and the materialism of the other. But for me this inventory is valuable above all in the way in which it allows us to measure the constructional and perceptual strengths and weaknesses of a given system. We're all idealists, all materialists; and the final judgment or label is simply a matter of ideology, or, if you prefer, of political commitment.

In my own case, the list of language conversions, after some initial Sartreanism (and no doubt Poundism), would be fairly long: structuralism, Greimassian semiotics, Frankfurt School dialectics and sentences (but also Proustian sentences), Heideggerianism, Deleuzianism, Lacanianism (cum Mallarmé). . . . It is clear that these are not all really styles as such: Algirdas Greimas's sentences did not form the mind (but perhaps you can say that he translated it into visual diagrams); Claude Lévi-Strauss is a fine writer, but of an old-fashioned belle-lettristic type which no one wants to imitate any more. Nor does the list really convey any unprincipled pluralism, despite the appearances: my tolerance for other conceptual languages is not inexhaustible, and it seems to be mainly Franco-German. I draw the line at most Anglo-American idioms, such as British empiricism or Wittgensteinianism: but an even more fundamental line has to do with Marxism and/or politics, and I would certainly be willing to subscribe to Alain Badiou's four truth conditions—four modes of access to the Absolute—politics, art, love (he means sexuality, gender, and psychoanalysis) and science (mathematics)—provided I was allowed to omit the science!

Still, the continuities between these things remain to be explored: why did so many Sartreans convert to Greimassian semiotics, for example? This mysterious affinity evidently has something to do with the way in which phenomenology offered some initial space for detecting the omnipresence of ideology, which Greimassian analysis (the semiotic square, for example) then offered to sort out into its component parts and its mechanisms. Alternately, it would be productive to follow the dialectic through these bewilderingly different languages and to see if their fascination and what is (for me) empowering, productive, and usable in them has anything to do with its secret workings.

The interviews, then, are mainly interesting for me to the degree to which they put me on the track of some inner unity between all these interests, whether they are intellectual or aesthetic flirtations or deeper passions and commitments. (Sometimes such relations are so deep you fail to notice them yourself: Doug Kellner once pointed out the omnipresence of Karl Korsch in my *Marxism and Form*. I must have thought it was so obvious I didn't have to mention it; and the same goes for Fernand Braudel in *The Political Unconscious*.)

But this can be a problem in itself: "perché vuol mettere I suoi idée in ordine?" (Why do you want to put your ideas in order?) as Mussolini once said to Pound. What does it mean to take this kind of satisfaction in the underlying unity of your interests if not as the sign and affirmation of precisely that personal identity and that unification of subjectivity that we are not supposed to harbor any longer in the age of Fourier's butterfly temperament. Multiple subject positions, parcellization, schizophrenic fragmentation (of the ideal type)—all seem to shift the emphasis from Identity to Difference, and to cast doubt on the kind of thematic or conceptual unification we used to pursue. I guess I prefer to think of the matter in aesthetic terms, in terms of stylistic variety: "There should be something to eat and drink on every page," Gustave Flaubert once said; it is an excellent rule for including as much dissonance and heterogeneity as you can take. Maybe Fourier was onto something when he said that people could not concentrate more than two hours on a single activity: something that explains the now canonical length of movies (since the sound era at least) and that has certainly been scaled back to fifty or sixty minutes when we come to lectures and maybe even interviews or conversations as such.

But now I had better come to what is for me the structural flaw (I'm not sure I want to call it a contradiction) in the interview as a form. It has to do with the transformation of concepts into opinions, the processing of episteme into doxa (to use Plato's language), the way in which intellectual commitments are transformed into so many optional thoughts or "ideas" that can be compared or contrasted with others of the same type, which one can swap like stamps or baseball cards, or ferociously defend like your favorite clothing style or haircut. Indeed, in the old days, the most important qualification for a teacher or a news commentator or a cultural interpreter was to have strong opinions that could be trotted out on all occasions and put forcefully enough to intimidate the student, consumer, or public. It's wrong to say that people like that knew everything or pretended to: no, but they had opinions on everything and were never at a loss. I think this fashion has passed in the academic world, and that that kind of journalism has also disappeared; but the mode is still alive on the talk shows, where opinions are still admired.

But what is the opposite of opinion? Plato thought it was the truth, but critics of sheer opinion today would probably not want to follow him in this in a postmodern age, in which "truth" so often seems to take the form of one more dogmatic opinion. I postponed the discussion by speaking of "intellectual commitments" a moment ago in order to avoid dealing with this question: now I must try to say what it is that has deeper roots than sheer opinion (and perhaps even a wholly different soil or source). The pragmatists called it belief, but that also seems to postpone the problem in a different way; while the equally facile alternative of "ideology" does so by leading us back to something more on the order of error, if not of opinion itself, albeit opinion with its substructure in the unconscious (images of embedding and depth seem inescapable in this particular context). But I have also previously called such convictions "interests," thinking of that key moment in *Dr. Faustus* when Zeitblom asks Adrian whether he knows anything stronger than love, and receives the answer, "Yes, interest." The connotations of interest in that sense of attention and curiosity and the investment of time and vital energies (rather than their dividends) then perhaps leads us on to the more satisfactory existential accounts of the "originary project": of my choice of being and of commitment which turn this matter of "truth" or Platonic "knowledge" in the direction of activity and the imagery of rootedness or the Unconscious into a relationship to Being itself. This may still be relativism, but it is a relativism of absolutes and of ontological commitments, and not of opinions or even of ideological symptoms.

At any rate, the interview as a form inevitably turns the former into the latter and flattens interests and commitments out into a stream of intermittently entertaining (or boring) thoughts. It is certainly a form in its own right, and when skillfully executed offers the pleasures peculiar to it (as the Aristotelians might put it), but they are pleasures more closely affiliated with curiosity and gossip than with practice and the project. I say this only to specify and differentiate, and not to moralize, as Martin Heidegger does about gossip, which I myself somewhere (talking about Marcel Proust) went so far as to characterize as Utopian. Well, it is certainly collective.

But these mild pleasures have to be paid for by a deterioration in the language itself, which is to my mind even more serious than anything that happens in the transubstantiation of episteme into doxa, although it can be said (by those in a hurry) to amount to the same thing. This is the immobilization of the very process of formulating into the final form of a slogan: the final crystallization of the opinion-commodity into a catchphrase that can be appealed to in any context, and reused over and over again without any tangible wear and tear. In the individual interview, this process is triumphant, a genuine discovery procedure from which something definitive emerges. Unfortunately, after several versions of this, the discovery is reduced to a tiresome repetition, which can at best send us back to the original moment of production and at worst stand as the symptom of some fatuous self-satisfaction.

For the interviewee, however, this formal requirement encourages bad habits indeed and turns the mind in the direction of concentrated formulations from which thinking only slowly recovers, if at all. The logic of the stylistic *trouvaille* is, to be sure, at one with commodification and fashion as such, whose relations with the modern and modernism have often been noted. Beyond that, however, it can be identified as a form of reification—or to use a more recent version, of thematization—in which a former idea has been turned into an idea-object, or indeed a word or theme: that final expression, as Ludwig Wittgenstein said of the truth, with which we agree to stop.

Unfortunately, the rhythms of intellectual reification are at one with the public sphere itself, which demands a constant traffic in such tokens, which it calls ideas. What would be the point, indeed, of holding an interview designed to avoid ideas? The named idea, like the various forms of money itself, is the indispensable unit of circulation of the public sphere, very much including the educational institutions, whose interminable debates about pedagogy turn over and over again on the problem of making students "think," which is to say, on avoiding just such thematized opinions and stereotypes, just such interiorized prejudices and commonplaces, in the first place. If this is understood as a tension that can never be resolved, however—as an interminable alternation between the wandering mind and the stylistic or linguistic freeze frame—then the customary search for a resolution might be converted into a method for perpetuating the alternation itself and keeping the whole process going, as something we have to use cleverly since we cannot do away with it, at least in this society.

For to nonthematized ideas would correspond anonymous subjects, one would think: an intellectual Utopia achieved as much as the abolition of intellectual private property as by the eclipse of the public sphere as a separate realm altogether, reabsorbed back into sheer immanence. Whether this is a prospect intellectuals can fantasize with relish and gusto, I leave decently unexplored in a collection destined for them, where the anti-intellectual or populist note would certainly be ungrateful.

The fluctuations in the content of these interviews also tells me something about the ambiguities of my own work, or at least of the more current readings of it, which seem to alternate between an interest in its Marxism and a curiosity about the phenomenon of postmodernity it only later on began to describe. The first interview, by Jonathan Culler and his colleagues at *Diacritics*, was largely concerned with Marxism as such, with its literary critical possibilities, its contribution to methodology, and also to the kind of politics my own version of Marxism seemed to imply. Later on, it is only in the non-Western interviews, by Paik Nak-chung and by Sabry Hafez and his colleagues Abbas Al-Tonsi and Mona Abousenna, that these preoccupations return with any direct force, as though possibilities were sensed in those situations that had become obsolete in the standard Western ones. As for China and Brazil, the two places in which my work has always aroused the greatest interest (something I have been very gratified by), I'm sorry to say that after the publication of *A Singular Modernity* (2002), in which the very concept of "alternate modernities" was dismissed, my Chinese and Brazilian readers seem to have parted company with me, accusing me of being yet another Western or first world theorist preaching to the rest of the world and seeking to impose Western theories on it. I must still feel, unfortunately, that the only possible "alternate modernity" open to us today is called socialism, and that merely cultural versions of these forms of difference are not very helpful. But perhaps what pained my critics more was less the attempt to impose my Western thinking on them than my expectation that they would develop alternatives that might reenergize us in the West or the first world: an expectation perhaps too hard to live up to.

As for the cultural alternatives, the basic positions on this seem to me wonderfully dramatized in the engagement with Stuart Hall, for whose intellectual generosity I am grateful, and whose insistence on resituating these issues within specific national situations I much appreciated. This fundamental engagement is then played out in a different way in the opposition between economics and politics I tried rather heavy-handedly to explain in the interview with Sabry Hafez: I hope to return to this "explanation" in another place and eventually to clarify it. The interview with Sara Danius and Stefan Jonsson also sets an agenda of unfinished business that is for me still, some ten years later, a work in progress: the ideas of cognitive mapping, of narrative, and of allegory.

As for postmodernism and postmodernity, unsurprisingly it is in the context of the arts that its questions are most extensively rehearsed: in the interview with Anders Stephanson (for an international journal of the visual arts, *Flash Art*) and in that with Michael Speaks (for the distinguished architectural journal *Assemblage*). Such questions, I believe, are very far from being exhausted, despite the rather facile consensus in some quarters that postmodernism is over (or ended with 9/11). But my theory always distinguished between the immediate stylistic features of postmodernism and the characteristics of the postmodern situation, in which a whole variety of social phenomena, such as the status of culture itself and the role of the aesthetic, were modified beyond recognition. It is very hard to see how the latter could have come to an end without a different form of capitalism (or indeed some wholly different reorganization of the economic infrastructure) taking its place. As for postmodernism as an artistic movement or moment of some kind, I cannot particularly see that the features I enumerated twenty years ago have been superseded. What I refuse to admit in any case is the return of anything like an old-fashioned modernism, save in the form of its simulacrum; but on that *A Singular Modernity*, published later than most of these interviews, stakes out a position I would still strongly endorse.

With the comprehensive interview with Xudong Zhang we return to the question of Marxism and postmodernism, now encapsulated in the conception of "cultural studies" as an acknowledgment of the postmodern conflation of high and mass culture, as well as the Marxian commitment to the context and to history. I would now only want to correct the impression that I see myself as an authorized spokesperson for that form of cultural studies that has since been institutionalized as a university discipline in the United States. Perhaps I have as many second thoughts about disciplinary institutionalizations as I do about interviews: both smack a little too much of reification for my taste. And yet we can scarcely function without such institutions as a source of power and legitimation. This is, no doubt, yet another version of the standard complaint about what the academy does to everything it assimilates; yet the question about cultural studies also includes the unresolved concern for the future of critical thinking generally, as well as an anxiety about the immediate future of literature as such and its effectivity.

In the final interview with Srinivas Aravamudan and Ranjana Khanna—the one most nearly contemporaneous with the publication of this book itself—I have welcomed the chance to reformulate the older themes of these exchanges in terms of the new situation of globalization, which I now understand to be the same as postmodernity, or if you prefer, to be the latter's other, infrastructural face. The fact of globalization—its release of explosive new forces, the appalling new clarity with which it reveals American power and American capitalism, its demand for a productive rethinking of all the old theories of "culture and society" and indeed of "Western civilization" itself—now inaugurates an exciting set of new intellectual tasks, and indeed for the reinvention of the vocation of the intellectual as such. It is good provisionally to end on such an exciting prospect.

I am deeply indebted to Ian Buchanan for all the work he has put into the collection of these ancient texts and their editing; this book would not exist without his enthusiasm and commitment. I must also thank Roland Boer, Peter Fitting, Koonyong Kim, Reynolds Smith, Ranjana Khanna, and Srinivas Aravamudan for their help and encouragement, as well as the original interviewers for their stimulation.

Durham, North Carolina

March 2006

# Interview with Leonard Green, Jonathan Culler, and Richard Klein

**GREEN:** *What do you take to be the political significance of books like* Fables of Aggression *or* The Political Unconscious? *As a Marxist, do you see the main function of such works as critical and interpretative? I am thinking of Marx's eleventh thesis on Feuerbach: "The philosophers have only interpreted the world, in various ways; the point is to* change it." *I am also thinking of a recent article by Terry Eagleton, in which he raises the following issue: "For the question irresistibly raised for the Marxist reader of Jameson is simply this: how is a Marxist-structuralist analysis of a minor novel of Balzac to help shake the foundations of capitalism?"*

**JAMESON:** Read carefully, Terry's question is not so much a critique addressed to my own work as such, as rather the expression of an anxiety which everyone working in the area of Marxist cultural studies must feel, particularly when it is a matter of studying the past. The anxiety is a significant one, which should be looked at in some detail.

It would be too facile (but not wrong) to return the compliment by replying that Balzac, of all writers, has a privileged and symbolic position in the traditional debates of Marxist aesthetics: so that to propose a new reading of Balzac is to modify *those* debates (symbolically much more central in Marxism than in other ones, and involving political and epistemological consequences which it might be best to spell out more substantively in my response to your second question). So one type of political consequence that emerges from work like this can be located within Marxism, as part of

This interview first appeared as Leonard Green, Jonathan Culler, and Richard Klein, "Interview: Fredric Jameson," *Diacritics* 12:3 (1982), 72–91. © The Johns Hopkins University Press. Reprinted with permission of The Johns Hopkins University Press.

its redefinition, its self-definition, and so forth, something which may not particularly interest your readers.

On another level, however, such studies of "classical" texts are to be taken—to use the fruitful Althusserian concept—as an *intervention* in the standard university teaching of what is called the "canon." So at this point the question opens up into the more general problem of a Marxist pedagogy. I'm tempted to sketch a position on this last in terms of something like a practical double standard, since I tend to make a rough distinction between the functions of graduate and undergraduate teaching in this respect. The former involves something like laboratory experiments in the study of cultural dynamics and, insofar as this is loosely analogous to "scientific research," needs no particular justification in terms of immediate "relevance" (but we can come back to this type of study later on). But such graduate research could be described (going fast) as a pedagogy of form, as opposed to some more properly undergraduate orientation towards content.

Let me explain this last briefly: the opposition is not really that of theory versus practical criticism, although that is the stereotype that comes to mind. Rather, in undergraduate work one does not really confront the "text" at all; one's primary object of work is the *interpretation* of the text, and it is about interpretations that the pedagogical struggle in undergraduate teaching must turn. The presupposition here is that undergraduates—as more naive or unreflexive readers (which the rest of us are *also* much of the time)—never confront a text in all its material freshness; rather, they bring to it a whole set of previously acquired and culturally sanctioned interpretive schemes, of which they are unaware, and through which they read the texts that are proposed to them. This is not a particularly individual matter, and it does not make much difference whether one locates such interpretive stereotypes in the mind of the student, in the general cultural atmosphere, or on the text itself, as a sedimentation of its previous readings and its accumulated institutional interpretations: the task is to make those interpretations visible, as an object, as an obstacle rather than a transparency, and thereby to encourage the student's self-consciousness as to the operative power of such unwitting schemes, which our tradition calls *ideologies*. The student's first confrontation with a classic, therefore—with *Heart of Darkness*, with Jane Austen, with Vonnegut or with Hemingway—will never really involve unmediated contact with the object itself, but only an illusion of contact, whose terminus turns out to be a whole range of interpretive options, from the existential one (the absurdity of the human condition), across myth criticism and its more psychological form (the integration of the Self), all the way to ethics (choices and values, the maturing of the protagonist, the apprenticeship of good and evil). These various liberal ideologies (and they obviously do not exhaust the field) all find their functional utility in the repression of the social and the historical, and in the perpetuation of some timeless and ahistorical view of human life and social relations. To challenge them is therefore a political act of some productiveness. The reading of novels is to be sure a specialized and even an elite activity; the point is, however, that the ideologies in which people are trained when they read and interpret novels are not specialized at all, but rather the working attitudes and forms of the conceptual legitimation of this society. One may of course come at these ideologies in other, more specifically political (or economic) situations; but they can just as effectively and sometimes even more strikingly be detected and confronted in that area seemingly so distant from and immune to politics which is the teaching of culture.

This would then be a more general description and defense of the political uses of an intervention in the realm of teaching and studying the literary and cultural classics of the past. To be sure, if that were what I myself was primarily engaged in, the choice of Balzac is a singularly ineffective one for an Anglo-American public, where different kinds of school classics or specimens of the canon would be obviously a far more important strategic terrain. But, to speak the language of reification and specialization, I'm in French, and the mission of intervening in English departments, while very important, interests me personally less than some others. This answer has already been too long, but let me briefly spell out what those might be.

I happen to think that no real systemic change in this country will be possible without the minimal first step of the achievement of a social democratic movement; and in my opinion even that first step will not be possible without two other preconditions (which are essentially the same thing): namely, the creation of a Marxist intelligentsia and that of a Marxist culture, a Marxist intellectual presence, which is to say, the legitimation of Marxist discourse as that of a "realistic" social and political alternative in a country which (unlike most of the other countries in the world) has never recognized it as such. This is the perspective in which I would want my own efforts to be understood, and I suppose my own particular contribution to such a development would mainly lie in showing the capacity of Marxism to engage the most advanced currents of "bourgeois" thinking and theory; but that is only one task among others.

A final remark on the problem of the "canon": European radicals, particularly in the mid-1960s, with the increasing emphasis on the university as an "ideological state apparatus," came to formulate a view of political intervention in which literature itself, as an institution, was an appropriate target for critique and occasion for consciousness raising. Something of this developed over here, but was absorbed into an old American tradition of anti-intellectualism or know-nothingism, which paradoxically was never really left-wing at all, but simply replicated the general attitude of a business society to culture generally. I think it may be worth pointing out that in the framework of the classical nation-state, culture and the national "canon" do play a centrally legitimizing role which surely cannot have an exact equivalent in the superstate, which is also essentially a postcolonial society. American literature has never been a national literature in that sense, since its most intense moments have always turned around the agonizing problem of what an American culture could possibly be in the first place and of what it might mean to "be" an American—questions which no European would ever have thought of raising in the context of the nation-state. Our critical relationship to "classics" and to cultural institutions generally cannot therefore be those of the various European lefts and demands fresh thinking, which will not simply reproduce the critical distance with which the European left deals with its own elite national cultures.

Still, all this is a part of a more general problem, which I evoked at the beginning of this discussion and which is to me the fundamental one, namely, the relationship to the past itself. I have already implied that our relationship to our own past as Americans must necessarily be very different and far more problematical than for Europeans whose national histories (the still vital myth of the Great Revolution or the Paris Commune in France, say, or the burning significance in the present of a historical moment such as "the making of the English working class") remain alive within contemporary political and ideological struggles. I think a case could be made for the peculiar disappearance of the American past in general, which comes before us in unreal costumes and by way of the spurious images of nostalgia art, and for which Franklin D. Roosevelt is as dead and unreal as George Washington or Cotton Mather. This has something to do with the triumphant and systematic way in which the American past, and most particularly its great radical traditions, have been stamped out in almost every generation: the 1930s was only the latest great period of militancy to have been obliterated from any living collective consciousness (with the result that the militants of the 1960s were effectively denied any sense of a still vital radical tradition). But there is another disturbing and significant factor which must now be introduced into the discussion: and it is the unique dynamics of this latest moment of capital—variously called consumer society, media society, multinational society, postindustrial society, the "society of the spectacle," and so forth—and which is characterized by a historical amnesia, a repression both of the past and of any imaginable *future*, far more intense than in any other social formation in human history. It may be possible, then, if the study radicals make of cultural artifacts from the past—such as Balzac, but also Hawthorne or Dickens—is ineffective, that this is less our personal fault or problem than it is a systemic one, and a pathological feature of contemporary society.

Here I would only observe, as far as I am personally targeted here, that *The Political Unconscious* gives a very incomplete picture of my own work, in which the archaeological analysis of dead classics plays a less significant role than the choice of examples in that book may suggest. The Lewis book (*Fables of Aggression*) is about "proto-fascism," a rather current topic, one would have thought; but it is true that Wynham Lewis is scarcely one of the livelier influences in contemporary culture (unlike a number of his contemporaries), and in any case I have never been able to transmit my enthusiasm for Lewis to *anyone*, I'm not quite sure why.

But the readers of those books may be unaware that my work, increasingly, turns around issues in contemporary cultural evaluation and turns on objects of study such as the media, film, mass culture, science fiction and utopian narrative, and postmodernism—all elements in the cultural and ideological foundations of contemporary capitalism, surely, whether or not one can shake them by way of their analysis.

GREEN: *Along these same lines, you have written: "If we want to go on believing in categories like social class, then we are going to have to dig for them in the insubstantial bottomless realm of cultural and collective fantasy. . . . After that, if one wants to stress the primacy of the political, so be it: until the omnipresence of culture in this society is even dimly sensed, realistic conceptions of the nature and function of political praxis today can scarcely be framed." Do you see any danger in such a formulation? Let me be more specific. Do you think that such a theoretical position opens the discussion of the "political" to the possibility of abysmal and endless deferment? In the academy, among professional intellectuals, where your work is most likely to be read, do you believe that the primary urgency is to make your audience aware of the "omnipresence of cultures"? I would have believed the contrary,*

*that the most resistance would be in the willingness to accept the omnipres-
ence of the "political," particularly in a Marxian sense of the political.*

**JAMESON:** My problem with this question and the preceding one turns on
the presuppositions which inform both and which seem to me misguided.
In both questions there is taken for granted a conception of the political
and of political action (let alone "the Marxian sense of the political") which
is not so evident to me; and in the present question, a certain notion of
culture is advanced which the very passage you quote is concerned to challenge. As far as "the political" is concerned, any single-shot, single-function
definition of it is worse than misleading; it is paralyzing. We are, after all,
fragmented beings, living in a host of separate reality compartments simultaneously; in *each one of those* a certain kind of politics is possible, and
if we have enough energy, it would be desirable to conduct all those forms
of political activity simultaneously. So the "metaphysical" question: what
is politics—the seizure of power? taking to the street? organizing? talking
socialism? resisting hierarchy and authority? demonstrating for disarmament or trying to save your neighborhood? fighting city hall?—this question is worthwhile only when it leads to the enumeration of all the possible
options, and not when it lures you into following the mirage of the single
great strategic idea. Still, we have to talk about each of these forms of political intervention separately, so that there is a supreme misunderstanding to
be avoided: namely, the misconception that when one modestly outlines a
certain form of political activity—such as that which intellectuals in the
university can engage in—this "program" is meant to suggest that that is
the *only* kind of politics one should do. I would not want anyone to suppose that when above I suggested a certain kind of political intervention in
the teaching of literature, I meant that this was all we should ever do. On
the other hand, it is worth asking ourselves what the mirage of the great
single-function political "line" or strategy draws its power from. And I
think, particularly for intellectuals, this mirage comes from impatience
with the mediated, with the long term; it gets its power from the desire
(quite proper to a business society, by the way) to show immediate results,
to feel some ego satisfaction, to make the tangible mark right now. That is a
pleasant luxury, a wonderful gratification, but it is not for us.

The tendency to think politics univocally (or monotheistically, as a more
theologically minded left might put it) then reproduces itself elsewhere, as
in the feeling that the word *culture* has a fixed meaning assigned in advance. But I would point out that the point of the text quoted was to suggest

that we needed a new conception of culture and of its space or function in this society. More modestly, my feeling was that for people in literary studies, the suggestion that we call our object of exploration "culture" rather than "literature" was already a subversive and a liberating displacement: not only the masterpieces of high culture but also mass culture; and not only printed or verbal texts but cultural production generally; and finally not only the formal characteristics of such cultural production but its relationship to social reproduction as a whole. Raymond Williams has systematically defended this particular move, this particular displacement, and I would think it might have even more resonance in the United States where "culture" does not yet even have that legitimacy as a concept which it has in Britain. On the other hand, if the term *culture* fails to convey such a shift, if I am wrong about the effects of this terminological substitution, if your reading is characteristic of most people's reactions to what I wrote, then one must perhaps conclude that the slogan has misfired, that all this is to be said in another way and that we should abandon the word *culture* altogether for some other, sharper formulation.

Yet, to dwell on the term a little longer, its effectiveness ought really to lie in its very ambiguity (or "polysemousness"). We can separate out three distinct meanings at once, although there are probably any number of other ones: (1) The anthropological concept, according to which a specific and systemic cultural organization (a "pattern," a "style," and/or a characterological configuration) has as its function the binding together and practical interrelation of the various elements of a particular social formation. The concept seems generally to have been reserved for simpler or precapitalist or organic and tribal societies, although we still find degraded remnants applied to "advanced" ones, as in notions of the German or the Russian national character, present-day America's "culture of narcissism," and the like. But since the problem of the economic determination of a society arises with particular force in connection with so-called primitive societies, and since "culture," where they are concerned, always very centrally includes religion, this conception of culture is a systemic one, in which the cultural instance is not only grasped in a far more all-pervasive way than in modern societies but also becomes the central mechanism of social reproduction itself.

(2) The specific use of the term *cultural* in a certain Marxist tradition, most notably the Soviet: here *culture* designates daily life and daily practices in general (or, if you like, the "superstructural" in general). This is of course an immediately central political area for any postrevolutionary

society, since what is now designated is a level of collective consciousness, issues of education and social reproduction, and most significantly what we might be tempted to call ideological attitudes: literacy, the relationship of the peasant to industrial and technological phenomena, the relationship of hitherto dominated classes to images of authority, sexual politics and gender attitudes including the place of the family, and so forth. This brief list is enough to suggest that when Lenin and others termed this or that problem a "cultural issue," they did not thereby intend to marginalize or trivialize such problems, but on the contrary to designate them as a crucial area for which some enlarged conception of political work and collective re-education had to be invented. Gramsci's notion of a struggle for *hegemony*, or more precisely, for the construction of a counter-hegemony, seems to me very obviously to designate this same area, whose problematic has now been widened to include "cultural" struggles that must precede and prepare a social revolution; while the Chinese conception of "cultural revolution" obviously also develops very squarely in this tradition, although to discuss it (and to show the originality of this conception, which can now be distinguished from its limited historical experience in revolutionary China) would take too much time here.

(3) The narrowest conception of *culture*, finally, in the spirit of the remark of [George Bernard] Shaw's character (as well, I'm afraid, as in the spirit of your question): "Life is not all plays and poems, Octavius." It is a historical fact that other Marxist traditions (Marx and Engels themselves, Lenin in his appreciation of Tolstoy, Lukács, Mao Zedong, and even, *a contrario*, by the lengths to which he went to control or repress it, Stalin himself) gave a value to culture, even in this narrowest of senses, which is far from being ours in a business society. But the point of the remarks you quoted had nothing to do with some nostalgic revival of this older Marxian "respect" for high or elite culture; rather, I meant there to suggest the possibility of a fundamental historical and systemic transformation of culture and its place in contemporary society. Although the scheme is a relatively abstract or dogmatic one, and although it certainly merits the characterization of "historicist" or "teleological" (see below), I have found it useful to insist on the conception of stages in modern capital, and most particularly on the notion that the very organization of first world society today must be thought of as a new and original moment of capitalism, if you like a third moment, beyond those conventionally designated as "classical" or market capitalism and the "age of imperialism" or the monopoly stage of capitalism. Without entering into this debate in detail, works like Ernest Mandel's

*Late Capitalism* suggest that it might be possible, in a specifically Marxist way, to reappropriate a periodizing concept which argued, against Marxism, that modern or postcontemporary society no longer obeyed the classical laws of capital, production, social classes, and their struggle and the like (concepts like the "affluent society," Daniel Bell's "postindustrial society," notions like media society, information society, even quasi-existential but Marxian concepts like Debord's society of the spectacle might be given as examples of this last move). What people like Mandel have shown is that very far from amounting to an untheorized deviation from the analyses in Marx's *Capital* itself, this new or third moment of capital can on the contrary be theorized as its purest realization, as a moment in which the Marxian dynamics are more global and operate in a far more classical fashion than in any of the earlier stages.

What follows, for the realm of culture, is something that can be described in two distinct formulations. We could say, following the initial Frankfurt School account of the "Culture Industry," that capital is in the process of colonizing that most remote part of the mind—the aesthetic—that traditionally seemed to resist its logic (being governed, as classical aesthetics taught us, by "purposefulness without a purpose"): on Mandel's account, then, consumer society would be a thoroughgoing push into this area of the mind—culture, the unconscious, whatever you want to call it—and a final rationalizing, modernizing, industrializing, commodifying, colonizing, of the non- or precapitalist enclave left surviving there.

But that does not mean the "end" of culture: on the contrary, it might just as plausibly be argued that the conquest of culture and its traditional spaces and instruments by capital now determines an enormous expansion in culture proper—its old semi-autonomy lost, its isolation a thing of the past (neither praxis nor knowledge, Kant told us), it now becomes coterminous with the social field as a whole, and everything becomes in that sense "cultural"—politics, economics, law, ideology, religion, daily life, sexuality, the body, space, et cetera, et cetera.

All I was suggesting in the remarks you found questionable was that it is hard to see how *any* politics could be projected or conceived which is unwilling to take into account the structure of this actual moment of capital; which is unwilling—at least provisionally, experimentally—to take into account the possibility that our older models of both politics and culture may no longer be completely relevant. I'm not pushing any particular model of a newer cultural politics; but it does seem to me that unless the question of the changing status and function of culture today is taken into account, an effective cultural politics can scarcely be devised. Taking the whole matter more narrowly, I was suggesting that it is rather premature to deplore the weakening of class consciousness in our society today. It is a class society, and thus "by definition," class struggle continues at every instant, as throughout the whole long "nightmare of history." The problem would then seem to be that we are looking for class consciousness in the wrong place (under barrels, as with Diogenes): surely it is to be found alive and well in collective fantasy, and in the ongoing stories and images people tell themselves about history, in their narrative anxieties about their future and their past. That is then the beating jugular of class society itself, the vein we keep looking for in the wrong place, a neglected yet central terrain of struggle.

GREEN: *Louis Althusser is one of the many acknowledged theoretical influences in your own writing. He plays a pivotal role in your widely read article "Imaginary and Symbolic in Lacan: Marxism, Psychoanalytic Criticism, and the Problem of the Subject." Indeed, Althusser's concepts of the "Real," "historical overdetermination, condensation, and displacement," and "ideology" seem already to contain the seeds of a theory of the "political unconscious." Do you think that Althusser receives the attention he deserves among American audiences, in relation to the rest of the contemporary French theoretical vanguard?*

*Perhaps I can make my question about Althusser more specific. Althusser's position, formulated in* Essays in Self Criticism *[1976], that history is a "process without subject or goal(s)," calls into question the anthropological and humanist categories of subjective presence and teleological dialectic. Early in his work, Althusser pointed the way to reading history as an articulated text by explicitly utilizing the psychoanalytic concepts of overdetermination, condensation, and displacement. The idea of "structural causality" emphasizes the articulation of differences which marks a society as a social structure. Given the decentering, stratifying play of Althusser's thinking, do you see your latest position in* The Political Unconscious *as a direct departure from Althusser's thinking? Does your emphasis on historical narrative as "a single great collective story" open itself to the criticism of being teleological in ways which Althusser's work helps to forestall?*

JAMESON: The question could also have been raised about other figures, most obviously Lukács, too. The preamble, however, would be the expression of a real sense of exasperation with the terms in which our relationship to such theorists (mostly continental) is generally staged. Leave aside the parochial American mesmerization with European theoretical products; it seems they themselves are now developing a similar mesmerization with things American, Californian, et cetera, so that we can now carry on our transatlantic discourse via the appropriate distorting mirrors (supplied, no doubt, directly from the lumber rooms of the Lacanian mirror stage). What bothers me, when we have to do with the Marxist tradition, is the transformation of these various thinkers—and not only Althusser or Lukács but also Gramsci, Benjamin, Brecht, Williams, Thompson, et cetera, et cetera—into brand names for autonomous philosophical systems. In this the Marxist tradition has itself been infected by the logic of commodity culture in general: where the organization of consumption around brand names determines a quasi-religious conversion, first to the great modern artists—you convert to Proust, or to D. H. Lawrence, or to Faulkner, or to Sartre, et cetera—all incompatible, but every so often one switches religions; and then in a later stage to the theorists, so that one now converts to Heidegger, or Ricoeur, or Derrida, or Wayne Booth, or Gadamer, or de Man. Now the social content of these "adherences" is perhaps a little more marked than in ordinary commodity consumption, and is a reality and not only an ideology: that is to say, your libidinal commitment to a certain make of automobile does not really determine a collective solidarity with the other consumers of that vehicle, but your cultural commitment to a "theorist" does really become a badge of small-group affiliation; and here we touch a social dynamic into which the political then begins again to rush and flow. In a privatized and atomized society of this type, small-group formation (with the attendant phenomena of belief, fanaticism, puritanism, theoretical asceticism, polemic self-definition against the various enemies, and so forth) is a very attractive way in which the pull of the collective is felt, and promises some salvation from the isolation of the monad. Nowhere is this kind of attraction clearer than in the Althusserian school itself, one of the most triumphalistic and aggressive small-group formations on the left in recent times (but let's not forget *Tel Quel*, *Screen*, and other successful theoretical small-group formations; in this country, those impulses seem to have been mainly absorbed into more traditional sectarian small groups, Trotskyist, Maoist, etc.).

Now, to begin an answer to your question, I was never very attracted to that feature of the Althusserian phenomenon, but it can be said to have ended for all practical purposes in 1968–1969 anyway. The Althusser who has meant something to me is not the rallying point of a small "fused group" or theoretical guerrilla band, nor the brand name for a whole new theory in its own right; but rather an interesting, fragmentary, sporadic commentator on Marx. None of his published works is really systematic; most are ad hoc interventions or summaries of ongoing work in seminars, the latter seeming to have been the principal form through which his thinking has been expressed. This is not therefore a rigorous philosophical "system" in any sense of the word; it must be approached through Marx, through the Marxist tradition, to which it represents an ensemble of contributions, some important and some more controversial. But to approach Althusser as a philosopher in his own right, that is, as the builder of yet one more new philosophical system, is a little bit like approaching Lacan without passing through Freud: grotesque and illusory pseudosystems are the result, and an unnecessary multiplication of intellectual entities. This said, it is certain that Althusser's work—which draws together in an explosive synthesis many of the great themes and preoccupations of "high structuralism"—has been neglected here precisely because of its sometimes strident foregrounding of the Marxist tradition. We have enough contact with Freudianism in the air to entertain a fitful practice of Lacan (although the problems in reading Lacan's own texts are even greater, owing to their similarly fragmentary or oral nature); but in the absence of any Marxist culture at all, Althusser's preoccupations seem remote. This is not the place to enter into details; but one would think that among the most interesting contributions of Althusser and his school are to be numbered an inquiry into the relationship between the "levels" of social life (sometimes called "structural causality" or "structure in dominance"), a whole new theory of ideology (drawing significantly on Lacan), a meditation on the relationship between social institutions and ideology (the so-called "ideological state apparatuses"), a new conceptuality, including notions like that of "intervention" and "problematic," and finally, for Marxology, a provocative conception of the relationship between early and late Marx, which is based on a complicated but significant distinction between ideology (what he calls "humanism," that is an anthropology which includes a presupposition about "human nature") and "science" (namely, a discourse so organized—it is a question here of *Capital* itself—as to exclude ideological propositions, even to exclude subject positions as such; and here, too, the conception of "science" has many resonances in common with Lacan's own rich meditations on that subject). We might also mention Althusser's rather striking use of the materials of the history of science (in particular the important modern French historians of science): this is, however, for me the most doubtful segment of the Althusserian legacy, and I myself tend to find the whole Althusserian epistemology ("theoretical practice," "the production of knowledge") problematical and unsatisfactory.

But I also happen to be Hegelian enough to think that one does not simply *refuse* a thought like this in toto (as E. P. Thompson does in *The Poverty of Theory*, thereby turning "Althusserianism" back into a system, and in the process endowing it with something of a demonic prestige), but that one goes all the way through it so as to emerge on the other side. If "Althusserianism" were a system, then my own procedure could readily be taxed with eclecticism. If it is a moment of Marxism (along with its "enemy brothers," the work of Lukács, say, or of existential Marxism), then a more selective approach is perhaps authorized.

The problem can perhaps be put in another way; namely, that for Marxism there is no purely autonomous "history of ideas" or "history of philosophy." Conceptual works are also, implicitly, responses to concrete situations and conjunctures, of which the national situation remains, even in our multinational age, a very significant framework. Understanding Althusser therefore means first and foremost understanding the sense and function of his conceptual moves in the France of the 1960s; but when one does that, then the transferability of those former thoughts, now situational responses, to other national situations such as our own, in the United States of the 1980s, becomes a problematical undertaking. Perhaps this is a good transition to your next question.

To be sure, I may have spoken about one "single great collective story"; but this will be a rather mythic notion unless the accompanying stress on the primacy of the conjuncture, the concrete uniqueness of the historical situation, is also maintained—the latter then seeming to break "History" into a series of discontinuous moments. In my opinion, the problem is better focused in terms of the nature of the dialectic itself than in those of this or that (representational or narrative) vision of history. Indeed, it might best be discussed in terms of dialectical language, which is an attempt to stretch terminology so that it registers difference as well as identity. The most banal example would be that of the terminology of social class: in a strict sense, for Marxism there is only one social formation in which social classes appear as such (capitalism), and in that exceedingly strict sense also, there are really only two social classes, namely, the bourgeoisie and the proletariat. What are often designated as social classes in other modes of production—as for example aristocracy and peasantry under feudalism—

are in reality something closer to *castes*. And yet the *Manifesto* affirms all history as *class* struggle: the point of this terminological slippage then is to affirm the analogous dynamic of other modes of production, while leaving room for a redefinition of the term on a different historical basis when we come to modern society. Dialectical terminology is therefore never stable in some older analytical or Cartesian sense: it builds on its own uses in the process of development of the dialectical text, using its initial provisory formulations as a ladder which can either be kicked away or drawn up behind you in later "moments" of the text. Taken this way, then, the dialectical "narrative" of history is a good deal more complicated and reflexive than my own slogan may have suggested.

**GREEN:** *But what about teleology?*

**JAMESON:** Oh, yes, I had forgotten that interesting feature of period Althusserianism—the "rigorous," quasi-religious *examen de conscience*, what may be called the ideological New Year's Resolution ("I promise to extirpate from myself all traces of teleology, historicism, humanism, representational thought, etcetera, etcetera, but especially to denounce them whenever they are observed in other people"). The issue of teleology is, I take it, intimately bound up with that of historicism; and much depends on how narrowly the target is construed. "Historicism" is on this view, if I understand it correctly, meant to designate any belief in a "stages" theory of history, generally itself grasped as having fatally Darwinian or evolutionist overtones or undertones. I've explained myself at some length on this and won't do so again right now, except to say that the qualitative and systemic differences between historical moments which a "stages" theory implies seem to me to be obvious (I *am* a historicist, in other words). I would go on to say that for purposes of action, one must probably try to forget that this is so, were it not for one signal political advantage to a stages theory (and in particular to the Marxian one, sometimes called the theory of "modes of production"), namely, that it incites us to imagine what a radically different social formation of the future might be like: an effort of the imagination I have tended to call, following Marcuse and Bloch, the Utopian impulse, without which political action seems to me impossible (and I might add that the failure of the Utopian imagination on the Left today, the nervousness with which people skirt the question of the nature of some possible and desirable "socialism" or "communism," seems to me a very great failure indeed).

But something else has to be said about the past in order to correct whatever facile assimilation may be made between a "Marxist historicism" and the older idealist and Germanic variety, for which the human past and the immense variety of human cultures was (within their libraries) an invigorating and exhilarating perspective. For Marxism, however, history is in Joyce's phrase a long "nightmare," and the past—in particular the textual and archival past, with its heaps of ideological potsherds—cannot be confronted without nausea. The "cultural" past (taking the term now in a narrow aesthetic sense) is most apt for a reception in which this affective component is reduced: one's strongest apprehension of it can be found, perhaps, in the contemplation of the remains of dead legal systems, with their ideological prolongation in the "visions" and "values" of archaic political systems. Yet this odor of death that "sears" us with a kind of "gray horror" when we reopen the coffins of these pasts does not spare the past of our own system either, and surely has something to do with the immense gap between the universalizing overtones of such political visions (including those of the bourgeois Enlightenment) and the masses of people for whom those slogans are not "ideas" at all but empty signs of exclusion and of authority, boundary lines, "no trespassing" warnings. For all those people—the vast majority of the human beings who have lived on the earth—such "ideas" are indeed ideology in the sense of false consciousness: and it might be well to stress the positive side even of this very narrow and negative conception of ideology, namely, in its very revulsion for such dead languages a certain vision of what living ideas and discourse might be, in some genuinely human society in which, as Gramsci put it, everyone would be an "intellectual" in that sense, and everyone would be at the center of the "production" of "ideas" because everyone would feel some control and productive power over the situations those ideas attempted to address or to analyze.

As for teleology, I imagine that it is generally understood to designate either a belief in historical predictability (Popper forbids it) or, what amounts to the same thing, a belief in historical inevitability. I must say that I think no one has ever believed such things and that they are an ideological straw- or bogeyman. (Hegelianism, it is true, includes the peculiar operation of considering the past to have been "inevitable" after the fact; but that is a way of framing historiography.) Marxists have been optimistic or pessimistic depending on the circumstances, but to attribute to them some peculiar "faith" of this kind is to project a thought of Otherness onto them in a peculiarly dishonest mirage. As a citation of authority, it might be well to ponder the concluding clause of the *Manifesto*'s description of history as class struggle: "an uninterrupted, now hidden, now open fight, a fight that each time ended, either in a revolutionary reconstitution of society at large, *or in the common ruin of the contending classes.*" What is "teleological" in Marxism might better be termed "antiteleological" in the following sense: inevitable is not the triumphant emergence from capitalism of "socialism" (about which we have just observed that nobody today seems to have any clear notion of what it might be), but rather simply the self-destruction of capitalism (as of preceding modes of production) under its own internal contradictions. A lot of people do "believe" this, and they are obviously not all Marxists (indeed, many of them are businessmen). But I will add a remark on the concept of contradiction itself, since that may allow us to pinpoint the weakest element in Althusserianism proper: the junking of the Hegelian dialectic had the ambiguous effect of seeming to discredit the materialist dialectic, so that many of the followers of Althusser graduated directly into post-Marxism. Althusser himself never went so far as to denounce the concept of "contradiction" as being fundamentally idealistic (after the fashion of, say, Lucio Colletti), but one understands from personal testimony that he was moving in this direction. I must therefore register my own feeling that no Marxism is possible without a conception of contradiction (that is, without a conception of the dialectic), just as no Marxism is possible without a vision of a radically different future.

But now I want to answer your question in yet a third way, at the risk of Ptolemaic or scholastic subtleties; and this will be a methodological answer, designed to mark the proper use of a "macronarrative" such as the Marxian "vision of history," and to demarcate that from the "archetypes" of a Jung or a Frye. I think a distinction must be made here between a diachronic framework (that is, a narrative of "universal history"), in which the essential categories of analyses—notably those of the modes of production—are laid out and articulated, and the moment of analysis of the text itself, which is *synchronic* and in which such "narrative" categories are called into play in the form of synchronic overlap, tension, contradiction, and the like. If these two moments in the operation are not separated, what results is a typologizing and classificatory affair, in which our principal business seems to be that of dropping a text into the appropriate box or historical "stage": this last seems to me of little interest at all, and if *that* is what people mean by "historicism," then historicism can cheerfully be abandoned.

**KLEIN:** *In the first chapter of* The Political Unconscious, *"On Interpretation," you write: "To imagine that, sheltered from the omnipresence of his-*

tory and the implacable influence of the social, there already exists a realm of freedom—whether it be that of the microscopic experience of words in a text or the ecstasies and intensities of the various private religions—is only to strengthen the grip of Necessity over all such blind zones in which the individual subject seeks refuge, in pursuit of a purely individual, a merely psychological, project of salvation." On the preceding page in a footnote, there is a lengthy quotation from Marx on Necessity, the realm of "the blind forces of Nature," that concludes: "Beyond it (the realm of necessity that includes both Nature and Man's social interchange with Nature) begins that development of human energy which is an end in itself, the true realm of freedom, which, however, can blossom forth only with this realm of necessity as its basis."

(1) How do you understand the possibility of Marx's imagining a "true realm of freedom," which "having an end in itself" entails the sort of autonomy and independence that is normally associated with the aesthetic doctrines you identify with bourgeois, individualist blindness?

(2) What do you mean by the "semi-autonomy" of structural levels, "which has to relate as much as it separates"?

(3) In order to argue against the organic continuity of expressive causality, you need to postulate, following Althusser, an interrelatedness between elements of all the elements in a social formation which is not that of identity or homology but one of difference. "Difference is then here understood as a relational concept, rather than as the mere inert inventory of unrelated diversity." How can difference be thought of as being relational without losing the force of separation, detachment, and independence, which is contained in the very notion?

JAMESON: I feel that it is misleading to frame this discussion in terms of the "individual subject." We have lately been caught in a double bind, in which two distinct conceptions of the individual subject have seemed to exhaust the possibilities: the one is the old Frankfurt School notion of the autonomous subject, the strong ego or personality (alienated and reified by late capitalism, but presumably alive and well in classical capitalism); and the poststructuralist ideal of the decentered subject, the "man without qualities" (Musil), the Reichian subject without "character armor," the Deleuzian schizophrenic subject. One can be attracted to either of these conceptions on the appropriate occasion and also be repelled by either; but everything changes, I would think, when a third term is introduced, namely, the reinvention of genuine collective life, in which, if one likes, the subject is therapeutically "decentered" by other people, but which amounts to a whole new mode of being in which people can live. The Marxian realm of freedom, designated by the quote at issue here, is a collective realm, in which a whole community is able to master "necessity" and to set its own collective priorities.

Let me go a little further than this and propose a philosophical (and therefore ideological) proposition which is nowhere in Marx, but which seems to me in the spirit of certain contemporary Marxist thinkers with whom I feel some kinship (most notably Raymond Williams and Ernst Bloch, in different ways, but also present in certain features of Sartre's work): this involves that currently very unfashionable and stigmatized thing called "ontology." I feel, in other words, that it may be productive to think in terms of a genuine transformation of *being* which takes place when the individual subject shifts from purely individual relations to that very different dynamic which is that of groups, collectives, and communities. Sartre was moving in this direction in his *Critique of Dialectical Reason*, without, however, ever proposing any definitive formulation of this specu- lative conclusion. The transformation of being, however, is something that can be empirically experienced (I hesitate to say "verified") by participation in any kind of group praxis—an experience no longer as rare as it was be- fore the 1960s, but still rare enough to convey a genuine ontological shock, and the momentary restructuration and placing in a whole new perspective of the kinds of private anxieties that dominate the monadized existence of the individual subject (still, essentially, our predominant experience in this society). Like Sartre (but for somewhat different reasons) I hesitate to as- similate this new form of group being to the category of social class (which remains an analytic category); but it seems at least minimally important to recapture the affirmation of the collective from its more notorious right- wing appropriations.

But unlike the previous question, this one (on difference) does very much concern aesthetics, or is at least best approached by way of the aes- thetic, and most notably the aesthetic of postmodernism, about which I would argue that relationship by way of difference is one of the constitu- tive features. To put it this way is to realize that the question asked in (3) is its own answer; the characteristics outlined thereby become an impera- tive: "think or perceive difference in such a way that it is relational with- out losing the force of separation," et cetera. This is obviously a difficult and unstable position to maintain: one has to avoid a kind of imperceptible high modernist assimilation of surface difference to underlying identity, at the same time that the relaxation of "relational difference" into simple inert differentiation and random heterogeneity is prevented. We forgot the words *totality* and *totalization* in the checklist of stigmatized concepts of an earlier question: it is arguable, I suppose, that earlier conceptions of totalization or totality (such as those of Lukács) aimed at some massive high modernist unification of a disparate field. I think that in Lukács's case that probably wasn't so, but in any case an equally strong argument might be made for a different conception of totality in our time (Althusser called it "structural totality," among other things) whose distinguishing mark is the overcoming of reification and fragmentation, not by way of the latter's stylistic obliteration, but by means of a conceptual or aesthetic tension able to hold fragments together, in their radical difference, in a single mental act. Three examples might be given, one being the current interest in the allegorical, which—an explicit repudiation of the aesthetic of the "symbol," with its organic unity—seeks a designation for a form able to hold radical discontinuities and incommensurabilities together without annulling precisely those "differences." A more graphic emblem of such a process can be found in the recent Nam June Paik retrospective at the Whitney Museum, in which hosts of closed frames (stacks of "discontinuous" TV sets with their "autonomous" images) are brought to life simultaneously. Such "texts" thus project an impossible new type of perception: you cannot simply follow one video image and ignore the others, nor can you watch them all at once (like David Bowie in *The Man Who Fell to Earth*)—something like the impossible synthesis of both those perspectives is what the text demands and withholds, and this can fittingly stand as an allegorical emblem for the motto, Difference relates. The third illustration that comes to mind is the practical political issue of micropolitics and alliance politics on the left, the problem of the relationship by difference between a host of groups organized around radically different concerns and slogans, which cannot be subsumed under any unified political "line" of the older type and yet which seek a conjunction of energies and which are palpably related in spirit to one another.

But as this may strike some readers as some rather modish endorsement of current forms of postmodernism, I would also like to say it in a very different language, that of a text which has always been very important to me, namely, Heidegger's essay the "Origins of the Work of Art." Heidegger there describes the effect and function of the "authentic" work of art as the inauguration of a "rift" between what he calls World and Earth—what we can rewrite in other language as the dimensions of History and the social project, on the one hand, and Nature or matter, on the other, ranging from geographical or ecological constraint all the way to the individual body. The force of Heidegger's description lies in the way in which the gap between these two dimensions is maintained: the implication is that we all live in both dimensions at once, in some irreconcilable simultaneity (and I would think that his distinction both includes and largely transcends more traditional categories like those of the "public" and the "private"). We are at all moments in history and in matter; we are at one and the same time historical beings and "natural" ones, living in the meaning endowment of the historical project and the meaninglessness of organic life, without any ultimate "synthesis" between these two dimensions ever being possible or conceivable. The Heideggerian formula thus first repudiates any such conception of a possible synthesis between History and Nature (such syntheses are called "metaphysics"), and at one and the same time repudiates a conception of the work of art which would aim at reuniting both symbolically, under some repression of History by Nature, or the reverse. The work of art can therefore never heal this fundamental "distance"; but it can do something else, and better—it can stage the very tension between the two dimensions in such a way that we are made to live *within* that tension and to affirm its reality. This has always seemed to me an extraordinarily suggestive conception of the inaugural "poetic" act, which Heidegger goes on to assimilate to the comparable philosophical act (the deconcealment of Being) and to the act of political revolution (the inauguration of a new society, the production or invention of radically new social relations). His examples are traditional ones (the Greek temple, the Mörike poem, the Van Gogh painting), but allow for very unexpected modern equivalents in a fallen society: our own great American poem, William Carlos Williams's *Paterson* enacts the Heideggerian project negatively, "producing the concept" of the inaugural American epic by a systematic demonstration of the latter's impossibility. Still, I think that this may be finally a more useful framework in which to grasp some of the more stimulating and *enabling* consequences of the notion that difference can relate.

GREEN: *Those who might have doubts about the unity and singleness you sense in the historical narrative might well harbor similar suspicions of another central category in your critical scheme—the "Real." Could you talk about the necessity and importance of this category to your thinking? Again, Lacan and Althusser seem to be centrally behind your insistence of thinking the "Real" as a materialist category.*

*(1) One clear criticism of the "Real" derives from a mistrust of transcen-*

*dental signifieds. Even if the "Real" is an "absent cause," that which "resists symbolisation absolutely" and must be apprehended through its textual effects, is it not open to the criticism of belonging to a nostalgia for things simply as they are, things in themselves, of history before the text, history as plenitude?*

*(2) From another perspective, your layering of the real and the textual, of history and its narratives, has met with criticism from another quarter. Is there something dangerously convenient about holding the "Real" in reserve as "absent cause"? In effect, does such a deferral of the historical "referent," the "Real," allow the intricacies of the latest rhetorical criticism while holding the materialist "Real" in perpetual reserve?*

**JAMESON:** The two questions cancel one another out, one would think. The first confronts me with the classic poststructuralist objection (the "referent" does not exist), while the second accuses me of dangerous complacency precisely with respect to that same poststructuralist position. In fact, the "model" here is that of the analytic situation, as the source of this terminology in Lacan might suggest. The "Real" is the moment of truth, the moment of anxiety, in which the analysand approaches the painful and unwanted truth of his or her situation—not because he or she suddenly glimpses or "discovers" the truth in some full representational way, but rather because of the gradual weakening of defenses, character armor, *mauvaise foi*, rationalization, and the like. This process has its equivalent in the political realm, in the realm of ideologies, where a conjuncture (and at the outer limit a polarizing, revolutionary situation) causes the (usually liberal) ideological system of defenses to crumble and confronts us with anxiety of choice and commitment. It is this process which is meant by the imperfect language of an "asymptotic approach to the 'Real'; and just as the analyst can describe it abstractly (or "scientifically"), so can the historian or political analyst, provided it is understood that there is a vast gap between that conceptual or abstract shorthand and the *experience* of the process itself (and also, of course, that the abstract analysis can be wrong or incomplete).

**GREEN:** *Let me raise a question about yet another of your central themes, the Utopian. How do you respond to those who question, as question they must, the apparent transcendentalism of what seems to be a recuperation of history as History, "transparence," "cure," and "plenitude"? Is the Utopian yet one more transcendental vision, the resting place of materialist heterogeneity, col-*

lective unity, and self-transparence? Given the reigning theoretical mistrust for the safety of origins or their mirrored fulfillments, why does the Utopian remain such a vital theme in your work? What urgency does it satisfy?

(1) I would like to get at this question from a slightly different angle. You seem to mistrust the Althusserian dichotomy of science and ideology. But is it possible that, while you question Althusser's notion of science, you introduce your own epistemological anchor, a sort of epistemological guarantee, in the form of the Utopian? "It is in detecting the traces of that uninterrupted narrative, in restoring to the surface of the text the repressed and buried reality of this fundamental history, that the doctrine of the political unconscious finds its function and its necessity."

(2) Perhaps more practically, what space does Utopian unity leave for cultural difference? What tolerance might there be in the totalized vision for racial, sexual, or ethnic diversity?

And after the history of our own devastating epoch, of all that we associate with names like Stalin or Pol Pot, one might strongly argue that if there is a Utopian aspect to revolution, it is powerfully sustained by its own negative, a death instinct and will to domination. What sustains your will to believe in the romance of Utopia? Some would argue, in this light, that Marxism is a relic of an impossible politics, that we can no longer believe in the unity of such categories as "mode of production" and "class conflict."

JAMESON: I've made a beginning with this question above, in a previous answer. Let me resume that more programmatically by saying that the fashionable current slogan of a "crisis in Marxism" is generally misdirected. I don't mind using the language of "science" and "ideology" in something like an Althusserian sense (although I don't always feel his account of "science" is as powerful or persuasive as his account of "ideology"): I bring this up in order to suggest that contrary to conventional wisdom (even the conventional wisdom of your question which raises some doubt as to the viability of categories like "mode of production" or "class struggle"), the "scientific" side of Marxism has never been richer or more creative. "Scientific" here designates the analysis, after the fact, of existing or past conjunctures; it involves the explanatory power of Marxism as an analytical instrument (very specifically including class analysis); and today, in the midst of a worldwide and national economic crisis, and with the almost complete collapse of "liberalism" as an ideology, it should not seem necessary laboriously to defend this proposition. I would guess that many more people today are willing to entertain specifically Marxian explanations for the current crisis than would have been the case ten years ago, say. To give you an example which draws on your own question, there exist properly *Marxist* analyses of Stalinism, as well as of premature or abortive revolutions such as those in Kampuchea or Afghanistan. (On the former, I would recommend you to the history of the Soviet revolution by Charles Bettelheim.) These analyses are more powerful than any liberal analyses since they do not rely on Lord Acton's dictum, on theological conceptions of the sinfulness of human nature, or on reifications of phenomena like "power" or "bureaucracy," but are rather *totalizing* models of the social formation as a whole, in which the objective *conditions of possibility* of the enormities of Stalinism are located in the economic base. The "crisis in Marxism" is thus not a matter of the loss or discrediting of its instruments of analysis and of its unique explanatory power; it is rather a matter of a crisis in Marxist *ideology*, a crisis in the properly Utopian conception of what a radically different society should be and of the nature of the new social relations that might be imagined in such a system.

This is the effort for which I have reserved the term *Utopian*, not in Marx and Engels's original debunking sense, but in the sense of a properly Marxian effort to debate alternate forms of social life—something being done far more vigorously among the feminists or in the environmental movement than among us, among other things because of excessive nervousness about "actually existing socialism" and excessive intimidation by the Gulag Industry and post-Marxism generally. On the other hand, if the term *Utopian* remains misleading, then let's replace it with something else. Yet some of the terms of your question imply that such "Utopian thinking" has already been done, and that we might consult a secret blueprint somewhere to show up its inadequacy in areas like "racial, sexual, or ethnic diversity," say. But no blueprint exists, and it is obvious that such issues come at the very top of the agenda. I have the feeling now that I should go on to say some very obvious things, namely, that revolutions in underdeveloped countries (whose results have been what Rudolph Bahro calls "actually existing socialism") are obviously bound to have very different contradictions than what might be imagined for advanced industrial countries (where such revolutions have never taken place); and also that the violence of revolutionary movements has always historically been a response to counterrevolutionary violence, either from within or from without, from the surrounding world system in which such revolutionary enclaves have developed (something as true for the great bourgeois revolutions as for modern socialist ones). But perhaps I don't need to go on in this vein.

What I would prefer to stress here in conclusion is something which does not seem to me to have attracted very much attention, namely, the existence of something like a fear or an anxiety of Utopia which is common enough (and even very understandable) within present-day society. I take the current attacks on Utopia (and "current" is a matter of politeness, since the conceptuality of all this goes back to the hoariest Cold War literature of the 1950s and even beyond) not so much as theoretical argument—in any case these positions have become doxa and received opinion rather than thinking—but rather as the expressions and the symptoms of some deeper terror which must confront everyone on the occasion of any fundamentally radical change or conversion. Just speaking now on the level of individual experience, it is clear that all of our habits and values have been developed within the constraints and the alienations of *this* society, even where the individual is concerned to resist those constraints—and perhaps especially in this last case. We are indeed far more vitally informed and defined by our anxieties than we like to think: they make up the very texture of our lives, including everything that is most precious about our individual or private existence (and this very specifically includes the very *category* of the "private" or the "personal" or of "experience" itself). To grasp this in its enormity means deepening analyses such as those Benjamin made of the relationship between urban sensory shock and Baudelaire's modernism; and coming to a more disturbing sense of the omnipresent symbiosis in late capitalism between the destructive or negative stimulus and that cultural transformation of it into "pleasure" or "thrill," which is increasingly the way in which the human organism has found it possible to survive in a forbiddingly inhuman environment and to make the latter livable. Getting rid of that environment therefore means getting rid also of a whole range of intensities and gratifications in terms of which we individual subjects of late capitalism have become accustomed to defining our own "identity."

To imagine losing all these anxieties therefore places the imagination before a frightening stillness—what William Morris meant, I think, when to *News from Nowhere* he gave the revealing subtitle, *An Epoch of Rest*. It is indeed hard to imagine how anything would survive of our current passions in such a situation—whose radical differences range all the way from the disappearance of material anxieties about money, unemployment, housing, and medical care to the sudden and unaccountable absence of the commodity form, the abolition of the split between "public" and "private" (and between "work" and "leisure"), and, no doubt, the libidinal transformation of the body itself.

"Utopia" must therefore necessarily be the occasion of great anxiety for the privatized individual subject: something that obviously needs to be taken into account, not merely in evaluating current anti-utopian ideologies but more practically in progressive political action as well.

GREEN: *The theme of "reification" is indispensable in your work. In your postface to* Aesthetics and Politics *you call reification "a disease of that mapping function whereby the individual subject projects and models his or her own insertion into the collectivity. . . . The reification of late capitalism—the transformation of human relations into an appearance of relationships between things—renders society opaque: it is the lived source of the mystifications on which ideology is based and by which domination and exploitation are legitimized." If reification is a disease, the disease which determines the opacities of ideology, what is the cure? Is it not the very inescapable representational nature of ideology which renders it infirm, incapable of transparent appropriation of the real, history, and truth?*

*The question I am asking leads to this: Can you clarify your intentions in the two following passages? "Totality is not available to representation, any more than it is accessible in the form of some ultimate truth (or moment of Absolute Spirit)." And, "If the diagnosis is correct, the intensification of class consciousness will be less a matter of populist or ouvrierist exaltation of a single class by itself, than of the forcible reopening of access to a sense of society as a totality, and the reinvention of possibilities of cognition and perception that allow social phenomena once again to become transparent, as moments of the struggle between classes."*

JAMESON: I use the word *reification* in a rather idiosyncratic way, which may not be clear. The term is generally associated with the Lukács of *History and Class Consciousness* and can, I think, be interpreted as a far vaster category than that designated by the same word in Marx himself (social relations coming to be felt as the relations between *things*); and in particular as the place of a kind of synthesis between Lukács's Weberian heritage and that of Marxism proper. This is at least how I use the word, so that it stands essentially for social and psychic fragmentation—that of specialization, of the division of labor, of the labor process itself (Taylorism, Fordism), but also for the gridwork of Cartesian extension, for the abstraction of Cartesian space, as well as the kinds of perceptual specializations that accompany this last, for a new parcellization of the psyche as well, and thereby of the body itself and its sensorium, and a whole new dimension of conceptual abstraction (to all of which might be added descriptions like that of Foucault of the infinitely divisible gridwork of power, which are also very consistent with this general process and enrich our understanding of it in this or that local direction). This process, which I have described in positive terms, is also a negative and violent one, being accompanied by the destruction of communal space and the emergence of private property, and the destruction of older forms of collective life (most notably the village) and the atomization of people thrown onto the market. Insofar as the description is a binary one, it corresponds to the old *Gemeinschaft/Gesellschaft* distinction (which had its own influence on Weber and Lukács) and may thus seem nostalgic or Utopian in the bad sense (so here I pick up, more concretely, an issue raised in the previous question as well). This would be the case only if it were a question of two modes of production—that of capitalism, and the totality of what preceded it (largely lumped together as precapitalist). But the usefulness of the concept of mode of production is that it designates a whole variety of precapitalist forms, all different from one another, and with no particular Utopian privileges. Something can be learned from all of those modes of production about our own specific alienation and reification, our own loss of the collective; on the other hand, in themselves, the various precapitalist modes of production were all far more immediately violent, involving sheerly physical kinds of exploitation and repression, than capitalism itself (which has its own specific list of horrors, from enclosure and imperialism to high-technology torture). So the more general category of "reification" does not necessarily, I think, trigger the nostalgic reflex.

I don't, if I follow the line of the question properly, feel that "representation" is the fundamental key to ideology in general and the cardinal ideological sin. (But to argue this out would involve introducing another issue, that of "narrative," which is, I think, generally what people have in mind when they rehearse the usual poststructuralist "critique of representation.") The question is not so much as to whether representation is noxious but rather as to whether and under what conditions it is *possible* at all: and it was this issue that I sought to address in the passages you quote. In a society colonized by reification—that is, by fragmentation, by an infinite divisibility of social relations, space, and consciousness (and the unconscious) itself—in a society whose mode of reification has become dialectically intensified and raised to a whole new level in the world of the media image and the simulacrum, the attempt either cognitively or imaginatively to *totalize* becomes one of the preconditions for *political* action, let alone aesthetic production or theoretical analysis. Such an attempt no doubt involves the reconquest of certain forms of representation; on the other hand, my remarks on "difference" above may suggest that I'm not exactly proposing a return to old-fashioned Lukácsean realism as this is stereotypically understood.

GREEN: *I don't think I am alone in this observation; one cannot read* Fables of Aggression *or* The Political Unconscious *without noting a certain stubborn density in your prose. As well, one feels at times to be pushing against an almost encyclopedic accumulation of knowledge in your work. The combination makes for rewarding but also difficult reading. What do you think the manner of your writing might reveal about your relationship to the institutions that materially sustain your work? What might it say about the nature of your audience? I imagine we are back to our first question on the politics of your work, having, however, opened the scope to include the political space of the institutions which make this work possible.*

JAMESON: I'm in a poor position to judge the difficulty of my own work or to defend its stylistic qualities, particularly since with more time and work no doubt even the most complicated thoughts might have been made more accessible. If one defends difficulty *a priori* (as I have allowed myself to do occasionally), this can be taken as an ominous pretext for all kinds of self-indulgence. But in a general way (and leaving myself out of it), it is always surprising how many people in other disciplines still take a relatively belle-lettristic view of the problems of culture and make the assumption—which they would never make in the area of nuclear physics, linguistics, symbolic logic, or urbanism—that such problems can still be laid out with all the leisurely elegance of a coffee-table magazine (which is not to be taken as a slur on good cultural journalism, of which we have little enough as it is). But the problems of cultural theory—which address the relationship between, let's say, consciousness and representation, the unconscious, narrative, the social matrix, symbolic syntax and symbolic capital—why should there be any reason to feel that these problems are less complex than those of bio-chemistry? As I've already suggested above, my thinking on this takes the form of a double standard, a distinction between graduate and undergraduate teaching; and maybe this is what you mean by the role of the institution (a nicer way of putting all this than the conventional reproach of being "academic"). I believe that there is room, alongside what I would call the teaching of "content," for something like formal "laboratory experiments" or theoretical research. The texts that incorporate this kind of research have their own specific public, and there is no reason to suppose they have to be of general interest.

Then there is the question of what has today come to be called "theory": an explosion of very different and specialized codes, which one cannot ignore and which have to be addressed in one way or another. If one is content to remain within a single one of these codes, one can minimally assume a certain familiarity with that specialized private language: if you have to address a whole range of them, the problems of reference increase to that degree, so that you find yourself, or better still, I find myself in the sometimes comical position of having to expound a theory and awaken a certain interest and enthusiasm for it, only in a later moment to take a polemic and critical distance from it. Add to this the fact that my own code—which we've loosely been calling the "dialectic" here—notoriously sees connections between everything, with the result that one develops the unfortunate mental habit of supposing you can't say anything without first having said everything in advance. But the dialectic *is* a different way of thinking about things; and its problems are not reduced, as in other specialized codes (semiotics, phenomenology, etcetera) to the learning of a specialized lexicon. We spoke about reification and fragmentation a moment ago: the intensity of *that* then becomes the measure of the difficulty of making connections again.

Coming back to myself, I will observe that I have written more popular pieces and lectures, whether successfully or not I cannot judge. But popular pedagogy and journalism is a matter of great skill, and I don't see why everyone should be supposed to have that particular talent. I would also like to observe that while I don't share the widely spread and self-serving attitude that today criticism and theory are as "creative" as creative writing used to be, still there is the private matter of my own pleasure in writing these texts; it is a pleasure tied up in the peculiarities of my "difficult" style (if that's what it is). I wouldn't write them unless there were some minimal gratification in it for myself, and I hope we are not yet too alienated or instrumentalized to reserve some small place for what used to be handicraft satisfaction, even in the composition of abstract theory. What is socially offensive about "theoretical" texts like my own is, of course, not their inherent difficulty, but rather the signals of higher education, that of class privilege, which they emit.

GREEN: *How does the "field" look for Marxists in American universities today? Are there jobs? Are younger Marxists getting tenure? Do you believe that anything like a "community" of Marxist academics exists in America?*

JAMESON: The current situation for Marxist or radical academics is I think defined by three parameters, exclusive of the financial and budget crisis itself, which is the obvious outer constraint of the situation. First, it does not (yet) seem to have been possible, after the failure of the Vietnam War, to restore a genuinely McCarthyist purge-type atmosphere (which is not to say that it will remain impossible to do this). Second, one has the feeling that university administrators generally are consciously or unconsciously conditioned by one overriding concern: that the 1960s (in the obvious senses of the reference) shall never return. The 1960s, however, evolved in such a way that the traditional ideological markers ("are you or have you ever been a member," etcetera) became disjoined from the "disruptive" activities of radical troublemakers on campus who had no affiliation with or interest in the older ideological institutions: and this makes for a certain ambiguity at the present time and perhaps indeed explains in part why a simple old-fashioned McCarthyist solution is unworkable. But undesirables can be fired for all kinds of administrative reasons whose political intent is hard to demonstrate (legally). The third parameter is, however, a great renewal of interest in Marxism in all fields, at least on the graduate level: this essentially reflects an impatience and a fatigue with a great many formalisms, and also the disintegration of the dominant liberal ideology which has been with us since the New Deal. So many academic departments feel the pressure of student demands in this area (the famous academic marketplace, after all!), and the working solution seems to be a pattern in which you hire junior professors to satisfy that student interest, but dismiss them at the moment of tenure; it is a solution which is also financially attractive, for obvious reasons.

I have mentioned the "legitimation crisis" of our hitherto hegemonic ideology, namely, liberalism (something that ranges from the exhaustion of Keynesianism to the political disarray of the New Deal coalition, and which drags all kinds of hitherto unexamined presuppositions and values down with it in its ruin). This situation has clearly opened a space for the vigorous development of all kinds of right-wing ideologies, from which some revitalized corporatism may be expected to emerge: what must not be forgotten is that it opens up a very significant new space for Marxism as well. But it is important not to confuse the critique of liberalism with attacks on liberal allies and what used to be called "progressive elements in the middle classes": there is a historical lag here, and people in this country—from government functionaries to voting Democrats of all kinds—have still largely been formed by the ideals of the New Deal tradition, as is still clear in the kinds of popular front alliances which continue to be vital in disarmament or antinuclear movements, in feminism, in the resistance to American military intervention abroad, and so forth. What one wants to show about the persistence of such ideals is not that they are "wrong" and ideological, petty bourgeois, and the like, but rather something very different, namely, that they are *unrealizable* within multinational capitalism.

This said, I think it would be a mistake to defend the place of Marxism in the American university system on the basis of (an otherwise admirable) liberal tolerance and pluralism. There is a far more powerful justification to be made for the intellectual role of Marxism than this, and it has to do with what has been termed reification in an earlier section of this interview, namely, with the increasing specialization and fragmentation of the disciplines. Many intellectuals deplore this irreversible development, by which increasingly small segments of reality become the provinces of specialized codes or private languages (whose jargon and lexicon are perhaps not even so forbidding as the sedimentation in each of them of voluminous disciplinary traditions—both key texts and a history of key *problems*—which no lay person has the time to master). The mainstream academic "solution" to this crisis has been, under whatever slogan, the notion of "interdisciplinary" programs, whose results have until now notoriously been disappointing indeed. Over against this, I think it is crucial to insist on the fact that Marxism is the *only* living philosophy today which has a conception of the unity of knowledge and the unification of the "disciplinary" fields in a way that cuts across the older departmental and institutional structures and restores the notion of a universal object of study underpinning the seemingly distinct inquiries into the economical, the political, the cultural, the psychoanalytic, and so forth. This is not a dogmatic opinion but simply an empirical fact: if middle-class thought can devise, I don't say a better, but simply *another*, vital ideal of the unity of knowledge, then fine, let it do so: but it has not done so, and its historic attempts in this direction—positivism was one, American pragmatism another, semiotics only the latest in this series—have not finally been very impressive. I remember an article by Stephen Toulmin a few years ago in the *New York Review of Books* in which he had occasion to deplore the cosmetic excision of "Marxist" passages from English translations of the work of Lev Vygotsky and other Soviet scientists: those passages, he said, were not simply ideological lip service to the regime; they formed an integral part of the scientific text. And then he observed this, which seems to me of the greatest relevance to the present discussion: whether we like it or not, he said, we need to take into account the possibility that Marxism is a better ideological and conceptual framework for scientists to work and do research in than those generally available in the West. At any rate, some such position would seem to me to be a stronger and less defensive framework in which to argue the importance of Marxism in the university than one which appeals to charity, tolerance or guilt.

Your question on the "community" of Marxist intellectuals has a national and also an international dimension; I suppose the answer is that such a community does not really exist here yet, for many reasons of which I will note two. First, the intellectuals who identify themselves as Marxist are only a small part of the more generally radical community as a whole, and there is no little tension between these two categories, not least because of the things associated with "Marxism" and "Marxism-Leninism" in the 1960s. Second, Marxist academics are as fragmented, as vulnerable to the departmental specializations, as anyone else, if not more so: the humanities versus the social scientists, not to speak of the linguistic contexts, Latin American versus North American, European versus postcolonial, et cetera, so that, above and beyond the increasing difficulties in getting a grasp of someone else's discipline, there is in operation a certain disciplinary rivalry or incomprehension, which, coming back to ourselves, always thumps down hardest on "culture," since in a business society that is universally agreed to be the most frivolous of the "disciplines," from a political or any other standpoint.

**CULLER:** *One might argue that the most politically effective movement in literary criticism has been that of feminist criticism, which has succeeded in opening up the literary canon, introducing new sorts of courses—on women writers—to educational institutions of the most diverse sorts, and thus affecting thinking beyond that of specialists in research universities. Three questions:*

*(1) What do you think about the actual and potential impact of feminist literary criticism?*

*(2) Is there a lesson here for other sorts of criticism that seek political impact? Feminist criticism has, in its theoretical discourses, been extremely heterogeneous. Is this related to its institutional success?*

*(3) If we take feminist criticism as the example of critical thought, with a Utopian dimension which has affected the institutions within which it is lodged, can you envision comparable effects that your own mode of criticism might achieve?*

**JAMESON:** Obviously we have learned many things from feminism, but people have also been changed by the very changes in social temperature from which the feminist movements themselves sprang, so all this is hard to sort out. I have to say that much of the political force of feminism comes from its collective dimension, its status as the culture and the ideology of a genuine social group; and this ties back also about the political problems raised today by the dynamics of microgroups or small-group politics. The weakness of a Marxist intelligentsia over against these collective realities is the classical weakness of the well-known "free-floating" intellectual, defined "by definition" as someone who has no group affiliation or who has lost some initial group connection. Perhaps I could put it more pro-grammatically by asking with what organic social group the straight white male intellectual has any particular affinities; modify any of the qualifiers and you get minimally the possibility of being an intellectual *and* having a group identity (qua gay or black or woman or ethnic)—although that does not really cure the ancient malaise of the "intellectual" either in the long run. At any rate, the question of the effectiveness or power of an ideology (or philosophy or method or whatever) can never be kept separate from the matter of its collective dynamics and underpinnings. (The other solution for such intellectuals is evidently to form small sectarian groups, organized around ideological "lines," which then *substitute* for the missing "knowable community.")

I have myself been particularly interested in some of the new paradigms of cultural history projected by various feminisms; and also concerned that the rather tense "dialogue" between Marxism and certain of those femi-nisms not degenerate into a sterile quarrel about what the "real" ultimately determining instance is (class or sex?). It seems to me very plausible, for example, that certain moments of cultural history are determined, at least in part, by a whole male backlash and instinctive defense of privilege, that is, by a fear of feminism and the production of various new kinds of ideo-logical defenses against that social threat (including, of course, new and more attractive images of what "women's place" should be and why they should be happy to stay put in it). Historical paradigms of this kind have al-ready shown us a great deal about the cultural past (and present) which we didn't see before (or didn't want to see before, to limit the pronoun to men). All I would want to add to this is the reminder (Althusserian overdeter-mination!) that these do not have to be single-shot or monocausal models. Just as it seems very possible that at a given moment, cultural production is dominated by an anxiety about the loss of gender privileges, so, too, it seems equally plausible to me that such an anxiety—with its own fantasies, representations, symbolic expressions or obsessions, and the like—can be grasped as a multipurpose "apparatus" through which many other anxieties equally find their own expression—and those would continue to include class anxieties, anxieties about the future, the unconscious "management" of class struggle, and so forth. At other historical moments, this hierarchy of the investments of anxiety might well be arranged differently, and class representations might well be called on to articulate, at the same time, in an overdetermined fashion, the at the moment weaker gender (or racial) anxieties which a dominant group also feels. What I have sometimes called the "political unconscious" demands the exploration of all these multiple determinations on the occasion of this or that unique historical conjuncture; it was never meant to exclude any of them (such as gender or race) or to limit its explorations to the thematics of social class (do I really have to say this?). So the thematics of feminism do not have to be taken as an alternative interpretive code, provided we are united, if not by some achieved vision of a future utopian community, then at least by the necessity of developing one.

# Interview with Anders Stephanson

**STEPHANSON:** *Your argument about postmodernism has two levels: on the one hand, an inventory of constitutive features, and on the other, an account of a vaster reality which these features are said to express.*[1]

**JAMESON:** The idea is to create a mediatory concept, to construct a model that can be articulated in, and descriptive of, a whole series of different cultural phenomena. This unity, or system, is then placed in a relation to the infrastructural reality of late capitalism. The aim, in other words, is to provide something that can face in two directions: a principle for the analysis of cultural texts, which is at the same time a working system that can show the general ideological function of all these features taken together. I'm not sure that my analysis has covered all the essentials, but I tried to range across a set of qualitatively different things, starting with the visual, passing through the temporal, and then returning to a new conception of space itself.

Since our first concepts of postmodernism have tended to be negative (i.e., it isn't this, it isn't that, it isn't a whole series of things that modernism was), I begin by comparing modernism and postmodernism. However, the object is ultimately a positive description, not in any sense of value (so that postmodernism would then be "better" than modernism) but to grasp postmodernism as a new cultural logic in its own right, as something more than a mere reaction. Historically, of course, it *did* begin as a reaction against the institutionalization of modernism in universities, museums, and concert halls, and against the canonization of a certain kind of architecture. This entrenchment is felt to be oppressive by the generation that comes of age,

---

This version of the interview first appeared as Anders Stephanson, "Regarding Postmodernism: An Interview with Fredric Jameson," *Social Text* 17 (1987): 29–54. An earlier and shorter version appeared as "An Interview with Fredric Jameson by A. Stephanson on Postmodernism," *Flash Art* 131 (1986): 69–73.

roughly speaking, in the 1960s; and, not surprisingly, it then systematically tries to make a breathing space for itself by repudiating modernist values. In the literary context, values thus repudiated include complexity and ambiguity of language, irony, the concrete universal, and the construction of elaborate symbolic systems. The specific features would of course have been somewhat different in other arts.

**STEPHANSON:** *You begin the exploration with an analysis of depth and surface in painting.*

**JAMESON:** I wanted to focus on a certain flatness, not to be confused with the way in which modernist painting famously reconquered the surface of the painting. I describe this in terms of the disappearance of a certain depth, a word I wanted to function in a deliberately ambiguous way. I meant not only visual depth—which was already happening in modern painting—but also interpretative depth, the idea that the object is fascinating because of the density of its secrets, which are then to be uncovered by interpretation. All this vanishes. Similarly, because the idea of interpretive depth is a subtheme of the relation between postmodernism in the arts and contemporary theory, I tried to show how this goes along with a new kind of conceptualization which no longer involves *philosophical* notions of depth, that is, various hermeneutics in which one interprets an appearance in terms of some underlying reality, which these philosophies then uncode. Finally, historicity and historical depth, which used to be called historical consciousness or the sense of the past, are abolished. In short, objects fall into the world and become decoration again; visual depth and systems of interpretation fade away, and something peculiar happens to historical time.

This is then accompanied by a transformation of the depth of psychological *affect* in that a particular kind of phenomenological or emotional reaction to the world disappears. Symptomatic here is the changeover from anxiety—the dominant feeling or affect in modernism—to a different system to which schizophrenic or drug language gives the key notion. I am referring to what the French have started to call *intensities* of highs and lows. These have nothing to do with "feelings" that offer clues to meaning in the way anxiety did. Anxiety is a hermeneutic emotion, expressing an underlying nightmare state of the world; whereas highs and lows really don't imply anything about the world because you can feel them on whatever occasion. They are no longer cognitive.

**STEPHANSON:** *You speak here of "the hysterical sublime" and "the exhilaration of the gleaming surface." In the "dialectical intensification of the autoreferentiality of all modern culture," we face a complete lack of affect punctured by moments of extreme intensity.*

**JAMESON:** Dialectically, in the conscious sublime, it is the self that touches the limit; here it is the body that is touching its limits, "volatilized," in this experience of images, to the point of being outside itself, or losing itself. What you get is a reduction of time to an instant in a most intense final punctual experience of all these things, but it is no longer subjective in the older sense in which a personality is standing in front of the Alps, knowing the limits of the individual subject and the human ego. On the contrary, it is a kind of nonhumanist experience of limits beyond which you get dissolved.

**STEPHANSON:** *Whereupon we reach the temporal aspect.*

**JAMESON:** Yes. The visual metaphoric depth gives way to a description of temporal disconnection and fragmentation, the kind of thing embodied, for example, in John Cage's music. Discontinuity in sound and time is then seen as emblematic of the disappearance of certain relationships to history and the past. Analogously, it is related to the way we describe a text today as the production of discontinuous sentences without any larger unifying forms. A rhetoric of texts replaces older notions of a work organized according to this or that form. Indeed, the very language of form disappears.

**STEPHANSON:** *During the 1960s, I was once told that the average camera movement—a change of view, a zoom, a pan—did not go below something like one per 7.5 seconds in an ordinary thirty-second commercial, the reason being that this was considered the optimum of what human perception could handle. Now, it is down to something like 3.5 or less. I have actually timed commercials in which there is about one change every two seconds, fifteen changes in a matter of thirty seconds.*

**JAMESON:** We are approaching a logic of subliminality there, and your example effectively illustrates this new logic of difference to which we are being programmed—these are increasingly rapid and empty breaks in our time. Each training in an increased tempo is a training in feeling that it is natural to shift from one thing to another.

**STEPHANSON:** *Nam June Paik's video art is, as you say, a valuable post-modernist place to explore this problem.*

**JAMESON:** As a kind of training in a new logic of difference. An empty formal training or programming in a new way of perceiving difference.

**STEPHANSON:** *What exactly is that new way of perceiving difference?*

**JAMESON:** I tried to put this in the slogan "difference relates." The very perception of breaks and difference becomes a meaning in itself; yet not a meaning that has content but one that seems to be a meaningful, yet new, form of unity. This kind of view does not pose the problem, "How do we relate those things, how do we turn those things back into continuities or similarities?" It simply says, "When you register difference, something positive is happening in your mind." It's a way of getting rid of content.

**STEPHANSON:** *From this diagnosis of the temporal you proceed to the spatial.*

**JAMESON:** I then link these two sets of features (surface and fragmentation) in terms of the spatialization of time. Time has become a perpetual present and thus spatial. Our relationship to the past is now a spatial one.

**STEPHANSON:** *Why does it necessarily become spatial?*

**JAMESON:** One privileged challenge for modernist language—take that of Marcel Proust or Thomas Mann, for example—always involved temporal description. That notion of "deep time," Bergsonian time, seems radically irrelevant to our contemporary experience, which is one of a perpetual spatial present. Our *theoretical* categories also tend to become spatial: structural analyses with graphs of synchronic multiplicities of spatially related things (as opposed to, say, the dialectic and its temporal moments), or languages like Foucault's, with its empty rhetoric of cutting, sorting, and modifying, a kind of spatial language in which you organize data like a great block to be chopped up in various ways. Indeed, this happens to be how I "use" Foucault, with limitations that will probably infuriate his disciples. Much of Foucault was already familiar: the binary opposition between center and margin was largely developed in Sartre's *Saint Genet*; the concepts of power had emerged in many places, but fundamentally in the anarchist tradition; and the totalizing strategies of his various schemes also have many analogies from Weber on. I propose, rather, to consider Foucault in terms of the *cognitive mapping* of power, the construction of spatial picture models, and the transfer of conceptions of social power and its forms onto powerful spatial figures. But then, of course, once put that way, Foucault's own figures—the grid, for example—become starkly relativized and cease to be theories as such.

**STEPHANSON:** *Where does "hyperspace" come into the spatial argument?*

**JAMESON:** Normal space is made up of things, or organized by things. Here we are talking about the dissolution of things. In this final moment, one cannot talk about components anymore. We used to talk about this in terms of subject-object dialectics; but in a situation in which subjects and objects have been dissolved, hyperspace is the ultimate of the object-pole, and intensity the ultimate of the subject-pole, even though we no longer have subjects and objects.

At any rate, the motion of spatialization replacing temporalization leads back to architecture and new experiences of space which I think are very different from any previous moments of the space of the city, to name one example. What is striking about the new urban ensembles around Paris, for example, is that there is *absolutely no perspective at all*. Not only has the street disappeared (that was already the task of modernism), but all profiles have disappeared as well. This is bewildering, and I use existential bewilderment in this new postmodern space to make a final diagnosis of the loss of our ability to *position ourselves within this space and cognitively to map it*. This is then projected back on the emergence of a global, multinational culture that is decentered and cannot be visualized, a culture in which one cannot position oneself. That is the conclusion.

**STEPHANSON:** *To be more specific, you use, very elegantly, John Portman's Bonaventure Hotel in Los Angeles as an example: a mirror facade, a self-enclosed structure in which it is impossible to orient oneself. Yet the new commercial spaces around Rodeo Drive are the very opposite of what you describe: quaint squares, readily visible spaces where things can be purchased in quite obvious and conventional ways.*

**JAMESON:** But that is the Disney version of postmodern architecture, the Disneyland pastiche of the older square or piazza. I picked emblematic things and not, by any means, everything that can be analyzed in that vein. These other examples do not exemplify the hyperspace, but they are certainly exemplary of the production of simulacra. Disney's EPCOT is another excellent example.

**STEPHANSON:** *In other words, you are referring to his compressed version of the world: little toy countries where you can orient yourself in no time at all.*

**JAMESON:** I suppose you can orient yourself because walking paths are available. But where you actually are is a real problem, for you may in fact be in the Florida Everglades, and in this case you are not only in a swamp but also in a simulacrum of a different geographical complex altogether. Disneyland is, on the whole, supremely prophetic and paradigmatic of these multiple shifting and dissolving spatial levels.

**STEPHANSON:** *The emergence of postmodernism is materially tied in your analysis to the rise of American capital on a global scale, dated to the late 1950s and early 1960s. However, the United States was then actually beginning to experience a relative decline in its postwar dominance: other nations were coming back economically, and there was an upsurge in third world liberation movements and the return in the first world of oppositional ideologies fashioned very much on the depth model (Marxism for one).*

**JAMESON:** Notions of the discontinuity of culture and economics can account for some of that. The setting in place of American power is one thing; the development of a culture which both reflects and perpetuates that power is a somewhat different matter. The old cultural slate had to be wiped clean, and this could happen in the United States instead of Europe because of the relative absence of the persistent background of an ancien régime culture over here. Once modernism broke down, the absence of traditional forms of culture in the United States opened up a field for a whole new cultural production across the board. Individual things could be pioneered in Europe, but a system of culture could only emerge from this American possibility. The moment American power begins to be questioned, a new cultural apparatus becomes necessary to reinforce it. The system of postmodernism comes in as the vehicle for a new kind of ideological hegemony that might not have been required before.

**STEPHANSON:** *Isn't this view close to straightforward functionalism or instrumentalism?*

**JAMESON:** Yes and no. There is certainly a way in which this system—from the export of American television shows to so-called high cultural values, above all the very logic and practice of "American" consumption itself—is as effective a vehicle for depoliticization as religion may once have been. There had to be channels of transmission, which are laid in place with communications systems, televisions, computers, and so forth. Worldwide, that was really only available in the 1960s. Suffice it simply for a power elite to say: "Well, in this situation we need a cultural system which has to correspond to changes that are taking place in people's lives and offer a kind of content." The new life experience embodied in postmodernism is very powerful precisely because it has a great deal of content that seems to come as a solution to existential problems.

A lot of other discontinuous systems are going on here too. Some of the social effects of American hegemony are not felt until the 1960s—the Green Revolution in agriculture, for example—so it's wrong to see this merely in terms of political power. Much of the social resistance of the 1960s comes when people—peasants, for instance—begin to realize what the neocolonial systems are doing to ways of life that had been exploited before but left relatively intact. The emergence of resistance does not necessarily mean merely rolling back American influence; it can be a symptom of the disintegrating effects of that influence on deeper levels of social life than the political one.

**STEPHANSON:** *When you depict the capitalist destruction of Van Gogh's world of peasant shoes and Heidegger's country pathway, you do so in terms of Tafuri's account of the modernist project in architecture: the aim of ensuring that the future holds no surprises, the idea of "planification" and elimination of future risk. This seems a valid point. However, you skate over rather easily the modernizing features of Marxism itself, the results of which are clear and obvious in the unthinking destruction of the environment in Soviet-style societies. Planification with a vengeance, which actually prepares the grounds for future disaster. The obliteration of Heidegger's pathway can thus be seen as an integral feature of any modernizing ethic.*

**JAMESON:** Plainly, in an advanced society, our immediate oppositional tendency is to talk about restraining technological progress. I am not sure poor societies always have that option. Some of these features, what is happening to cities like Moscow, are part of what could be called the cultural debt crisis. Think of the 1960s and 1970s, when the Soviets were sucked into the world system and began to believe that they had to have tourists and build big hotels. One has to distinguish between the Promethean scenario—the struggle with nature—and other kinds of commodification that they really get from us or that they imitate in a lot of ways.

STEPHANSON: *Yet Stalin was a great admirer of American technology and Taylorist efficiency. The fact that the Soviets engage in this sort of destruction is not only rooted in their wanting to catch up with the West or having to compete with the West but also is embedded in a certain kind of Marxist theory. By delineating the problematic in an exclusively capitalist domain, you render yourself open to the objection that a strong element of conquering nature and older "logics" exists in Marxist as well as capitalist thought. Marcuse's analysis of Soviet theory is surely unequivocal on this point. If your argument, in short, is built on the idea of the relentless ordering of the world in terms of the commodifying logic of capital, it must also be clear that certain Marxisms are far from innocent.*

JAMESON: I agree. But the emphasis on production and productivity and on catching up with capitalism is at least part of the competition in which capitalism has ensnared these underdeveloped countries: they have to catch up. Therefore we have a very elaborate dialectical process where these societies have found it necessary to go beyond self-sufficiency or autarchy to generate modernization for many pressing reasons, like armament.

STEPHANSON: *Yes, but the conception of modernity is there from the outset.*

JAMESON: That is indeed an ideological conception, and it no doubt needs to be rethought.

STEPHANSON: *Your model goes from the microlevel, assorted things here and there, to the macrolevel, represented by Mandel's concept of late capitalism. These "homologies" between the three moments of capital and the three moments in cultural development (realism, modernism, and postmodernism) lend credence to descriptions of your position as unreconstructed Lukácsianism. It does seem to be a case of expressive causality, correspondences and*

*all. However, it is difficult to see how one can preserve a consistent politi-*
*cal commitment if one adopts poststructuralist fantasies of pure contingency*
*and nonrelation. In a nutshell, a certain amount of reductionism is neces-*
*sary. Hence objections to the actual concept of the three stages of capitalism*
*aside, I think the idea of this kind of model is perfectly proper. Problems arise,*
*however, with the meditating instances, the way in which you jump from the*
*minute to the staggeringly global.*

**JAMESON:** But Lukács takes a moralizing position on modernism that is
neither historical nor dialectical. He thinks it is something essentially morally wrong that can be eliminated by an effort of the will. That position is
very different from my presentation of something that seems *more* morally
horrendous, namely postmodernism. As for expressive causality, I find it
paradoxical that a discontinuous and dialectical model of something can
be criticized for being an idealistic continuity that includes a telos. Each of
these moments is dialectically different from each other and has different
laws and modes of operation. I also make a place for overdetermination;
that is, some things are enabled by developments in the cultural realm that
tie into others at certain conjunctures. I don't think that's what one would
do in a model of "the Spirit of the Age." For example, the notion of hegemony is not normally thought to be Hegelian. In talking about a certain
kind of cultural hegemony, I have left a space for oppositional, or enclaves
of, resistance, all kind of things not integrated into the global model but
necessarily defined against it. I can see how in some very loose and general
sense one can make the sort of characterization you made, and in the same
loose and general sense it wouldn't bother me. If we talk about the specifics,
however, I would certainly want to see what reprehensible things "expressive causality" ended up doing before I endorsed it. On the other hand, as
you say, any attempt to be systematic potentially attracts those criticisms
because the whole point is to make a reduction in the first place.

**STEPHANSON:** *What distinguishes your concept of postmodernism is the*
*fact that it does not designate it as a stylistic mode but as a cultural domi-*
*nant. In that way it bears little relation to the ideas of everyone from Tafuri*
*to Lyotard.*

**JAMESON:** Two points here. First, it's important to understand that this
notion of a dominant does not exclude forms of resistance. In fact, the whole
point for me in undertaking this analysis was the idea that one wouldn't be

able to measure the effectiveness of resistance unless one knew what the dominant forces were. My conception of postmodernism is thus not meant to be monolithic, but to allow evaluations of other currents within this system—which cannot be measured unless one knows what the system is.

Second, I want to propose a dialectical view in which we see postmodernism neither as immoral, frivolous, or reprehensible because of its lack of high seriousness, nor as good in the McLuhanist, celebratory sense of the emergence of some wonderful new Utopia. Features of both are going on at once. Certain aspects of postmodernism can be seen as relatively positive, such as the return of storytelling after the sort of poetic novels that modernism used to produce. Other features are obviously negative (the loss of a sense of history, for example). All in all, these developments have to be confronted as a historical situation rather than as something to be morally deplored or simply celebrated.

**STEPHANSON:** *Moralizing aside, is postmodernism not predominantly negative from a Marxist perspective?*

**JAMESON:** Think of its popular character and the relative democratization involved in various postmodernist forms. This is an experience of culture accessible to far more people than the older modernist languages were. Certainly, that cannot be altogether bad. Culturalization on a very wide front might be deplored by people for whom modernism was a very sophisticated language to be conquered by dint of self-formation, of which postmodernism is then a bastardization and vulgarization. Why this should be condemned from a leftist standpoint is, however, not clear to me.

**STEPHANSON:** *In that sense, no, but as you yourself have emphasized, simple opposition to totality in the name of some celebrated fragmentation and heterogeneity render the very idea of critique difficult.*

**JAMESON:** Yet even heterogeneity is a positive thing: the social rhetoric of differences is reflected in this, which in itself is surely not a bad thing. The point is that many of these seemingly negative features can be looked at positively if they are seen historically. If one views them as items in a defense of postmodern art, they don't look the same. Postmodern architecture is demonstrably a symptom of democratization, of a new relationship of culture to people, but this does not mean that one can defend or glamorize the buildings of postmodernists simply because they are populist buildings.

**STEPHANSON:** *It is obvious, nevertheless, that postmodernist discourse makes it difficult to say things about the whole.*

**JAMESON:** One of the ways to describe this is as a modification in the very nature of the cultural sphere: a loss of the autonomy of culture, or a case of culture falling into the world. As you say, this makes it much more difficult to speak of cultural systems and to evaluate them in isolation. A whole new theoretical problem is thereby posed. Thinking at once negatively and positively about it is a beginning, but what we need is a new vocabulary. The languages that have been useful in talking about culture and politics in the past don't really seem adequate to this historical moment.

**STEPHANSON:** *Yet you retain the classical Marxist paradigm: the master narrative underneath this search for a new vocabulary is very traditional.*

**JAMESON:** Traditional in a sense, but it implies a third stage of capitalism which is not present in Marx.

**STEPHANSON:** *Nor indeed is the second one, "monopoly capitalism," which was invented by the Second International and bought wholesale, with very bad results, by the Third.*

**JAMESON:** The Marxist framework is still indispensable for understanding the new historical content, which demands not a modification of the Marxist framework, but an expansion of it.

**STEPHANSON:** *Why is that clear?*

**JAMESON:** Contemporary Marxist economics and social science is not a rewriting of nineteenth-century Marxism. This can be dramatized, as Mandel does, by saying that it is not that reality has evolved away from Marx's model or that this is no longer the capitalism analyzed by Marx, but that it is a much purer version of that model, that, as Hegel put it, today reality much more closely begins to approximate its own concept. A feature of this third stage is that the precapitalist enclaves have systematically been penetrated, commodified, and assimilated to the dynamics of the system. If the original instruments of Marxism are unserviceable, it is not that Marxism is wrong now, but that it is *truer* now than in Marx's time. Hence we need an expansion, rather than a replacement, of these instruments.

**STEPHANSON:** *The old Lukácsian model of truth and false consciousness is, I suppose, one casualty in this regard.*

**JAMESON:** In the more interesting parts of Lukács, that is not in fact the model. Let me put that in a more practical way. Obviously, there is false consciousness, and there are moments when one wants to denounce certain things as sheer false consciousness; this is essentially a political decision and part of a struggle that has to be waged. In ideological analysis, on the other hand, the denunciation of works of art for embodying false consciousness was possible only in a more heterogeneous class situation, in which the working classes were a nation within the nation and did not consume bourgeois culture. When one takes a stand in such circumstances, one can see that certain kinds of objects—Proust's writings, for example— are decadent in the sense that it is not the mode in which either experience or artistic form makes any sense to people who work. From that viewpoint one can denounce the decadence and false consciousness which Proust undoubtedly embodied. But now, when these class differences are no longer secured by social isolation and the process of massive democratic culturalization continues, there is no space outside for the left to occupy. My position on ideological analysis of works of art today is, therefore, that you don't denounce them from the outside. If you want to denounce their false consciousness, you have to do it from the inside and it has to be a *self-critique*. It is not that false consciousness doesn't exist anymore—perhaps it is everywhere—but we have to talk about it in a different way.

**STEPHANSON:** *You propose, then, to preserve "the moment of truth" in postmodernism. What exactly is it?*

**JAMESON:** I am using contemporary German post-Hegelian language here. Ideological analysis from that vantage point means talking about the moment of truth and the moment of untruth, and in this case I am trying to say that insofar as postmodernism really expresses multinational capitalism, there is some cognitive content to it. It is articulating something that is going on. If the subject is lost in it, and if in social life the psychic subject has been decentered by late capitalism, this art faithfully and authentically registers that. That is its moment of truth.

**STEPHANSON:** *Modernism, as you have argued, emerges at that same time as mass culture, to which it is thus inextricably linked. Postmodernism can* *then be seen as the collapse of these two into one again. Terry Eagleton has re-formulated this as a kind of sick joke on the historical avant-garde, in which the attempt by the avant-garde to break down the boundaries between art and social life suddenly becomes a reactionary implosion.*

**JAMESON:** It's not a matter of becoming that, but being *revealed* as that. The other version of that account, which I find very persuasive, is that of Tafuri in connection with architecture. He tries to show that the pro-topolitical aesthetic revolution first laid out in Schiller—that is, "We must transform our consciousness through a heightened aesthetic experience, and that will in itself constitute a revolution that makes political revolution (and the Terror) unnecessary"—is virtually taken over word for word by Le Corbusier: "We change the space we live in and then we don't need political revolution." The protopolitical impulse of modernism, according to Tafuri, is necessarily always predicated on exclusion, for the radical new space of the modern thing must begin by a gesture of excluding the old fallen space that is to be revolutionized. Implicit here is the belief that this new space will fan out and transform the old space. Instead, it simply remains an enclave space; and when the existential and cultural, spatial, revolution fails to take hold in this fallen, outlying world, the building or work of art becomes an isolated monument, testifying to its own sterility or impotence. It ceases to be a revolutionary gesture. So what Eagleton is ironizing is, in Tafuri's account, already implicit in the first modernisms.

**STEPHANSON:** *There is a misreading of your reading of Tafuri which seems to say that by calling for a "properly Gramscian architecture" you are simply calling for some cleared enclave of resistance; but that is not quite what you are arguing.*

**JAMESON:** In my appeal to a Gramscian architecture, I also mentioned Lefebvre. I was thinking not of an architectural practice as such, but of an awareness that the locus of our new reality, and the cultural politics by which it must be confronted, is that of space. We must therefore begin to think of cultural politics in terms of space and the struggle for space. Then we are no longer thinking in old categories of critical distance but in some new way in which the disinherited and essentially modernist language of subversion and negation is conceived differently. Tafuri's argument is couched in cultural terms, but what matters in any defeat or success of a plan to transform the city is political power, control over speculation and land values, and so on. That's a very healthy awareness of the infrastructure.

STEPHANSON: *How does this differ from traditional politics?*

JAMESON: The difference is that the political is projected onto at least two levels: the practical matter of this place, this terrain, and these resistances; and then above and beyond that, the cultural vision of Utopian space of which this particular enclave is but a specific figure. All of which can be said in a more banal way in terms of the decay of the very concept of socialism, which we can observe everywhere (in all three worlds). It is a matter of reinventing that concept as a powerful cultural and social vision, something one does not do simply by repeating a worn-out name or term. But it is a two-level strategy: the specific space or place *and* the global vision of which the first is only one particular manifestation or local fulfillment. Add to this the fact and problem of the new global systemic space, and we have a demand made on the political imagination that is historically unparalleled. Let me put it this way: There exists today a global capitalist, or late capitalist, culture which we call, as is now apparent, postmodernism. It is a tremendously powerful force which, in sheer gravitational attraction and capability of diffusion, is known, or used to be known, as cultural imperialism. Nothing like a global socialist culture exists as a distinct oppositional force and style to this. On the other hand, when one proposes such a political project to some of the interested parties, they rightly begin at once to worry about the dissolution of the national situation and culture which has generally played such a powerful role in socialist revolutions. What is wanted, therefore, is a new relationship between global cultural style and the specificity and demands of a concrete local or national situation.

STEPHANSON: *Is the spatial aspect not really what Social Democrats in Europe have been concerned with, sometimes successfully, for a long time?*

JAMESON: The problem with the Social Democratic governments is that they've gained power in a nation-state whose economic realities are really controlled by the international market. They are therefore not in control of their own national space. Ultimately, I am talking about a global space which is not abstract or speculative. I am talking about the fact that the proletariat of the first world is now in the third world and that production is taking place around the Pacific basin and beyond the national boundaries.

These are practical realities, and the control of national space may itself be an outmoded idea in a situation of multinationals.

STEPHANSON: *Indeed, one may take your macroanalysis to mean that the task of radical first world intellectuals is a kind of "third-worldism." This, to my mind, recalls various "bribery theories" of the 1960s—using the absence of movement among the Western working class as a justification for fixation on other, and less quiescent, continents. Eventually these positions were discarded, and rightly so.*

JAMESON: The attractiveness of "third-worldism" as an ideology rises and falls with the condition of the third world itself, but the political movement going on today—such as there is—lies in places like Nicaragua and South Africa. Surely, then, the third world is still very much alive as a possibility. It is not a matter of cheering for third world countries to make their revolution; it is a dialectical matter of seeing that we here are involved in these areas and are busy trying to put them down, that they are part of our own power relations.

STEPHANSON: *But that tends to end up in moralism: "We shouldn't do this and we shouldn't do that in the third world." Once one has realized that, what is there to do? No particular politics follows as far as the first world itself is concerned. One tends to end up with Paul Sweezy's position that the only thing to do is prevent interventions in the third world. This strikes me as a bit barren.*

JAMESON: Well, what are the alternatives? We are talking about culture, and culture is a matter of awareness; and it would not be bad to generate the awareness that we in the superstate are at all times a presence in third world realities, that our affluence and power are in the process of doing something to them. The form this awareness takes in American culture has to do not only with foreign policy but also with the notion that the United States itself is a third world country because of unemployment, nonproduction, the flight of factories, and so on.

STEPHANSON: *Why does that make us a third world country? It seems like the definition of a first world country.*

JAMESON: If the third world is defined, as it sometimes has been, as the development of underdevelopment, it does seem clear that we have begun to do this to ourselves as well. In any case, the apparent return to some finance capitalism with dizzying edifices of credit and paper no longer reposing on the infrastructure or "ground" of real production offers some peculiar analogies to current (poststructuralist) theory itself. Let's say that here the first world—if it does not revert back into third world realities—unexpectedly, and in a peculiar dialectical reversal, begins to touch some features of third world experience: perhaps another reason third world culture has lately become one of our passionate interests.

**STEPHANSON:** *In arguing against condemnation and celebration, you wish to encourage a critique that goes through postmodernism in a sort of "homeopathic" way.*

**JAMESON:** To undo postmodernism homeopathically by the methods of postmodernism: to work at dissolving the pastiche by using all the instruments of pastiche itself, to reconquer some genuine historical sense by using the instruments of what I have called substitutes for history.

**STEPHANSON:** *How is this "homeopathic" operation to be understood more specifically?*

**JAMESON:** The figure of homeopathic medicine here does not imply that the culture functions only in that way, but it is often the case. Modernism, for example, was an experience of nascent commodification that fought reification by means of reification, in terms of reification. It was itself a gigantic process of reification internalized as a homeopathic way of seizing on this force, mastering it, and opposing the result to reification passively submitted to in external reality. I am wondering whether some positive features of postmodernism couldn't do that as well: attempt somehow to master these things by choosing them and pushing them to their limits. There is a whole range of so-called oppositional arts, whether it's punk writing or video art, that really try to use postmodern techniques—though for obvious reasons I dislike the term *technique*—to go through postmodernism and beyond it. It's certainly wrong to go down the list of contemporary trends and, once again, in typical left-wing fashion, try to find out which is forbidden and which is progressive. The only way through a crisis of space is to invent a new space.

**STEPHANSON:** *Despite the disappearance of a sense of history, there is no lack of historical elements in postmodern culture.*

**JAMESON:** When I talked about the loss of history, I didn't mean the disappearance of images of history, for instance, in the case of nostalgia film. The increasing number of films about the past are no longer historical; they are images, simulacra, and pastiches of the past. They are effectively a way of satisfying a chemical craving for historicity, using a product that substitutes for and blocks it.

**STEPHANSON:** *But historical images are, in a way, always substitutes.*

**JAMESON:** That is not the way Lukács analyzed the historical novel in its emergent form; he thought of it as an approach to knowledge. I would also argue that something like science fiction can occasionally be looked at as a way of breaking through to history in a new way; achieving a distinctive historical consciousness by way of the future rather than the past; and becoming conscious of our present as the past of some unexpected future, rather than as the future of heroic national past (the traditional historical novel of Lukács). But nostalgia art gives us the image of various generations of the past as fashion-plate images that entertain no determinable ideological relationship to other moments of time: they are not the outcome of anything, nor are they the antecedents of our present; they are simply images. This is the sense in which I describe them as substitutes for any genuine historical consciousness rather than specific new forms of the latter.

**STEPHANSON:** *The cannibalizing of styles is part and parcel of this type of "historicity."*

**JAMESON:** This is what architects call historicism, the eclectic use of dead languages.

**STEPHANSON:** *I first became aware of this a couple of years ago with regard to fashion, when the 1950s was being mined, along with its ideological orientation: the schlock of the Eisenhower epoch, fascination with television series of that period, and so forth. Now, when that seems exhausted, there is excavation of the 1960s, not the politicized 1960s, but the 1960s of the go-go girls. One can imagine that even the militant 1960s can be used for stylistic innovation, rather in the manner in which Macy's department store instantly transforms East Village vogues into commercial values.*

**JAMESON:** Perhaps one could write a history of these nostalgias. It would be plausible to say that in a moment of exhaustion with politics, the images that are cannibalized and offered by nostalgia film are those of a great depoliticized era. Then, when unconsciously political drives begin to reawaken, they are contained by offering images of a politicized era. We are all happy to have a movie like *Reds*, but is that not also a nostalgia film?

**STEPHANSON:** *Perhaps, but nostalgia is difficult to avoid in popular depictions of the past.*

**JAMESON:** A historical situation is at stake, and one can't wish this postmodern blockage of historicity out of existence by mere self-critical self-consciousness. If it's true that we have real difficulty imagining the radical difference with the past, this difficulty cannot be overcome by an act of the will or by deciding that this is the wrong kind of history to have and that we ought to do it in some other way. This, for me, is the fascination with novels such as Doctorow's *Ragtime*. Here is a radical left-wing novelist who has seized the whole apparatus of nostalgia art, pastiche, and postmodernism to work himself through them instead of attempting to resuscitate some older form of social realism, an alternative that would in itself become another pastiche. Doctorow's is not necessarily the only possible path, but I find it an intriguing attempt to undo postmodernism "homeopathically" by the methods of postmodernism: to work at dissolving the pastiche by using all the instruments of pastiche itself and to reconquer some genuine historical sense by using the instruments of what I have called substitutes for history.

In your terms this might be another version of "third-worldism" in the cultural sense. We come back to looking for some alternative place which is neither the past of the first world, the great moment of modernism, nor its present, which is that of schizophrenic textuality.

**STEPHANSON:** *But how is it possible, in a mode of cultural expression that by definition is superficial, to say anything about deep structures? After all, the essence of Marxism is to reveal something about what "really is."*

**JAMESON:** Doctorow is still my best example, for by turning the past into something which is obviously a simulacrum, he suddenly makes us realize that this is the only image of the past we have; in truth, a projection on the walls of Plato's cave. This is, if you like, negative dialectics, or negative theology, insistence on the very flatness and depthlessness of the thing which makes what isn't there very vivid. That is not negligible. It is not the reinvention of some sense of the past wherein one would fantasize about a healthier age of deeper historical sense: the use of these very limited instruments shows their limits. And it is not ironic.

**STEPHANSON:** *But how does one use the perception of difference to get somewhere else? If you resort to homology, you've basically done the same thing that you criticise in* Reds, *but not in Doctorow's work.*

**JAMESON:** The problem of homologies (and the unsatisfactory nature of these parallels or analogies between levels) has been a constant theoretical concern for me. Something like the homology does seem difficult to avoid when one attempts to correlate distinct semiautonomous fields. I've played with alternative concepts: Sartre's notion of the *analogon* and Peirce's concept of the *interpretant*. Both of these stress the operation of reading analogies off the allegorical object, rather than discovering them ontologically, as "realities" in the world. And each seems, in addition, to contribute a little towards clarifying the process I've called cognitive mapping, the invention of ways of using one subject and one reality to get a mental grasp of something else which one cannot represent or imagine. As an emblem of this process, I might offer the picture of those hypersterilized laboratory chambers into which enormous gloves and instruments protrude, manipulated by the scientist from the outside. The normal body is doing one thing, but the results are taking place in another space altogether and according to other dimensions, other parameters. It must be a bewildering set of tasks to exercise, as far from our normal bodily operations as the deductive or abductive appropriation of the banana is for the laboratory monkey. But, if it were possible, this would give you an idea of the new kinds of representational processes demanded here.

**STEPHANSON:** *The personal "style" so typical of modernism has, according to you, become a mere code in postmodernism.*

**JAMESON:** This is another feature first explored by poststructuralism, namely, the eclipse of the old personal subject and ego. Modernism was predicated on the achievement of some unique personal style that could be parlayed into the subject of genius, the charismatic subject, or the super-subject, if you like. Once that subject has disappeared, the styles linked to it are no longer possible. A certain form of depersonalization thus seems implicit in all of this: even when modernism itself is pastiched, it is only an imitation of style, not a style.

Still, I always insist on a third possibility beyond the old bourgeois ego and the schizophrenic subject of our organization-society today: a collective subject, decentered but not schizophrenic. It emerges in certain forms of storytelling that can be found in third world literature, in testimonial literature, in gossip and rumors, and in things of this kind.[2] It is a storytelling which is neither personal in the modernist sense nor depersonalized in the pathological sense of the schizophrenic text. It is decentered, since the stories you tell there as an individual subject don't belong to you; you don't control them the way the master subject or modernism would. But you don't just suffer them in the schizophrenic isolation of the first world subject of today. None of this reinvents style in the older sense.

**STEPHANSON:** *Some years ago, in a wholly different context, you called the brushstroke the very sign of the modern genius, pointing specifically to de Kooning's metabrushstroke as the last gasp of some individualizing art.[3] Yet, the next morning, neo-expressionism brought back this megabrushstroke with a vengeance. Would you then say that this was pastiche, not the surviving element of some older modernism?*

**JAMESON:** Some of it is merely a pastiche of modernist subjectivity.

**STEPHANSON:** *On the other hand, certain of these painters, Immendorf for instance, were quite explicitly political, with interesting stories to tell.*

**JAMESON:** A lot of it is European or comes from the semiperiphery of the American core (Canada, for example). It would seem, for instance, that neo-expressionism flourished particularly in Italy and Germany, the two Western countries that experienced the historical "break" of fascism. Here one could argue with Habermas, who sees the German version of neo-expressionism as reactionary. We, on the other hand, could perhaps use it in other ways, not classifying it as a morbid attempt to reinvent a subjectivity, which in the German tradition is tainted anyway.

**STEPHANSON:** *And now we see the return of minimalism, blank surfaces, and "neo-geo" forms looking rather like 1960s and early 1970s to me. The cannibalization of styles has apparently been "revved up," conceivably ending in some furious, vertiginous act of biting its own tail.*

*You suggest an interesting connection between Tafuri's rigorous anti-Utopianism—his almost Adornian negative dialectics of architecture—and Venturi's celebration of Las Vegas: the system, for both, is essentially a massively all-encompassing one which cannot be changed. The difference is that Tafuri's stoically refuses it, while Venturi invents ways of "relaxing" within it.*

JAMESON: For Tafuri, Venturi is himself part of an opposition whose other term is Mies van der Rohe. The one solution is that of absolute Mallarméan purity and silence; the other is the abandonment of that final attempt at negative purity and the falling back into the world. The problem with Venturi's architecture or his "solution"—characteristic of many poststructuralisms today—is the appeal to irony, which is a modernist solution. He wants to use the language of the vernacular of Las Vegas, but, being engaged in art and aesthetics, he also has to have some kind of minimal distance to it. All of this art, as Tafuri says, is predicated on distance, and distance is always a failure: since it distances itself from what it wants to change, it can't change it.

STEPHANSON: *This reminds me of your criticism of Lyotard's concept of postmodernism: he claims to have eliminated the master narratives, but then smuggles them back in again.*

JAMESON: His most famous statement on postmodernism is that it should prepare the return of the great modernisms. Now does that mean the return of the great master narratives? Is there not some nostalgia at work here? On the other hand, insofar as the refusal of narratives is viewed as the place of the perpetual present, of anarchist science, to use Feyerabend's term (the random breaking of paradigms, and so on), we're in full postmodernism.

STEPHANSON: *So the master narratives in that sense are not dead.*

JAMESON: All one has to do is look at the reemergence of religious paradigms, whether it is in Iran or liberation theology or American fundamentalism. There are all kinds of master narratives in this world, which was supposed to be beyond narrative.

STEPHANSON: *The appropriation of modernism in the United States, when it comes, is quite different from the European predecessors. Though in itself a depoliticized art, postwar modernism here is nevertheless employed in very instrumental ways.*

**JAMESON:** The political elements of "original modernism" in its historical emergence were left out in this process of transplantation so that the various modernisms have been read as subjectivizing and inward turning. Other features vanished too. The whole Utopian and aesthetico-political element in modern architecture, Le Corbusier for example, is no longer visible when we are talking about great monuments and conventions imitated in the schools. At the same time, one must say that this modernism was no longer being produced: there was not a living modernism that could have been encouraged in a different way.

**STEPHANSON:** *Somewhere you mention Habermas's defense of the return of a completion of high modernism and point out that this seems to be a defense against a political reaction which in West Germany is still really antimodernist. In this country, the situation is in fact the opposite, is it not? The Hilton Kramers here are obviously not defending radicalism. Defense of postmodernism—one thinks of Tom Wolfe—can, on the other hand, also be associated with right-wing politics.*

**JAMESON:** The modernism Hilton Kramer wants to go back to is the subjectivizing modernism of the 1950s, the American reading of modernism that has been sullied and has lost its purity and so must be recovered. However, Habermas's modernism (I hesitate to call it the genuine article) is seen in the context of 1910 and is therefore something very different. Modernism elsewhere died a natural death and is thus no longer available, but in Germany modernism was of course cut short by Nazism; thus there is an unfulfilled character to that project which I presume someone like Habermas can attempt to take up again. But that option is not viable for us.

**STEPHANSON:** *The coupure in the "dominant" occurs, as you outline it, in the late 1950s or early 1960s. Art becomes completely enmeshed in the political economy of its own sphere, which in turn becomes part of a greater economic system. Emblematic among the pictorial artists here is Warhol, with whom you contrast Van Gogh in the initial delineation of modernism/postmodernism. Warhol is perhaps almost too obvious an example. How does a contemporary of his like Rauschenberg fit in?*

**JAMESON:** Rauschenberg is transitional, coming in at the tail end of abstract expressionism, but now in his most recent stuff is developing a whole panoply of ways of doing postmodernism. His new works are all collage surfaces with photographic images, including, symptomatically, both modernist and postmodernist ones in the same at work. The other thing about Rauschenberg is that he works a lot in third world countries where many of these photographs are taken.

In dealing with postmodernism, one can isolate people who made some pioneering contributions, but aesthetic questions about how great these contributions are—questions that can legitimately be posed when you're dealing with modernism—make little sense. I don't know how great Rauschenberg is, but I saw a wonderful show of his in China, a glittering set of things that offered all kinds of postmodernist experiences. But when they're over, they're over. The textual object is not, in other words, a work of art, a masterwork like the modernist monument was. The appreciation of the work no longer requires the attachment of some permanent evaluation of it as with the modernist painters or writers, and in that sense it is more of what I sometimes call a disposable text. You go into a Rauschenberg show and experience a process undertaken in expert and inventive ways, and when you leave it, the event has ended.

**STEPHANSON:** *What was the reaction of the Chinese audience?*

**JAMESON:** Fascination, puzzlement. I tried to explain postmodernism to my Chinese students, but for a general Chinese audience, it would simply be "Western art." Yet it must be understood in our historical context: it isn't just modern art in general, but a specific moment of it.[4]

**STEPHANSON:** *How are the traditional ways of apprehending art changing with all the great social transformations now going on in China? Is there any attempt to rejuvenate modernist notions of creativity, to replace tradition with Western subjectivity?*

**JAMESON:** It is not being replaced in that way. There is considerable translation of Western best-sellers, but also of high culture; translations of Faulkner's *The Sound and the Fury* and Alice Walker's *The Color Purple*, but also lots of Arthur Hailey. Maybe I can explain it in terms of theory: The Chinese are now interested in two kinds of theory: Western theory and traditional Chinese theory. It is felt that both of these are levers that can get them out of the kind of essentially Soviet cultural theory in which they were trained in the 1950s. As Deng You-mei, one of the most interesting Chinese writers, said to me: "We are not much interested in Western modernism as such. We are bored by novels that don't tell stories." In other words, the elaborate symbolism you find in James Joyce or Virginia Woolf doesn't do anything for them. Right after the fall of the Gang of Four, it was important to recoup some of what had been forgotten, but when I got there in 1985 and thought I was bringing news about Kafka, they told me they knew it already; it had interested them at the end of the 1970s, but not anymore. Deng You-mei said, "What you have to realize is that for us realism is also Western. Our realisms come out of the Western traditions; certainly the dominant realism of the 1950s was the Soviet one. We think there is something different from both modernism and realism and that is traditional Chinese storytelling."

This is the third world's input into the whole poststructuralist debate on representation, which is loosely assimilated to realism over here: if it is representation and realism, it's bad, and you want to break it up with the decentered subject and so on. But these Chinese strings of episode narratives fall outside this framework. They are an example of going back to the sort of storytelling that one finds both in the non-West's discovery of its own way of telling stories and in a certain form of postmodernism. So one has to rethink this question of realism and representation in the Chinese context. I took a tour through some famous grottoes with stalactites. Imagine the bourgeois public that hates modern art, and here in the same way you have a guide with a little light projector who proclaims: "Look at these rocks. There is an old man, three children, there's the goddess, et cetera." And you think: this is the most rudimentary form of what we denounce as representation in the West, a public that thinks in these terms. But China developed, alongside this popular realistic or representational perception, a very different kind of spatial perception in the evolution of the written characters. It is possible, therefore, that an oppositional culture in China might take the form of a revival of certain kinds of popular ways of seeing things, ways which would not necessarily have the same social meaning for us.

**STEPHANSON:** *What about allegory here? You have referred to allegory in the third world novel as well as with regard to postmodernism.*

**JAMESON:** That was one attempt to theorize the radical-difference of third world cultures from our own. In nonhegemonic situations, or in situations of economic or cultural subalternity, there tends to be a reference to the national situation that is always present and always felt in a way that it cannot be in the dominant culture of the superstate. But this type of analysis is not intended as a program for art, to the effect that we should now begin to write allegories.

**STEPHANSON:** *The Chinese cave mentioned before cannot be described as one of "hyperspace."*

**JAMESON:** Nor does it really betoken any radical cultural difference. This is exactly what the American tourist would do with the caves in Louisville, Kentucky. Whether a revolutionary peasantry or an American tourist looks at these is not relevant to that conception. If, as Bourdieu has explored, people have no institutional reason to justify the aesthetic operation to themselves, namely, by feeling that a little artistic training is somehow good and a sign of social distinction, then they have to have another reason for doing it, which ends up being to see likenesses. Seeing likenesses in this basically mimetic sense is not inherently a sign of the people or the popular either, but it is certainly an interesting index of the relationship of culture to people for whom culture is not a socially signifying property or attribute.

In postmodernism, on the other hand, everyone has learned to consume culture through television and other mass media, so a rationale is no longer necessary. You look at advertising billboards and collages of things because they are there in external reality. The whole matter of how you justify to yourself the time of consuming culture disappears: you are no longer even aware of consuming it. Everything is culture, the culture of the commodity. That's a very significant feature of postmodernism, which accounts for the disappearance from it of the traditional theories, justifications, and rationalizations of what we used to call aesthetics (and of concepts of high culture).

**STEPHANSON:** *Postmodern art may in some sense be disposable texts, but its monetary value is of course anything but disposable and transient. Warhol, it should be underlined, does not appear in the model as an originator, as traditionally understood. Your object is the system of culture, not the evaluation of contemporary artists.*

**JAMESON:** In trying to theorize the systemic, I was using certain of these things as allegories. From this angle it makes no sense to try to look for individual trends, and individual artists are only interesting if one finds some moment in which the system as a whole, or some limit of it, is being touched. Evaluation does come into play, since one can imagine a much less exemplary postmodernist exhibition, and one would then have to say that that painter is not as good as Rauschenberg. But this is not the same kind of use of aesthetic axiological evaluation that people felt they were able to do when they were handling modernism, for example, making relative assessments of Proust against Mann.

All the great modernists invented modernism in their own fashion. It is likewise clear that no one postmodernist can give us postmodernism, since the system involves a whole range of things. Warhol is emblematic of one feature of postmodernism, and the same goes for Paik. Both artists allow you to analyze and specify something partial, and in that sense their activities are surely original: they have identified a whole range of things to do and have moved in to colonize this new space. However, this is not original in the world-historical sense of the great modernist creator. If one artist actually embodied all of these things, Laurie Anderson, for example, he or she would no doubt be seen as transcending postmodernism. But where Wagner, in the *Gesamtkunstwerk*, may have done something like that in a key moment of modernism, Laurie Anderson's *Gesamtkunstwerk* does not do that for a nonsystematizable system, a nontotalizable system.

**STEPHANSON:** *This leaves no great space for criticism of individual works. What is the task once one has related the part to the whole?*

**JAMESON:** If they are no longer *works*, in other words. This is particularly true for video, which one usually sees in batches. You have put your finger on the fundamental methodological problem of the criticism of postmodernism. For to talk about any one of these postmodernist texts is to reify it, to turn it into the work of art it no longer is, to endow it with a permanence and monumentality that it is its vocation to dispel. A critic who is supposed to analyze individual texts is thus faced with almost insuperable problems: the moment one analyzes a single piece of video art one does it violence; one removes some of its provisionality and anonymity and turns it into a masterpiece or at least a privileged text again. It's much easier to deal with it in terms of trends: "Here's a new trend (described as such and such), and here's another." But the whole language of trends is the dialectic of the older modernism.

**STEPHANSON:** *We are returning here to the problem of evaluation.*

**JAMESON:** The Cubans, who have a different system, point out that our sense of value, in a good as well as bad sense, is given to us by the art market. One possible opposite of this would be a situation—I'm expanding on their argument—in which only a few styles would be permitted. But in a country like Cuba, which is devoid of an art market but exceedingly pluralistic culturally, where everything from Socialist Realism to Pop Art to Abstract Expressionism can be found, there is no mechanism that can identify this as being more advanced than that. One begins to sense then that the art market has an almost religious-ontological function for us. We don't have to face this radical plurality of styles of "anything goes" because somebody is always around to tell us that "this is a little newer and more innovative than that." Or more valuable, since I now think our value system depends on that transmission of the market mechanism.

**STEPHANSON:** *So how do the Cubans evaluate?*

**JAMESON:** It is a real problem; they don't know. They confront the death of value (in Nietzsche's version, the death of God) much more intensely than we do. We still have these marvelous theological mechanisms by which we pick things out and sort them. They face the more interesting problem of what the value of art would be in a situation of complete freedom, in the Nietzschean sense: freedom, that is, to do anything you want. Value then enters a crisis, also of the Nietzschean type. This is not the case when there is still a market, or when only a few styles are permitted and anyone who pushes against the paradigm can be identified. There you still know where you stand in terms of value.

**STEPHANSON:** *You say somewhere that the dialectical imagination to which Marcuse refers has atrophied. Yet at the same time you say that a constitutive feature of mass culture is that it satisfies a deep Utopian impulse in the consumer. If the Utopian imagination has been atrophied, the Utopian impulse has not?*

**JAMESON:** Marcuse, ironically, was the great theorist of the autonomy of culture. The problem is that aesthetically he reverted in a much simpler manner to the autonomy of Adorno's modernism. But Adorno's great aesthetics—the aesthetics one writes when it is impossible to write aesthetics—involves time and death and history: experience is historical and condemned to death in a sense. Marcuse's concept finally simplified that complexity out of Adorno, taking up an older modernist model which is not now helpful. His notion of the Utopian impulse is a different matter. The objection there is that he falls back on a position in which the autonomy of art still permits a kind of full expression of the Utopian impulse, which is what I would deny.

**STEPHANSON:** *Adorno's negative dialectics is criticized in your account for allowing no resistance to the overall system. Nothing, seemingly, is to be done. You point to the similarities here with the poststructural tendency to see the system as complete and completely unchangeable in its systematicity; and I suppose one could indeed say that about Foucault et al., at certain times. The result is pessimism, and it matters less that the first model is dialectical and the latter is one of heterogeneity and contingency. Yet a quick reading of Fredric Jameson leaves one with a distinct residue of pessimism as well.*

**JAMESON:** The whole point about the loss in postmodernism of the sense of the future is that it also involves a sense that nothing will change and there is no hope. Facile optimism is, on the other hand, not helpful either.

**STEPHANSON:** *In "going through" poststructuralism and postmodernism and preserving its moment of truth, you are intermittently very hard and negative, quite rightly emphasizing the politically unsavory effects.*

**JAMESON:** There one can make a distinction. A difference exists between the production of ideologies about this reality and the reality itself. They necessarily demand two different responses. I am not willing to engage this matter of pessimism and optimism about postmodernism, since we are actually referring to capitalism itself: one must know the worst and then see what can be done. I am much more polemical about postmodernist *theories*. Theories which either exalt this or deal with it in moral ways are not productive, and *that* I think one can say something about.

**STEPHANSON:** *The reconquest of a sense of place here, the attainment of a new cartography, is primarily a call directed to the left itself. We are not referring to any great political practice, but we are arguing with the 1,500 people who happen to be deeply influenced by Deleuze and Guattari, for a large proportion of intellectuals of self-professed radical persuasion would no doubt describe themselves as heavily influenced by poststructuralist ideologies.*

**JAMESON:** That's why it's worthwhile to get a systemic sense of where all these things come from so that we can see what our influences are and what to do about them. The proliferation of theoretical discourses was healthy because it led to some awareness of their political consequences. In moments of economic crisis or intervention abroad, people can determine more clearly what any given theory does or allows them to do. It is a matter of theoretical and historical self-knowledge, and what I am engaged in is in fact a struggle within theory as much as anything else. If I were making videos, I would talk about this in a different way.

**STEPHANSON:** *In that respect, yours is a systematic project of building "totalizing" models, something which, to understate the case, has been fairly unpopular among the Western intelligentsia in the past decade. Are people perhaps more receptive now to "model building"?*

**JAMESON:** They are more receptive to the historical features of it, to the idea of thinking historically. They are not necessarily more receptive to the Marxist version of this historical inquiry, but perhaps they are willing to entertain even that on some supermarket-pluralist basis.

**STEPHANSON:** *The historical dimension counteracts the postmodernist immersion in the present, the dehistoricizing or nonhistorical project. In that sense it goes outside the postmodern paradigm.*

**JAMESON:** That is essentially the rhetorical trick or solution that I was attempting: to see whether by systemizing something which is resolutely unhistorical, one couldn't force a historical way of thinking at least about that. And there are some signs that it is possible to go around the ahistorical, to outflank it.

NOTES

1. See Fredric Jameson, "Postmodernism, or, The Cultural Logic of Late Capitalism" which first appeared in *New Left Review* 146 (1984): 52–92. It was later, in 1991, reprinted in extended form as the first chapter of the book of the same name, published by Duke University Press.

2. See Fredric Jameson "Modernism and Imperialism," in *Nationalism, Colonialism, and Literature*, by Terry Eagleton, Jameson, and Edward W. Said (Minneapolis: University of Minnesota Press, 1990), 43–66; Fredric Jameson, "On Literary

and Cultural Import-Substitutions in the Third World: The Case of the Testimonio," *Margins* 1 (1991): 11–34; Fredric Jameson, "Third-World Literature in the Era of Multinational Capitalism," *Social Text* 15 (1986): 65–88.

3. See Fredric Jameson, "Towards a Libidinal Economy of Three Modern Painters," *Social Text* 1 (1979): 189–99.

4. These remarks were made in 1986.

# Interview with Paik Nak-chung

**PAIK:** *This is your first visit to Korea, but you have been a week in Seoul, and perhaps we may begin with some of your impressions and thoughts on Korea.*

**JAMESON:** Well, I don't know that you necessarily want my physical impressions of the city, but this is a very stunning landscape and a wonderful time to be here. These gingko trees, which must be very specific to Korea, are just electrifying to see, especially at this time of the year and with the mountains surrounding the city. So all that's very impressive. I feel I've learned a lot on this trip, and I have now a great deal to think about and to sort out. Above all it has become increasingly clear to me the degree to which Korea has been in effect repressed from the political consciousness—certainly of the United States, and surely of the first world. We know about our guilt in situations like India and Vietnam, obviously; some of us are aware of guilt in the Middle East and to a certain degree in Ireland—at least our British comrades are, or should be. Those are political wounds that are visible. But we don't remember not merely what happened to Korea in the past but continued involvement of the entire life of this country in the Cold War–derived presence of the United States. I've been to a number of third world countries, but this is the only one I think whose productivity is such that, as I understand it, if the two Koreas were unified, you'd be more powerful in all kinds of ways than any European nation-state, and in any case you have a much older history. But the surprise is the way in which a country with this enormous industrial prosperity and productivity is still profoundly political. The third world countries I've visited have been essentially very

The (interview was conducted by Paik Nak-chung in Seoul on 28 October 1989. It first appeared in Rob Wilson and Wimal Dissanayake, eds., *Global/Local: Cultural Production and the Transnational Imaginary* (Durham, NC: Duke University Press, 1996), 348–71.

poor, desperate countries, from Nicaragua to the Philippines and Palestine, and so on, whereas we are accustomed to think that prosperous first world countries depoliticize gradually, cease to be political in the classical way. Here it makes a very odd impression to find a bustling, prosperous industrial country in which everyone has both suffered politically and is politically conscious. So what I want to reflect on and what I want to take away as something I've learned is not the idea that Korea would be an aberration or an exception in that respect, but perhaps that it is the classical example of how politics functions and that it is the rest of these countries, both first world and third world, that are in some respects exceptions.

**PAIK:** *I would like to come back later to this question of Korea's being apparently exceptional but essentially typical or classical. But now I want to ask your impressions about the conference you've just been participating in, the "International Conference on Marxism and the New Global Society."*

**JAMESON:** Well, there are very few world conferences of Marxist intellectuals and scholars. My presence is something of an oddity because I come out of Marxist philosophy and cultural studies more than sociology or economics, although I sometimes feel that Marxists are often as bad as bourgeois scholars in the way in which they allow themselves to become compartmentalized—Marxist economists don't have a clue as to the importance of culture, and Marxist cultural critics don't interest themselves in economics, and so forth. Here I felt an atmosphere of greater exchange, but I did think that the conference tended to be deflected into two ways that weren't necessarily directly related—one, the obligatory review of what's happening in all the communist regimes or communist parties today and, second, on Marxist theory itself, how it is flourishing today and how is comes to terms with these things. I think there was something of a conflict of directions, as I may say, with some people attempting to demonstrate that Marxism was dead, and the rest of us trying to show that Marxist theory was very vigorous indeed. For me, the most important thing is what eventually the students will get out of this and what kinds of new approaches or avenues open up for them when the symposium comes out in Korean as well as in English. I had hoped for a more vigorous participation by the Soviet group. It may be that they are still sorting their thoughts out. I agreed with what one of the Soviets said, that we will eventually have very interesting and innovative interpretations of Marx from the Soviets; we don't have them yet, but that's not surprising. But then there must also be a background to this that I am not aware of, the experience of the Soviet group here in Korea. I don't know how often they come, and so I think there is a whole area here which is very important for you and for them that I don't perceive.

**PAIK:** *Your presentation was titled "Postmodernism and the Market." Whereas most of the participants, being economists and sociologists and so on, seemed to be mainly interested in the introduction of the market mechanism into socialist economies, and thus tended perhaps inadvertently to support the thesis that planning is out and we should all adopt the free market system, you concentrated on the market ideology and strongly argued that this was incompatible with Marxism or socialism or any idea of people controlling their own destinies. And I think your characterization of the market ideology as a "Leviathan in sheep's clothing" was not only a telling polemical point but well worth the name of a "dialectical image." But I am afraid your point didn't seem quite to get across to most of the other participants.*

**JAMESON:** I think there were two points of difference between my approach and that of many of the others. The first is, as may be predictable from my background and training, that my emphasis was on ideology and culture and the role of the image of the market in contemporary politics, and I think those of us in cultural studies are more keenly aware that today in media society these images and ideologemes are very powerful objective political forces and have to be addressed. But I find that my colleagues in the social sciences are very often more naive, old-fashioned philosophical realists in that they think reality is out there and you either talk about the market or about planning; but that there is also an idea of the market or an idea of planning which has a force different from but as important as the thing itself they don't always grasp. The second point of difference I would say is that with a few exceptions—and there were exceptions, in particular my friend Alain Liepietz, who is I think one of the most interesting economists at work today—most of the Marxist scholars had a conception of an objective scholarship which ruled out the matter of socialist politics as a perspective in a conference of this kind. That's something that I can't do, and my contribution was directed very much towards the matter of some future contribution to socialist or Left politics in this conjuncture. So certainly, insofar as the other participants didn't share that perspective, they didn't quite know what to do with my suggestions, or were (if they were antisocialists) delighted that the market ideology was triumphing in this particular way that I described.

**PAIK:** *This brings us to the problem of postmodernism, a subject which seems to have occupied you a great deal over the past few years. Now would you briefly explain your notion of the postmodern in a way which would be helpful to many Korean readers not familiar with your work and yet would also contribute to the ongoing debate?*

**JAMESON:** Yes, and I gather it is also my vision of history and my notion of this current stage of capitalism as a postmodern one that may make my position a little bit unclear. Although postmodernism is a cultural word and has generally been taken to describe first of all the style of certain forms of contemporary architecture and after that certain kinds of image-production and other kinds of cultural products—and while I believe that these cultural changes are significant and important symptoms and clues as to the underlying thing itself—I really use the word *postmodern* as the name for a whole mutation or transformation in this current stage of capitalism which I distinguish sharply from the two previous stages. To be very general about it, after the political triumph of the middle classes we have some first stage of a national capitalism, a capitalism of a classical type in which exchange and production take place within the borders of individual advanced countries, and then, towards the end of the nineteenth century, the second stage (which has been classically called by Lenin and others the monopoly stage or the stage of imperialism, since those two things seem to come at once), the amalgamation of businesses into large national monopolies and then the carving up of the world into a set of spheres of influence controlled by classical colonial powers. To each of those corresponded a certain set of cultural forms and forms of consciousness. Very crudely, the first stage of national capitalism corresponds essentially in literature and culture to what one may call the moment of realism, dominated by essentially realistic forms and artistic languages and, of course, by the common sense of philosophical conceptions. The moment of monopoly capitalism or of imperialism, however, seems to me the moment in which modernism as such emerges, and that moment has been particularly interesting to me as a literary critic; but my premise has been that that stage seems to have come to an end, probably after the work of reconstruction after World War II was completed. There have been all kinds of economic symptoms as well as cultural ones that indicate this and foretell the emergence of a whole new moment no longer characterized by colonization of the old imperialist type but by decolonization and necolonialism, by the emergence of great multinational corporations, the spread of business to parts of what had hitherto been thought to be the third world (and obviously the Pacific Rim is the most famous example of this internationalization of capitalism), and also the transformation of a whole range of cultural forms, which are therefore no longer modern. Now one other cultural but also economic and industrial, technological feature one must mention is, of course, the media and television. As far as terminology is concerned, one can talk about media society or multinational society—these are all various words for the postmodern. Daniel Bell's famous "postindustrial society" is another—it's of course a conception that claims that class struggle is over and that our new "mode of production" is dominated by knowledge rather than profit—something not terribly plausible for anybody who reads the newspapers; but it does rely on the notion that we are entering a new kind of industrial production which is not classical, second-stage industrial production, but is now based on computers, information, scientific research: something one could also call a postindustrial production, with automation and cybernetics. McLuhanism would probably identify the newspapers as the technological correlative of the first or national stage of capitalism, radio and film—probably silent film—as the correlative of the second; while we ourselves have television and the Internet. So my premise has been that we should explore both culturally and infrastructurally, socially and economically, this whole new third moment of capitalism. If those of us who believe that this third stage is at hand are correct, then that means that a certain number of classical forms—of politics, of aesthetics, but also of psychology and a whole range of other things—are no longer really valid, and that we need new ones which are not the traditional ones. This doesn't mean, as some people have said, that Marxism is over, but that there certainly needs to be a vigorous response from the Marxist tradition to this transformation which is in fact, in my opinion, implicit in Marxist theory. Ernest Mandel in the book I draw on here, *Late Capitalism*, takes the following position: everybody says Marx's *Capital* describes an older form of capitalism, obviously today things are very different and he couldn't have foreseen them, and so on; no, on the contrary, he argues capitalism today is a purer form of capitalism than the very uneven situation about which Marx wrote, and there is a way therefore in which the ideal model of *Capital* may correspond better to our situation than it did to that of the nineteenth-century British and continental one.

**PAIK:** *One of the points I tried to make as discussant on your panel was that if you were at all correct in your main thesis—and many of the phenomena you cite are obvious even to someone living far away from the most advanced societies of this era—then perhaps it raised a whole set of really old questions as part of the needed new response. I mean concepts like "nature" and "human nature" may acquire a new relevance which perhaps you haven't quite done justice to. For instance, you speak of the "obliteration of nature" in this postmodern era. First, I'd like to know more precisely what you mean by this, whether it isn't something of an exaggeration, whether nature is a thing that can be obliterated. Secondly, insofar as something of this sort has advanced to any serious extent, then I wonder if it doesn't call for a new attitude on our part to the old categories of "nature," "human nature," and so on.*

**JAMESON:** First of all, let me try to make a little clearer my position on the disappearance of nature. I think when one talks about the obliteration of nature, in some deeper practical way what one means is the end of traditional agriculture—that is, the industrialization of agriculture and the transformation of peasants or farmers into agricultural workers. This is the essence of the Green Revolution; it involves junking all the traditional modes of extraction plus the forms that went with that village or peasant life and introducing the application of chemical fertilizers to the soil as an industrial unit. I think that would be the most basic sense of the abolition of nature. Pollution, although it's horrifying and dangerous, is maybe simply a spin-off of this new relationship to nature. We had a number of papers at the conference on ecology and ecological politics and so on, and I think we all have to be very concerned about those things, but our experience in the West—that is to say, my observation of these things in the West—is that ecological politics tends to be bourgeois politics, that lower-class people are interested in other issues that are sometimes incompatible with ecology. I think that many things can be achieved ecologically, but they have to be part of some larger collective political project, which has not yet been forged. And it would involve the control of big business; it seems clear to me that a capitalist country, even if it passes some laws about pollution, about the emission of chemicals from the smokestack, is very unwilling to put together the kind of bureaucracy necessary to police all those things. It's either not able to afford to do that, or it isn't really interested in doing that. It also seems to me fairly obvious that, whatever the record of the Soviet Union up to now, such controls would be much easier to achieve under a socialist system.

Now the other place where nature exists is, I think, the unconscious. That is to say, in classical German aesthetics from which all this comes— Lukács used to argue (as Terry Eagleton has again done recently) that Marxism itself could be seen as coming out of Schiller's aesthetics in some way— for classical German aesthetics, art or culture was the one sphere that was not colonized by either knowledge production or commodity production; and I think one could include in that all the things that Freud described in terms of the unconscious. That is, there has been a place in human nature which includes the aesthetic and the realms of desire and the deeper personality and so forth, which has been in a sense outside the range of forces of older forms of capitalism or of the social system itself. Today I think one of the characteristics of the postmodern is very precisely this penetration and colonization of the unconscious. Art is commodified, and the unconscious is itself commodified by the forces of the media and advertising, and therefore it is also in that sense that one can claim a certain kind of nature is gone. Now, Sartre, who has had I think a certain importance here in Korea as well, always used to make fun of the more conservative or nostalgic defenses of nature, and Sartreanism is at least one version of the expression of a great optimism about the triumph over nature and the release of human life from its traditional limits, a release that allows human beings to construct their own selves and their destinies. And I think it's proper to insist on that feature of all this too—that is, there is a certain freedom involved in being no longer constrained by traditional forms of human nature. On the notion of human nature itself, I guess I remain somewhat ambivalent; I suppose I think that it has a great political value when it is oppositional and that notions of human nature should be oppositional notions. When they become dominant and normative notions, then one must be much more suspicious. But then in that case what I would like to suggest is—and this is very consistent with the whole postmodern period where people lament the disappearance of the older, inner-directed personality, the acquisitive individual, the centered subject, and all those things—that instead of replacing those with the rhetoric of psychic fragmentations, schizophrenia, and so on, one should return again to notions of collective relations, but collectivities of new types, not of traditional kinds. That would, it seems to me, be a way of looking at human nature as a social thing that would be in my opinion the most productive socially and culturally, and politically as well.

**PAIK:** *I share your ambivalence towards the concept, and I'd even stress the importance of maintaining that ambivalence, but I think denying the concept altogether like Sartre is something else—something quite different from Marx's attitude as well. I, for one, find quite convincing Norman Geras's argument in his book* Marx and Human Nature *that Marx at least never meant to say that there was no such thing as human nature; he just happened to work at the moment when it was the oppositional attitude to attack the existing concepts of human nature. But now the point that I want to raise is whether we haven't reached, precisely because of the phenomena you refer to, a point where the oppositional attitude now is rather to bring forward again the notion of human nature—in a new way, of course. I mean, with the commodification and mediatization of almost the entire human universe, there is the danger that anything the market or the media say will go for human nature, and you have to stand up somewhere and say that man isn't like that, all this is "against human nature," that the desires mobilized by the mediatized market are false desires, faked desires, and so on. And in the ecology session we were talking about the need to reintroduce use values into the critique of political economy. Now if you are going to bring in the concept of use value and still make some kind of science of the critique of political economy, you'd have to find a way of quantifying the use values, and you obviously couldn't do this unless the beings to whom those values are useful have a certain "nature"—changing, to be sure, but changing in a certain given way.*

**JAMESON:** Well, that was the scandalous position taken at the very beginning of the postmodern by Marcuse. His notion that there were false desires, false forms of gratification and even happiness was taken poorly by a great many populist Leftists, since it suggested that the philosopher-king could decide that lots of working-class people watching television only thought they were happy but were not really happy after all. But I think there remains a great deal that's powerful in Marcuse's way of thinking. My position, however, is a little different. I very much take the point of everything you are saying, but I think it goes back to a notion which has been lost (and this ties into my political perspective which I mentioned in the beginning)—the loss not only of a vision of socialism but of a vision of the transformation of human beings that was a crucial part of socialists. That was, I think essentially a modern matter, a modernist matter; the moderns in their various ways and all the great classical socialisms had a picture of the transformation of human beings in a future society—of a certain utopian transformation of the self as well as of the social world—and therefore their conception of human nature was a conception of new human possibilities in the future. That's what one finds in the early Marx, even though Marx is of course notoriously reluctant to spell these things out. But that evocation of the potentialities of human beings under radically different circumstances—if one could recapture *that*, then I think one would have the right set of coordinates on a possible human nature in the terms of which judgments could be made on what the Frankfurt School calls degradation of culture, the commodification, repression, Gramscian subalternity and the like. Nature must stand in a dialectical relationship with Utopia and with the time of the future, rather than involving a deduction of a static human nature here and now which is somehow being commodified or vulgarized by contemporary society.

**PAIK:** *Let's now come to the question of periodization—of realism to modernism to postmodernism, which as you say you base on Mandel's scheme concerning capitalism. The difficulty I have with this periodization is that it lumps together under "realism" two periods which someone like Lukács would consider crucially different. As you well know, Lukács finds most of the great realists before 1848—and 1848 for him is the great watershed. Of course, he finds exceptions like Tolstoy who comes later because he is a Russian, and so on, but given your periodization, the distinction he is very keen on making between authentic realism and naturalism would be lost sight of.*

**JAMESON:** Lukács has meant a great deal to me, and not least in thinking about these matters. I think that Lukács, although he is profoundly hostile to the modern, which he sees dialectically as the culmination of naturalism and symbolism, nonetheless provides some very interesting and suggestive descriptions of it. One can take those over and use them in other ways without his particular value judgments. Now, for him 1848 is important ideologically and politically in the sense that it means the emergence of the first glimpse of a possible working-class culture and therefore the first moment in which bourgeois universalism must then recognize its own class limits and class guilt or else must pass over into that other culture as Marx himself did. I think that the crucial account of the difference between Balzac and Flaubert in this respect is very important. All that is very powerful in Lukács. But as the Tolstoy example suggests, I think one has to understand this as a matter of the unequal rates of speed in the various national situations, and then also, not merely unequal rates of speed but also superimposed developments, so that a realistic art along with conditions that correspond to the older capitalism persist in the middle of a later kind of economic organization and culture, just as today (to come back to the stage I add on to Lukács, namely, postmodernism) it's plausible to argue that even in the third world one gets a postmodern veneer of some sort and certain kinds of postmodern production. Here, however, there persists productivity, and then one even has enclaves of older kinds of production too, and those things coexist both economically and culturally. So I think that complexifies Lukács's schema and makes it somewhat less peremptory and judgmental. He takes into account Tolstoy; the other very great realist author—for me almost the greatest, although in Lukács's sense a little tainted by naturalism—he never mentions at all, and that is Pérez Galdós in Spain, who is writing in the 1880s to the 1920s. But I think if one made this a little less rigid, one could accommodate some of these surcharges, discontinuities, and overlaps.

Now I also believe we have to rethink naturalism. I haven't found any theory of naturalism that is satisfactory to me. There is a return to some of the naturalist writers in the United States after a long period of neglect. I consider Dreiser a realist, but we have some very strange naturalists as well, like Norris. Some recent writers have begun to see naturalism as an interesting social but also psychic-formal symptom: there is a beautiful description by Gilles Deleuze, in his new books on film, of filmic naturalists (Buñuel and Stroheim) and their combination of deep psychic unconscious fetishism and attention to certain zones of the social, which also seems to me very suggestive in connection with Zola. The other thing about naturalism which is very important—you will tell me if this is wrong—but my impression is that when one is talking about the export of the Western novel and the arrival of the Western novel in the East or the third world generally, it is not Lukács's realism we are talking about, but it is Zola and naturalism. The naturalist novel was as powerful a Western and indeed a French invention and export as the automobile or the cinema. And therefore coming to terms with naturalism may involve doing more things than Lukács was willing to do. My understanding is that one of the reasons Lukács attacked naturalism so severely was that it was, for him, living in the Moscow of the 1930s, a code word for socialist realism, so that his attacks may have meant more in the situation of the Soviet Union than they did in the West, largely because Western literature had advanced beyond naturalism at that point.

**PAIK:** *To a student of English literature, which in a very inadequate way I am, the year 1848 is bound to be somewhat less significant than it is to Lukács, and also as an admiring reader of D. H. Lawrence, T. S. Eliot, and other moderns, I have strong disagreements with Lukács's specific discriminations—to which I could add some philosophical quarrels as well. But I think what is important is his attempt to distinguish those realist works which adhere to what you would call a totalizing vision—or, to draw on an observation in* The Political Unconscious, *those works that succeed in producing "the privileged narrative forms" in which the modernist "strategy of containment" does not operate—and those other works which fail to do so. Now, I think you are correct in saying that the naturalist novels have the greatest impact when they are introduced to the third world countries not previously familiar with the Western novelistic tradition, but I doubt that this invalidates Lukács's basic point. For one thing, I believe the naturalist novels have that kind of impact because they are perceived by the readers as addressing precisely those total questions, questions concerned with their whole destiny including the political destiny of the nation. And in this connection I recall a remark in the autobiography of Richard Wright, where he relates how deeply he was moved by reading the works of Dreiser, Norris, Sinclair Lewis, and so on, because they seemed to speak directly to his own life situation—which of course may be said to share many third world characteristics. Another point is that naturalism as something of a simplification of Lukács's realism would be more accessible in the initial stage of contact with the Western novel.*

**JAMESON:** I think you are right to insist on the category of totality. This is Lukács's great contribution to the study of novelistic form, I believe, and yet perhaps one can use it in other ways than he does. Surely looking at some of the classics of the modern, if you think of *Ulysses*—if there was ever an attempt to mold an image of social totality, it was that. So one can sometimes use Lukács against himself. I would like to do it like this. That is, I would like to say that the artist attempting (just to speak crudely) to produce a model of totality, not to say a representation of totality, is always working against certain given limits in his society which prevent its subjects from perceiving the social totality. A society grows more complex and as capitalism develops, the access to a picture of social totality is increasingly difficult, and it is according to that dialectic that one observes the transformations of art. In the realist period we have a socially simpler situation in which a vision of totality can be achieved with relatively more accessible narrative strands and constructs; in the modernist period, however—and one of the determining features of modernism is specifically to raise the issue of representation as the crucial one—there is a crisis in the possibility of representing the totality, whence these extraordinary modernist formal attempts to reinvent that in an imperialist world system where it is increasingly difficult to show how things fit together. Now in our global system I would say we've reached yet a third realm of difficulty; and here, if one had any political judgment to make on the current forms of postmodernism, it is that they have given this attempt up altogether—that is, they have now decided that representation is impossible, that totality doesn't exist, and consequently what made for the tensions and the ambitions of realism and modernism alike in their distinct situations is gone. I don't think that's necessarily a permanent thing; there will be political postmodernisms. There will surely be postmodernisms that attempt once again to rise to this task of somehow making a model or having a vision of a global system, and at the end of the essay "Postmodernism; or, The Cultural Logic of Late Capitalism," I propose a notion—the word has had some currency, I don't know if the concept has caught on—of what I call "cognitive mapping," which was meant to suggest that our task today as artists or critics or whatever is somehow to attempt to recapture or reinvent a new form of representation of this new global totality.

**PAIK:** *Lukács's contention was that the modernist writers, those you call the "high modernist" ones, had already given up on this attempt to capture the social totality. Now, you and I agree that he was unfair to many of these people, but his point seems more applicable, as you yourself suggest, to the postmodernist writers than to the high modernists. So in a way one might rephrase your point and say—I believe you have actually gone so far as to say "postmodernism is in some sense* more *modern than modernism"—but why couldn't one go a step further and say, postmodernism is a* purer form *of modernism than high modernism, indeed, in the same sense in which Mandel says late capitalism is a stage of purer capitalism than the previous ones.*

**JAMESON:** Well, that's an attractive formula that certainly allows us to rewrite Lukács to a certain degree since one can then transfer many of his critiques of modernism that one would not otherwise absolutely agree with and see those as prophetic of postmodernism. One always had the feeling in Lukács that he was preaching to these modernist writers and assuring them that the solution was either joining the party outright or at least having some sympathy with it (like Thomas Mann) as a condition of salvation. I don't know what would be our current recommendation, but certainly it seems to me implicit in this diagnosis that without some very keen sense of political and economic crisis itself, the postmodern artist cannot achieve this image of totality because there is no longer any point or motivation to do so. That is, this form of cognitive mapping is essentially politically, fully as much as aesthetically, motivated.

**PAIK:** *I think the main virtue of rephrasing it that way would be to salvage Lukács's main point, which is that the issue of his "realism" versus "modernism" remains the continuing and central struggle from the beginning of the capitalist age until it is overcome. And this has a special attractiveness for many of us Korean writers, because here we have the experience of the modern and postmodern pouring in at once, or almost at once, and primarily in the form of neocolonial cultural invasion. We realize, of course, that we can't deal with this situation simply by going back to our traditional forms or by adopting the older forms of Western art and literature such as the nineteenth-century forms of realism, but we are very committed that we should have some kind of realism in the sense of keeping alive this totalizing vision, which should pass through all these new influxes without quite submitting to them. So in that sense we are after something which may be called postmodern realism—but in this case changing the spelling a bit to indicate that we want to go beyond both high modernism and postmodernism. Maybe we need a new name altogether, but in this connection I came upon something in your essay on the Lukács-Brecht debate which I found fascinating. Well, let me read it to you from the volume* Aesthetics and Politics: *"In these circumstances, indeed, there is some question whether the ultimate renewal of modernism, the final dialectical subversion of the now automatized conventions of an aesthetics of perceptual revolution, might not simply be . . . realism itself! . . . In an unexpected dénouement, it may be Lukács—wrong as he might have been in the 1930s—who has some provisional last word for us today." Now, I find that very attractive.*

**JAMESON:** Of course, I wrote that before postmodernism had surfaced as a reality and a concept, so it would be perhaps a little more complicated now. My sense is this—I wish I could speak in any way about Korean literature, and I hope to remedy that ignorance insofar as we have translations, and we certainly need more of those—but my sense is that first of all there are ways in which a multidimensional third world social reality may be more interesting for an artist today than an increasingly one-dimensional first world one. That explains to me why in my observation—and I don't know whether this is so in Korea, but it is certainly so in China and in many other parts of the world—the most influential novelistic form anywhere is that of the Latin Americans, García Márquez in particular. Now, I would add—and I don't do this out of chauvinism or anything, but because I think it's significant—that in my opinion García Márquez also comes out of Faulkner, and that therefore Faulkner for a great many reasons has shown a new mode of narrative possibilities and certain kinds of realism, which has been maybe the most decisive global influence since the naturalists. At least this is the idea that I came to talk to Chinese writers about when I was in China a few years ago, who at the time were experimenting with a new kind of novel that they called the "roots" movement. My sense was this—and it's very consistent with Lukács's descriptions of the eighteenth and nineteenth centuries—that their forms of social realism before that had been static ones of the social surface and that one of the things that the Cultural Revolution did in China was to create a profound, deep sense of history and of historical scars and transformation; so that what they found in Faulkner and then in García Márquez was a new kind of narrative apparatus that allowed the writer both to register the social surface and also, like a seismograph, to pick up the ongoing influence of this deeper history. Now your history is obviously even more catastrophic and traumatic than that, and I would see that as being the fulfillment of Lukács's thesis: Lukács moves from the way in which the English eighteenth century perceives the surface of society to Scott's and Balzac's discovery of deeper history and how one integrates that. That seems to be what we are seeing recapitulated here on a much vaster scale, in the sense that you have postmodern realities as well as ancient peasant realities and all the strata in between. A Lukácsean realism would thereby be immensely more complicated.

**PAIK:** *Absolutely. Ours is surely another instance of Ernst Bloch's* Gleichzeitigkeit des Ungleichzeitigen *[syncronicity of the nonsynchronous], and while this could of course be simply an ephemeral moment before we are integrated to the one-dimensional global society, nobody who is seriously committed to praxis can accept that kind of defeatism in advance. So I would like to think that we do have a rare historical opportunity, which may no longer be available to the first world, for achieving and sustaining a totalizing vision. I find that in your reply to critics in the latest issue of* New Left Review[1] *you refer to the conditions of possibility for the kind of totalizing thought that would produce a concept like "modes of production"; and in* *many ways, García Márquez's Latin America, or even Faulkner who comes from a backward region—*

**JAMESON:** A backward region of the United States, yes, a third world part of the United States.

**PAIK:** *Very close in some ways to the conjunctures you mention in that article, like the Scottish Enlightenment or prerevolutionary France.*

**JAMESON:** Yes, absolutely, I agree with that.

**PAIK:** *Well, then, in this conjuncture of ours, the national struggle, the national question, and the concept of a national literature happen to be very important to us. But I believe these are terms which don't have much meaning to most of the intellectuals in the West. Of course, they shouldn't be meaningful in the old ways, but what would be your reaction to this?*

**JAMESON:** I've been very struck by this in Korea, and this is another matter that I must think more about. I guess my principal frame of reference for a positive conception of nationalism lies in embattled situations like that of the Palestinians, where nationalism is obviously progressive; but in terms of a postrevolutionary situation I have been most impressed with the role of nationalism in Cuba and the way in which a Cuban nationalism, a sense of Cuban exceptionalism, has gone hand in hand with the construction of socialism, has not been xenophobic, has been able, for example, to frame multiple personalities for the Cubans so that they feel themselves to be part of Latin America; they feel themselves to be part of that very different thing the Caribbean; they feel themselves to be a black country linked to Africa; and they feel themselves also very close to us the North Americans since we were in effect their last colonizers. So it seems to me that a powerful sense of the unity of the national situation does not necessarily involve xenophobia or narrowness but can be a whole opening to both political praxis and very vigorous kinds of cultural expression, something which seems uniquely the case here in Korea. I'm tempted to say if the first world doesn't understand this—and it's clear why, except for the strange case of Japan, the superstate in the United States or this new Europe has really no place for this kind of thing—then too bad for the first world: that is to say, there are realities that it needs to think about some more, and those are the index of its blind spots and its repressions and the things it doesn't want to know about in the outside world.

**PAIK:** *Would you care to comment on the relevance of this issue to the second world also? You've discussed Cuba, of course, but that's as much third world as second.*

**JAMESON:** Obviously the Soviet Union is a federation which has to think about these things in another way. Then one would have to compare the German example—but of course Germany has a tradition of having non-national states, Prussia was not a national state, so that, with respect the viability of the socialist Germany of the East, the German Democratic Republic, there are precedents in German history for non-national formations that maybe do not really exist in other parts of the world.

**PAIK:** *I think that's one of the major differences between the German case and the Korean, for we did have a unified national life for many, many centuries before the division in 1945. Another important difference would be that the division of Germany had at least some legitimacy or historical rationale in that it was punishment meted out to a powerful aggressor and in a way a measure to prevent the repetition of the same tragedy, whereas Korea was a victim of Japanese aggression—*

**JAMESON:** Jon Halliday has put that even more strongly in saying that the occupation and division that should have been visited on Japan were transferred to you.

**PAIK:** *Right. So there is a very strong feeling throughout Korea demanding reunification; I am sure I can speak for most Koreans, North and South, that we do have this feeling. But of course to have the feeling is not the same thing as to see the way to the thing or to have a theory for realizing it. Now, one of the difficulties is that the country has been divided for nearly a half century, and much more violently and rigidly, too, than the two Germanies, and as a result we have two very different social formations, perhaps even different kinds of nationalisms in spite of a very strong common national feeling. But in either case, I think the nationalism is a progressive one, even though there is involved a certain amount of xenophobia.*

*In any case, Korean nationalism has to be progressive because, for one thing, it has to take an oppositional stance towards the hegemonic powers that do not want to see the country reunified. Also, it's inherently impossible to get most Koreans to agree that any kind of reunification would be desirable. This is a point which so far hasn't received enough open debate in*

*Korea, but it is obvious, for instance, that a good many South Koreans would not want reunification on North Korean terms, at least insofar as these have become known to them, and the North Koreans would certainly oppose any idea of—well, we used to have the slogan of "Marching North and reunifying the country," and they would no doubt oppose that. So we need to work out a solution, a practicable response to the common national feeling which would serve the real interests of the Korean people, that is to say, the preponderant majority of the population both North and South. The problem is that while we are in many ways still a single nation with a long history of unified life and an acute sense of that history, we have had two virtual nation-states, or rather seminational states, for over forty years now, with two almost diametrically opposed social systems, and therefore with different individual and collective experiences. So how does one work out a solution which will satisfy both the common and the inevitably heterogeneous aspirations and yet manage to be practical? This makes the Korean case quite exceptional, but I think here we have rather a confirmation of your original point that Korea in being apparently exceptional may in fact be more typical, because we really face the same kinds of problems when we try to solve the difficulties facing the entire world today.*

JAMESON: It's as though you had two distinct opportunities for social transformation, as though it were given to Korea to have two lives at the same time, so to speak, which could involve a very rich set of possibilities.

PAIK: *But would you care to elaborate on your original remark about Korea's being not so much an anomaly as a classical example?*

JAMESON: I always try to make it clear, in my version of development or "stages" theory, that the stages coexist, overlap, and that one must not think of these things as separate. But in most theories of stages, one posits distinct kinds of politics that are relative to the stages themselves: wars of national liberation, and relatively nationalist struggles, that would be the stage of decolonization; socialist revolutions would be another type; now perhaps we can foresee struggles against a whole postmodern apparatus of domination or globalization that would again be distinct from those. And so what tends to happen as one looks around the world is that in poor third world countries one sees wars of national liberation with the nationalist dominant; in more advanced countries, labor struggles and issues of class domination. But in most places these seem to be separate, whereas in South

Korea they all seem to be taking place in the same social space. This is both an advanced and a third world country in some sense, the way places like Cuba and China are both second and third world countries. I think that's very interesting and it seems to me rather exceptional.

**PAIK:** *Korea is exceptional above all in being a divided country, and I think the division has—*

**JAMESON:** So that you are in a way both first, second, *and* third world—

**PAIK:** *Yes, yes, exactly. So the problems of all these worlds are concentrated here. Well, let me give you my sense of Korea's exceptionalism and typicality. You mention in your reply to critics "local struggles and issues are not merely indispensable, they are unavoidable; but . . . they are effective only so long as they also remain figures or allegories for some larger systemic transformation." Now, whether you take the level of South Korean society by itself or that of the two Koreas, the national struggle for reunification is an unavoidable, perhaps the unavoidable, local issue, but this particular national struggle happens to have certain inbuilt guarantees that it cannot succeed in the old-fashioned nationalist way—if only because we have more than one nationalism (perhaps it isn't even a case of two nationalisms, but something more like one and a half). And thus the social content of the nationalism or nationalisms becomes much more important than in a "less exceptional" national or decolonization struggle. At the same time, connections with larger worldwide issues turn out to be inevitable—for instance, in the fact that the two Koreas belong to different ideological blocs, and thus questions arising from the division of the world system into two contending blocs is superimposed on the local issue. And then, too, when you are to think of any concrete situation with any measure of concreteness, you have to look not only at the society within the national border and the world system as a whole, but also at the intermediate regional configuration. In our case it involves Japan and China, and the Soviet Union, and inevitably the United States.*

**JAMESON:** Yes, inevitably!

**PAIK:** *So even at the regional level you have practically every one of the prime agents in the world scene. And then, coming back to the question of division, in our case there is not only the regional but peninsular configuration to take into account—which is more than a configuration, I think it's actually* *a system of two sharply contending but sometimes perhaps also colluding state apparatuses. So one has to be able to think at once of the part (South Korea) and the whole (the contemporary world in its concreteness), and also to think of the Korean peninsula as both one and two—a dialectical feat which I assume everyone in today's world has to learn if he or she is to carry out the local struggle in the successful manner that you call for.*

JAMESON: Yes. I would like to say something more about this later, but I wish you would repeat here what you were telling me the other day about industrialization and Confucianism—that is, whether here and in Taiwan, Singapore, and so on, Confucianism as a substitute for the Protestant ethic is sufficient explanation for the tremendous industrial takeoff in these parts of East Asia.

PAIK: *No, I don't think it's a sufficient explanation, although I do agree that Confucianism had something to do with the kind of economic success that the so-called Asian NICs [newly industrialized countries] have had. Only, the curious thing is that people who are touting this Confucian ethic as a key to development are in many cases the same ones who were saying a few decades ago that East Asia—except for Japan, which had a feudal system like the European—was not successfully industrializing because of the Confucian ideology, the solution presumably being for us to turn into Christians as rapidly as possible. But as I say, I agree Confucianism was an important factor, especially in securing the relatively high level of national integration and education of the population in these societies. But I believe that even more crucial was the strategy of the global capital, and in this connection I recall an interesting remark by William Hinton criticizing Deng Xiaoping's strategy of development, which according to Hinton is an attempt to emulate South Korea, of course without giving up Communist party control; and he says this won't work because the primary reason for South Korea's success was the fact that China had gone socialist, and (says Hinton) if Brazil were a socialist country, Panama would now be an economic power.*

JAMESON: Very funny!

PAIK: *Of course it's an exaggeration, and Hinton probably meant it as such; I don't think Panama has the kind of infrastructure to make it another Taiwan or South Korea. But I do believe there is a valid point to it: I mean, the United States doesn't have the kind of strategic stake in seeing, say, Mexico or*

*Brazil become successful economies as it does in the case of South Korea; also the United States or a reigning multinational capital would be more afraid of Brazil developing a really successful national economy.*

**JAMESON:** Yes, and I think you also insist on the fact that division is very significant in South Korea or Taiwan, that perhaps it prevents the takeoff miracle state from becoming a nation which would then have power in its own right to pose dangers to—

**PAIK:** *That's right. On the one hand, the world capital cannot afford to have an economic debacle in these lands—not that it can afford a real debacle in Brazil or Mexico, either, but at least it could live with much more obvious failures there—and on the other hand, with the kind of built-in military and political dependency ensuing from division, it can tolerate a good deal of economic success on the part of these countries.*

**JAMESON:** Now, what I want to say about all this is, first of all, that my description of postmodernism in general, this whole moment in general, is characterized by a new significance of space as opposed to time or temporality in the modern. One of the most interesting newer forms of Marxism emerging is coming from radical geographers and is what I would call a spatial Marxism, an analysis of both the urban and of geography, and of geopolitics. It seems to me that that kind of spatial analysis is something to be developed and would be squarely in the line of what you are calling for here, because the way you are laying out the Korean situation is essentially in this newer sense a spatial dialectic.

**PAIK:** *That's very interesting, and I confess spatial Marxism is an area which is new to me. Up to now I've been rather uncomfortable with all this talk about space and spatiality in postmodernism as opposed to a presumed importance of time in high modernism, because at least one of the main tendencies of capitalism is to abolish space and turn everything into time—in the Marxian sense that finally all value is a matter of temporality. So the emphasis on space would be significant only if it is in opposition to this general trend, an attempt to recover the concreteness of space that capitalism makes disappear.*

**JAMESON:** Yes, that's precisely what I wanted to say. One of the features of this shift is that in the postmodern there is a new kind of dialectic between internationalism and regionalism; and it seems to me that's a new kind of link as well as an opposition that is that the attachment to the region very often meant a regressive politics, whereas today it may not, and it may in fact be very closely linked to a sense of the whole international dimension. It is an idea which suggests some of the benefits of this new kind of spatial thinking.

**PAIK:** *I see it does tie in very well with what we were discussing—not only about economic development but about nationalism as well. So perhaps we may now turn more particularly to the concept of "national literature," a topic of rather intense debate with us. Its proponents at least (including myself) see it as quite compatible with internationalism, indeed necessary to any desirable conception of world literature. I know you are not yet very familiar with how the concept actually works out in the Korean context, but I would like nevertheless to have some of your thoughts on it.*

**JAMESON:** This is a period in which the counterpart to multinational capitalism and its organization of global relations has to be, on the part of the Left and a progressive culture, an internationalization as well. I have pointed out that in Goethe's original description of "world literature," what seems to have been most prominent in his mind were the new media organs, like the journals that permitted contact between intellectuals in the various European countries, so that he, Goethe, would read the *Edinburgh Review*, the *Revue des deux mondes*, and be in closer touch with intellectuals in other national situations. "World literature" was then for him that set of relations, and not simply the emergence of great world classics.[2] If something like that could be imagined it would be a way of respecting the primacy of the national situation and also making it possible for an international network of intellectuals and cultures very much in the spirit of the dialectic I just mentioned between the regional and the international. It may be that today the powerful construction of a national culture is an act of internationalism rather than a withdrawal from the international situation. I tried in another place to push a slogan which was "the internationalism of national situations" and which proposed that our intellectual and cultural relations to each other *pass through* the primacy of the national situation understood in the larger sense, through the concrete regional situation, and that we would understand each other through those situations rather than in some timeless way from masterpiece to masterpiece. So if the Korean project is that of producing a "national literature," then the most important thing would be perhaps to think that such a literature has not yet existed, that the creation of a national literature in this new sense is a wholly new process that may not really have significant precedents, and that we are not talking about older forms of national culture at all but the forging of a whole new one in a whole new global situation, in which then that act may have a special paradigmatic value.

**PAIK:** *If such a project is to have any measure of success, don't you think we would need a more precise sense of the extent to which the so-called global capital is global, and where it is not yet that global after all—*

**JAMESON:** This is the matter of unevenness, the "synchronicity of the non-synchronous," which makes me think of a remark of Sartre's that has to do with publics. (We already are developing in the area of film, which is more immediate, a more sophisticated international public for the reception of a variety of cultures, but the literary is more difficult because of language and the problem of the translations.) But Sartre remarks in *What Is Literature?* that it's much better for the writer to have to address two or more publics at once: if you have only one public, then you know what they know, certain kinds of efforts need not be made; but to address several publics, a number of things have to be mobilized to explain what is not tacit knowledge and to transfer social meanings to publics to which they are alien. So there may be a sense in which a newly emergent global cultural public amounts to just such a chance for writers in a variety of national situations. I can imagine the life experience of a remote village that's still relatively traditional where today in 1989 people are living in ways that are still analogous to the 1920s or even the nineteenth century. Now I can see that writers of an older period, even if their project was only to register village life as such, would have described those realities differently than a writer today who describes the survival of this village life in a world from which most of it has vanished. That is to say, that the global perspective would transform the representation of those older and more traditional realities. In other words, part of the development of new realism may involve not so much a change in techniques and content as a shift in the whole perspective in which this content is embedded in our new global systems.

**PAIK:** *In other words, "cognitive mapping" is quite crucial.*

**JAMESON:** Well, that remains my thought.

**PAIK:** *Now, let's come to the old question of "what is to be done." Of course you've already mentioned cognitive mapping, and I was interested to see in your* New Left Review *reply that you sort of came out and admitted that this was translatable as "class consciousness"—*

**JAMESON:** But class consciousness on a new global scale, in ways we don't yet have the categories for.

**PAIK:** *Yes. But you must be aware that there are critics of your work who find it insufficiently related to concrete political practice. For instance, Neil Larsen in his very interesting introduction to the collected volumes of your essays* [The Ideologies of Theory] *remarks that while your notion of ideology is very fruitful, it leaves out or at least tends to neglect the canonical notion of "intervention" and thus limits the practical relevance of your work. Would you care to respond to that?*

**JAMESON:** Well, look, when one is talking about politics, one should always remember there are multiple politics—we are engaged in lots of them—and there is no single-shot definition of what is to be done that really is satisfactory. So on one level for me it's very important, as I tried to say at this conference, to participate in the reinvention of some conception of socialism which is appropriate to the new global situation. On the level of internationalism, it's important for us to forge a whole new network of intellectuals in the way that we are doing right now, a worldwide network of intellectuals—I think that's crucial. Larsen's objection surprises me in the sense that I have often said that there still existed ideology in the bad sense, false consciousness of the classic stamp. I've tried to insist a little more within the first world situation of media culture on ways in which the Utopian and symbolically political impulses were expressed in the media. Indeed, maybe now we've insisted so much on the Utopian dimensions of these things that we should insist more again on the more classical ones of mystification and false consciousness and so forth. The original study of the media on the Left essentially came from that perspective, because the media was seen as a very fundamental reason for the explanation of the failure of the working class to develop the appropriate revolutionary consciousness and to seize power in the West. That is, culture and consciousness began to be studied by Western Marxism essentially in the effort to explain the failure of a mass political movement and, of course, also the arrival of fascism.

I think we can't transfer these completely to the postmodern situation, but I would certainly hate to have us lose that negative and critical dimension that was present in those things. But it's much harder to sustain a kind of uncompromising negative critique of false consciousness in a situation in which—and I'm talking about the United States now—one doesn't really have the makings of a mass political movement in terms of which one could make that critique. So that obviously conditions what intellectuals in the United States can do, but I think there is for us in the first world a whole dimension of the critique of culture that must be sustained, and that's another very important task.

Finally, I thought that this was a moment—and I know a little bit for the visual arts and from contacts, friends, writers in science fiction—that this was a moment in which maybe again critics could, if not make suggestions to the artists, at least participate in the coming into being of new art. For a long time Stalinism and what resulted from that made us reluctant to offer any suggestions to artists; this may again be a period in which that kind of collaboration may be possible, as in hypothetical projects for different kinds of cultural politics. Meanwhile, it does not seem superfluous, particularly in the context of this particular discussion, to observe that a new emphasis on and a new openness to a properly global cultural production—to Nicaraguan poetry, say, fully as much as to US writing, to the modern Korean tradition as much as to that of continental and Western Europe—ought to function politically too, if only to sensitize its readership to the role of the United States in all these places and to form readers who are also militant opponents of North American interventionism. Indeed, Paul Sweezy recently, in a rather bleak mood, suggested that preventing intervention and supporting liberation movements in other countries was just about *all* the US Left could hope to accomplish nowadays: I hope there's more, but it should be clear that the study and teaching of so-called third world literature has a significant part to play in achieving that much. And finally, philosophically, the preservation and development of a dialectical way of thinking about things as over against a dominant positivism, or a one-dimensional technological thought, is also a very crucial matter.

**PAIK:** *Let me now end with a directly personal question. How do you feel this project of preserving a dialectical mode of thought is faring in your immediate surroundings? Do you feel it is going well, better than it used to, or that even this is being increasingly co-opted by the mediatized universe?*

**JAMESON:** I think it's dialectical to hope that one is often spurred on to make stronger statements in a situation in which one is in a minority and under adverse conditions. I've just gone back to the Frankfurt School and finished a long book on Adorno, about whom I think a good deal more positively than I have at some moments in the past, and this is a first attempt of mine to return to and describe a certain dialectic. I am teaching Marx's *Grundrisse* right now and working with Marx's own text and Hegel again. So I hope that part of my current work will lead me back to the dialectic itself and to newer ways of projecting it, and I think I wouldn't be doing so unless the dialectic seemed, so to speak, an endangered species.

NOTES

1. Fredric Jameson, "Marxism and Postmodernism," *New Left Review* 176 (1989): 31–46; reprinted in *"The Cultural Turn"* (Verso, 1998), 33–48.

2. Fredric Jameson, "Third World Literature in the Era of Multinational Capitalism," *Social Text* 15 (1986): 65–88.

# Interview with Sabry Hafez, Abbas Al-Tonsi, and Mona Abousenna

**HAFEZ:** *What is the impact of what you termed, in* Marxism and Form, *a Hegelian kind of Marxism on the development of the new critical discourse, particularly that which is written in English? Could you identify some of its tenets which have been assimilated in the contemporary mainstream criticism, or in other words, been accepted into the established critical canon?*

**JAMESON:** I don't think it's particularly important to retain the word "Hegelian." There are a number of other slogans for what's also sometimes called "Western Marxism," which has generally been defined by way of its difference from so-called "Soviet Marxism" or "dialectical materialism" as involving an increased emphasis on facts of consciousness and culture. There are many reasons why Marxists in the West have felt it important to do this, most obviously as an explanation for the failure of revolution in the West after the 1920s and the increasing role of cultural apparatuses such as, in our time, television and the media in the ideological policing of working-class people.

I will, however, say a few more things about the word *Hegelian*. The meaning of the word is obviously going to vary according to the stereotype one has about Hegel. I think that the polemics waged by Louis Althusser in the 1960s against Hegel are no longer of much significance for us for a whole set of reasons. In any case, what he meant by Hegel was idealism, and clearly I was not proposing a return to idealism. But a number of studies of Marx's own texts have shown that these texts are dialectical in a deeper

This interview was carried out in writing in the fall of 1989. It first appeared as Sabry Hafez, Abbas Al-Tonsi, and Mona Abousenna, "On Contemporary Marxist Theory: An Interview with Fredric Jameson," *Alif: Journal of Comparative Poetics* 10 (1990): 114–31. © The Department of English and Comparative Literature, The American University in Cairo. Reprinted with permission of the Department of English and Comparative Literature, The American University in Cairo.

sense than had hitherto been suspected, and that therefore they reveal not so much an influence of Hegel, but a development of what Hegel glimpsed in a whole range of new ways.

Let me simply say rapidly what I think the difference between a Hegelian and a non-Hegelian approach might be. Bourgeois philosophy imagines that its language is able directly to model the world, and therefore it seeks to immediately formulate the structure and nature of reality. In Hegel, there is always the sense that we never have immediate contact with the outside world, but that contact is always mediated by our own concepts which have their own logic and their own history. Therefore the task of philosophy is not a one-dimensional one in which we seek to register and represent reality directly, but rather to take two paths simultaneously. It must seek to characterize the outside world, in this case the structure of late capitalism, and at the same time it must seek to understand the limits of the concepts with which we do that understanding, and those limits are of course, at least in part, ideological and shaped by our formation within the very social world that we are seeking to understand.

Therefore, if one wanted to make a defense of this slogan of Hegelianism, as you seem to suggest I should, it would be that this approach obliges us to try to grasp the ideological limits of our own consciousness and its intellectual categories at the same time that it continues to grapple with the task of understanding the social and historical world which is outside us and which is our reality.

I would finally add that there are signs that a new way of reading Marx through Hegel is in a process of reappearing after the Althusserian period. Part of this may be understood to be reaction against Althusserianism in itself, and also against the much more recent British school of analytic Marxism. Some of it derives from the Frankfurt School, and from the so-called Capitalogic group in Germany and elsewhere, and it will receive a great new impetus when the work of the Argentinean philosopher Enrique Dussell, on Marx's *Grundrisse* and the unpublished manuscripts, is more widely known.

**HAFEZ:** *Perestroika has removed some of the psychological barriers against Marxism; how do you see the impact of such removal on the development of critical methodology particularly in the largely conservative English speaking world? Do you expect it to affect a transformation of the Marxist literary canon similar to that which was brought about by the Russian Formalists or the Frankfurt School, in other words, do you envisage a radical change in the*

*Marxist literary canon towards a wider awareness and less crudely utilitarian understanding of modernist culture in the West?*

**JAMESON:** I would have said that perestroika removed many of the political objections to socialism or communism. As for Marxism as a mode of thought, I think that your question is not dialectical enough. It is precisely in a conservative, English-speaking world that a more radical kind of Marxist thinking has had to develop in opposition to that hegemonic set of values and as a reaction against it. While we expect enormous things from the revival of Russian culture, Russian traditions, and the participation of the Soviet intelligentsia in international intellectual life, it seems to me that it will be a while before they have a distinctive contribution to make to Marxist studies. That they will make such a distinctive contribution I have no doubt whatsoever. Bakhtin is of course an enormous monument and resource for the Soviet intellectuals to draw upon. For the moment, according to my observations, they are busy assimilating intellectual trends in the West, and I would imagine the more crucial issue today is whether these Russian intellectuals will be interested in Marxism at all in the immediate future, let alone in making their contribution to it.

One should also add after the current events in Eastern Europe that there are really two possible outcomes for many of the Eastern European countries, most particularly the German Democratic Republic, only one of which is ever mentioned in the newspapers—that is, of course, the reversion to the market and the selling out of nationalized industries to private business, and less often invoked, the enlistment of cheap Eastern European labor for big business in Western Europe, particularly after 1992. The other possibility, particularly in the two Germanys, would be the renewal of a very sharp ideological debate on the nature of socialism. It seems to me that this is now the moment, after the end of the wall of violence and repression, for the Germans in particular to describe positively the benefits of a socialism which has most often been caricatured as being unproductive and inefficient, stagnant, and lacking the technological level of Western private business. Something is surely still to be said for the choice of other priorities which include full employment, free medical care and education, and cradle-to-grave security for its citizens.

**HAFEZ:** *The older Marxist criticism, which you once described as "genetic," emphasized the historical evolution of art from ritual and religion. How can the new Marxist criticism with its emphasis on dialectics and various forms* *of oral tradition and folk fantasia, which is clearly manifested in a literature such as that of Latin America and some third world countries, posit a new concept of criticism? Or form a new critical canon and how?*

JAMESON: The question is a very interesting one. Obviously the objections to genetic criticism were, to many people, what looked to be a crudely evolutionist perspective in which early forms of oral songs gave way to more complex modes of the imitation of reality. It's a perspective one finds, for example, in art critics like Arnold Hauser or even in non-Marxists like my teacher Erich Auerbach. I hardly think we wish to go back to that form of evolutionism, particularly since what has transpired for us in the whole new postmodern era is the notion that in many ways the oral traditions and what used to be thought of as simpler forms are more complicated and more interesting than our own bourgeois forms. In any case, for the socialist tradition all of this raises the crucial matter which Ernst Bloch, among others, characterized as that of the *Erbe*, "tradition" or the "heritage": how a new socialist culture, which necessarily emerges from a regime of high industrial production, is to assimilate the cultures of the past and of other modes of production, and in the process become a genuine world culture. Lukács, of course, thought that socialist culture should include the classics of realism and of older, middle-class culture. For many people in the West as well as the East for whom the classics of middle-class culture are perhaps in the postmodern period not so attractive, this has always seemed to be an unnecessary traditionalism. Bloch's vision was much vaster, and involved a new kind of pantheon of the forms of human cultural production which would, I think, be much more attractive to us in the postmodern era.

HAFEZ: *How can you explain the increasing interest of the exponents of modern critical discourse, from the structuralists to the Marxists, in the literature of the third world? Is this a reaction to overemphasizing the elaboration of literary structure and a return to the concept of value? Is it a result of the relative stagnation in certain Western literatures? Or is it part of the process of rejuvenation of Western modern critical theory and has nothing to do with the "third world" as such? Is it possible to transfer the socioeconomic demarcation coined by the dominant "first world" into the realm of literature without the danger of imposition and displacement? Is the concept of "third world" literature a descriptive or normative one? And what makes it different from other literatures?*

**JAMESON:** In my opinion, the new interest in the culture fully as much as the literature of the third world comes into being simultaneously with postmodernism. It certainly has something to do with the development of that literature and culture itself, which is very rich all over the world, and which seems to me to have gone beyond its original realist and modernist stages. This also has something to do, I think, with the impoverishment of culture in a kind of standardized media society like this first world one, which is therefore tempted to reinvigorate itself perpetually and to restore its vitality by infusions of a more vital culture from the outside. One could also go into any number of parallels with postmodernism itself, which I think must have something to do with the simultaneity of the economic situation all over the world but which are nonetheless paradoxical and certainly not be understood as any kind of convergence between these two very different movements. The return to storytelling would be one of those. The disappearance of, let's say, "centered" or anthropomorphic characters would be another one. What's generally called textuality is of course a feature of all kinds of texts today, including media texts. So that, I suppose, one could argue fully as much for a radical break of many contemporary third world writers and cultural producers with their own pasts as one could for analogies with forms developing in the first world. I suppose that one must also stress the significance of language in all this. My own feeling is that the literature is the least significant area of production in Western postmodernism, and that clearly has something to do with the standardization of our languages by way of the media. My sense is that in many third world traditions (one doesn't want to generalize, obviously), language, eloquence in the older sense, the word as such, retains a prestige and a power that it has lost in late capitalism in the West, and that the linguistic material available to third world writers is therefore much more fruitful.

I'm not worried about the transfer of Western critical theory to the third world or to its context. It seems to me that third world critics are perfectly capable of knowing what to use, what to modify, and what to reject—and indeed are bound to modify all these things ceaselessly, just as we ourselves have modified everything that came to us from Europe. Or if you prefer, North Americans could make a similar argument, and of course they have done so in previous periods of their own history, about the importation of theory from Europe—something which could be extended into a general paradigm of importation from the outside, in some distant analogy with the eclecticism of the Roman Empire. As a matter of fact, I feel certain that we both are and will continue to get an increasing amount of theoretical production and new conceptuality from the former third world as we have from Europe in the past. So that at that point, third world theory will really *be* third world theory.

I do think that there is something crippling in overstressing the way in which we're all locked into our national situations. That can be a very healthy realization—the battles that some critics have had over foreign theory also sometimes expresses a struggle between intellectuals, people, groups who feel that their function has been usurped by other groups, and of course those struggles are also not to be taken lightly. On the other hand, I think that we do have things to say to each other, and that one of our tasks at least is to create some kind of new global cultural network, one which is certainly not free of antagonism and tension, but which allows us to speak together more directly. It would therefore be unwise to exaggerate the degree to which our critical ideas only project our own realities and are absolutely unable to have any purchase on the various kinds of external other reality that come before us, culturally or otherwise.

**AL-TONSI:** *Could you specify your understanding of "history" or "historicism" and its relationship to your view of "totality"? How does your concept of the "historical" relate to the subject-object and individual-social dichotomies? Terry Eagleton's reading of these issues in your writings led him to qualify your Marxism as Hegelian. Do you endorse such a judgment?*

**JAMESON:** I've already said something implicit about historicism in my Hegel answer as well as about totality, but it might be worth saying all that in a somewhat different way and connecting it to the answer to the previous question, because I think that the best way of making one's own thoughts and interpretations situational is not to lock oneself into some diagnosis of ethnocentrism but rather to be aware of one's historical situation and the way in which that I won't say relativizes, but at least marks one's point of view. Therefore I think the question of foreign theory is much better dealt with in a historicist manner. That would imply that one went back and looked at the internal national socioeconomic situation in which certain kinds of theories arose (I'm thinking, obviously, of some theories of the French 1960s, but there would be many others and other countries to look at). One can then analyze the conditions of possibility for that theory to travel across into other national situations and to play a part. That would, I think, not relativize the value of these theories in any banal sense of the word. It would leave them with their power and validity intact, but it would reduce that value locally, just as Einstein's theory of relativity is said to transform Newton's general laws into the local laws of a small corner of a much larger universe. That kind of historicizing, I think, is therapeutic and an excellent way for intellectuals to bring themselves up against a renewed consciousness of their own concrete situation before they start to look out across at that of others. So I would very strongly endorse the matter of historicism. I think that the Althusserian attack on it was needlessly motivated by the anxiety that if a relativity of the historical situation prevailed, then the scientific value of Marx and Marxism would ultimately be lost. I think that there is little danger of this. Some of the classics of Marxism—Lukács as well as Gramsci—were always well aware that according to some of their own paradoxical formulations, Marxism was the theory of capitalism and would lose its validity or its "truth," so to speak, when that ended and gave place to something else. I would agree with that form of historicizing and relativizing, but I don't think it will affect the validity of Marxism today. We have grown increasingly suspicious of Hegelian notions of self-consciousness and reflection and reflexivity, and I share some of those doubts and suspicions, but if we don't want that, then we need to have some other form of self-critical distance and that can only be found, I think, in the historicist attitude towards our own present as history. Totality plays a part in this insofar as totality is the supreme instrument for grasping the nature of one's own current situation or that of other people. Unless one's cultural critiques and social diagnoses are governed by at least the regulative idea of totality of the connecting everything together and seeing all of those things as part of one enormous process, what comes out is unlikely to be anything more than opinions or journalistic impressions. I've made this defense of totality in a number of places lately for the obvious reasons that these are truths not merely forgotten but maybe absolutely repressed in our day. One of the basic lessons of the Frankfurt School was indeed that the social totality today is more total than it was—that is to say, that the very logic of late capitalism is an absolutely totalizing one which wishes to penetrate everywhere and to make links with everything. Thus it is not our own love for this kind of thinking which drives us towards it, but the nature of the object and of the system itself. Surely this is true in the various disciplines, all of which are straining at their seams and feel the vocation to include the totality in deeper ways. Unfortunately, in most postmodern disciplines, so to speak, or in most disciplines in the postmodern period, that effort to transcend disciplinary boundaries generally takes the form of simple transcoding, borrowing of this or that, the transformation of one concept in one field into another one, metaphorical and intertextual uses of language from other fields, and so on. This is because there are very few models of what a totalizing grasp of the transdisciplinary object or the social totality would be; and I daresay that Marxism is probably the only one that remains valid and vigorous in the contemporary world.

**AL-TONSI:** *Let's confront now the crisis of Marxist literary criticism as exemplified in the theory of reflection and the relationship between superstructure and infrastructure. Isn't the concept of mediation(s), after all, circular and unable to penetrate the problematic? Can't you see that such conceptual constructs (as mediations) join sometimes the very core of idealism, where perception (and it is not enough to qualify it as collective perception) is mixed up with the object? Do you agree that the concept of reflection constitutes a misreading of Marxist dialectics because it focuses on dualism and presupposes a homogeneous, leveled totality inside each and every superstructure and base?*

**JAMESON:** Yes, I think that the notion of reflection or correspondence has long since been blown away by most modern Marxist approaches. My own masters in this respect were the writers of the Frankfurt School, in particular Adorno, for whom the basic clue as to the historicity of a work and its deeper relationship to its social context lay in the form of the text and the generic innovation involved in it, rather than in its content. On the other hand, I think that the danger for Marxist criticism today is that, having modernized itself in respects such as these and shed its antiquated doctrines of reflection and correspondence, it may lose its identity altogether and fade away into other approaches. I think that Marxist criticism must hold to the conception of ideological analysis, albeit in as elaborate and complex modern and postmodern ways as you like, and it must remain committed to the problem of something like a context, that is something like a connection between the text, or the cultural artifact, and its larger situation. How to prevent that from falling back into the kind of dualism you rightly denounce is, of course, a fundamental problem, which I would be tempted to approach by way of the dynamic form that I mentioned a moment ago.

**AL-TONSI:** *I would like to inquire as to how you arrived at Marxism and Marxist criticism? Could you also elaborate on your concept and view of Marxist criticism?*

**JAMESON:** At virtually the dawn of my independent intellectual life, I found myself mesmerized by a sentence of Mallarmé that I later on used as the motto to my book *Marxism and Form*. It ran like this, "il n'existe d'ouvert à la recherche mentale que deux voies, en tout, où bifurque notre besoin, à savoir, l'esthétique d'une part et aussi l'économie politique" [There are but two paths into which our need divides: aesthetics and also political economy]. On a weak reading, this could mean little more than a "bifurcation" of needs into the body and the mind or soul, or somewhat less reprehensibly, into work and leisure time—these two zones being governed by economics and culture, respectively. I have read more into it, and trust it will not be a matter of self-indulgence (or at least not merely a matter of self-indulgence) if I think it useful to pursue the relationship between Mallarmé's notion and what I have come to discover is my own conception of Marxism itself (an area in which Mallarmé's judgment is borne out very paradoxically indeed, since as Perry Anderson has observed, the most striking and significant recent products of Marxist research and thought have tended precisely to be the twin distant poles of the economic and the aesthetic).

This will also be the occasion to reflect on judgments I have made on ethics, which have been widely deplored, Cornel West reminding me quite properly of the force of the ethical in practical politics, while Jonathan Arac wisely observes that my attempt decisively to separate the ethical from the political will confirm all the worst stereotypical fears about the "immorality" of Marxism itself. What I wanted to achieve in this radical separation was a valorization of collective thought and logic over that purely individual kind that seems to predominate in ethical theories; the effort seemed to me cognate with any number of versions of the end of individualism and the death of the subject (as well as to approach certain theological traditions which it seems to me a misnomer to call ethical and which also have to do with the extinction of pride or even of the centered subject itself), and finally, with the relative neglect of the originality of collective action itself (which I was tempted to distinguish from the individual in a well-nigh ontological fashion).

I want now to reassert this same position, but by enlarging it in a way that may make its consequences somewhat clearer in unexpected directions. For I have only very slowly come to understand that if it was a matter of making myself clear to other people, the word *political*—that I sought sharply to distinguish from the word *ethical*—was likely not merely to be ineffective but even counterproductive. *Political* for a Marxist public had to do with practice as such and with forms of activity in which long terms and short terms were uniquely coordinated, in ways it would be too complicated to explain here, but which seem to me to justify the claim for a uniquely Marxian conception of politics (based on the uniquely Marxian concept of praxis). But for most people, I suspect that politics splits apart into two lower-level meanings, the first having simply to do with any kind of group action against institutions; the second having to do with political philosophy.

It is this second meaning I want to dwell on here, with the result of reviving many of the older stereotypical objections about Marxism, in particular the one that accuses Marxism of lacking a tradition of political reflection and even of repressing politics as such. There is a way in which this stereotype seems to me not merely justified but deserving of a certain measured celebration. Political philosophy, indeed, and not merely the tedious handbooks of its specialists and interpreters, seems to me par excellence the realm of sheer opinion, which is to say, in some rather negative sense, of ideology itself. Of opinion I have always held that it is the least interesting kind of thinking or expression; this is of course in me nothing but an opinion, although it is strengthened somewhat by Hegel's endorsement, in whom it might be expected to be something else and something more substantial. At any rate one comes to Marxism at least partly with the conviction that convictions themselves are formed at some deeper place than sheer opinion by realities other than conscious choices—realities of social class and of the unconscious, which have sometimes been what the word *ideology* designated (when it was not precisely used to designate the conscious effects of those convictions or beliefs in the realm of sheer opinion—this duality being another way of characterizing what is potentially unstable not only in the traditional concept of ideology but in anything else that seeks to cover the same field by substitution and transcoding).

But if the source of opinion—and of sheer ideology in its unstable, conscious, epiphenomenal forms—lies in this deeper ontological relationship to the real (which can of course be modified and transformed, in ideological conversion, on the occasion of radically new kinds of class experience), then the surface play of ideological effects and opinions is insubstantial, for all its very real practical consequences, and a doubtful foundation on which to base either a theory or a practice. Such opinions are what are generally thought to be political; and their range is equally expressed by the procedures and mannerisms of the textbooks that designate either modes of argument (that is to say, essentially of rationalization)—decisionism, consequentialism, teleologism—or "positions," which strangely resemble their philosophical or metaphysical opposite numbers, the Weltanschauungen or worldviews, of which we are plausibly told that there is a finite number, and which then open out into a set of combinations which one can adopt at will and optionally, like moves on a chessboard. It is this optionality of the worldviews (idealism, realism, materialism) or of the political philosophies (libertarianism, petty bourgeois radicalism) that marks them most securely as sheer opinion: not in the sense in which people can be asked to change them without notice; but in the sense that they are not primary phenomena, but rather accidents of a different kind of substance. As effects, they offer a source of activity to the mind, which can explore its opinions and sometimes discover unsuspected ones; or interbreed them and evolve new species of ideology, or fresh combinations of older opinionated features. The work on this great variety of "self-expression," its simplification and organization according to easily graspable oppositions or combinations, is a very interesting pastime indeed; but it should be called typology rather than "philosophy" (political or otherwise) and has little content in its own right unless one is interested in experiencing the traditional anthropological wonderment at the variety of human thought and opinion.

This "opinion" of mine leads to two kinds of conclusions: first, that Marxism is not a political philosophy of that kind, and in no way "on all fours" with conservatism, liberalism, radicalism, populism, or whatever. There is certainly a Marxist practice of politics (alluded to above), but political thinking in Marxism, when it is not practical in that way, has exclusively to do with the economic organization of society, and how people cooperate to organize production. This means that "socialism" is not exactly a political idea; or, if you like, that it presupposes the end of a certain political thinking. It also means that we do have our homologues among the bourgeois thinkers, but they are not the fascists (who have very little in the way of thought in that sense, and have in any case become historically extinct), but rather the neoliberals and the market people: for them also political philosophy is worthless (at least once you get rid of the arguments of the Marxist, collectivist enemy), and "politics" now means simply the care and feeding of the economic apparatus (in this case the market rather than the collectively owned and organized means of production). Indeed, I will argue later on the proposition that we have much in common with the neoliberals, indeed virtually everything—save the essentials.

But these conclusions now lead me to a second and to my mind more interesting interpretation of Mallarmé's sentence by which I was so long fascinated: it has to do with the determination of form by content (and thus in some way with the dialectic itself). What I have been calling the intolerable optionality of ethical thought or political Weltanschauungen can now be expressed in a different way by suggesting that each involves a play of concepts that seems to have no deeper determination by its content, to know none of the constraints of the historical situation or the resistances of matter itself. The doctrine of form and content, however, coordinates action and history (or on another paradigm, base and superstructure), by reading the creativity and possibilities, the invention, of the active term in the light of the limiting factors of the inert term or the fundamental situation itself. Only a certain number of projects and outcomes are possible, and if there is an ontology of Marxism it lies in the fact that through praxis and its determinate failures one confronts the very nature of Being itself (provided you grasp Being as a historical and changing, evolving process). From the perspective of Marxism, which is neither an ethics nor a politics, ethics and politics are profoundly determined by a deeper content, which is to be found in ideological commitment, social class, historical experience. On their own terms, and viewed within the limits of the semi-autonomous fields, each has itself sought to constitute that limit, that deeper content that is not visible and falls outside the analysis. This is why ethics and politics are superficial "sciences" and why Mallarmé was correct to oppose them to political economy and aesthetics, each of which is profoundly marked by the drama of content and the experience of limits, of the impossibility of forms and the constraints of historical development. These two "sciences" are in this sense profoundly homologous, in that each one requires a constant and dialectical shuttling back and forth between the form and the reality itself, the "concept" and its material elements and social-historical derivations. The structural similarity is then further confirmed by the consummation of both in a certain Marxism, which alone and for the first time reveals and theorizes just this dialectic and this form of the content. (They are of course not the only "sciences" of this kind, as Mallarmé seems to suggest: one would at least minimally also want to include one he could not have anticipated, namely, psychoanalysis, and perhaps also anthropology.)

ABOUSENNA: *I am concerned with comparative literature and the relationship of culture and philosophy to literature. In my work, I have tackled these issues within a broad Marxist perspective based on the theory of civilization and adopting the recent view about the integrating processes now taking place in cultural development, particularly in the field of cultural creativity as a universal phenomenon. Within this global, universal perspective, cultural values retain their significance beyond the borders of the civilization that created them, serving as the basis for further cultural development. I have called this approach the civilizational perspective. In my comparative studies of Arabic and European literature, I have placed the culture of the Enlightenment at the core of a civilizational perspective that aims at establishing a dialogue between cultures on the basis of equality and productivity for a future civilization.*

*My question is the following: how can the global perspective transcend the social and ideological contradictions resulting from a class-divided society founded on property ownership and exploitation on the national as well as the international level?*

JAMESON: I think the question needs to be turned inside out; as formulated, it tends to suggest a relatively older liberal world vision, in which (no doubt following World War II) the global perspective was a benign one, of cooperation and the end of war and violence, whereas the national perspective included class tensions and antagonisms (not to speak of the violence of this or that nationalism itself). I would have thought we needed to reverse that perspective: the struggles within the nation-state—if they are not smothered or occulted in one way or another—are the authentic ones, which, when they are fought through, can alone be resolved. It is the global level and the new world sytem that is on the contrary negative, in the way in which it makes local and national autonomies impossible and locks populations into an economic machine over which they have no control. Indeed, to anticipate the next question, I would say that it is precisely because class tensions are concealed within the superstate that our (first world) literature and culture is lacking in vitality. But the new world system has only been in existence (or at least has only been visible as such) in the past ten or twenty years; so the other implicit question cannot yet be answered, namely, what relationship one can posit between politics at the internal level and some conceivable politics on the level of the global system as a whole. This is a period of enormous and unthinkable class restructurations on a global scale, in which the very positions of first and third world ownership, industry, workforce, et cetera, are being modified in unpredictable new ways, ways that leave politics problematic for the moment, but which also problematize the politics of culture. We need to feel our way towards some larger world cultural space—I have called it "an internationalism of the national situations"—in which the internal specificity of the national culture is respected at the same time that its subordination to the world economic system is intensified and lived as a constraint and a domination about which intellectuals and artists are lucid. The new global cultural perspective must pass through the national situation and its analogies with other such national situations; and not try to leap at once into the universal or into some "world literature" of an old-fashioned type.

**NASR:** *What steps are Western literary scholars taking to accommodate third world texts in a theoretical sense?*

**JAMESON:** So in effect I have already begun to answer this question about the status of third world literature in the West, at least as I see that status. I should say that this very issue seems to me the hottest current topic of debate among the more "advanced" Western theoreticians (along with the question of postmodernism, to which it is not unrelated). The urgency of it arises not merely from the disintegration of the canon but also from the enormous recent richness of third world literature and culture itself, which has (at least since the breakthrough of the Latin American "boom") begun to set its own agenda. Much is being done in the area of so-called postcolonial discourse (which seeks to study the formal effects on Western literature of the fact of imperialism itself) and also of so-called postcolonial literature, which seeks to study the newer third world texts themselves, across the barrier of classical non-Western languages that most of us cannot hope to appropriate, but which are themselves central facts and problems in those cultures. I myself speak from a perspective in which the relative sterility of the cultures of the three great first world or late-capitalist zones (Europe, the US, Japan) is acknowledged, and therefore in which the more vital cultural production of the other areas now affords us possibilities of analysis we cannot find in our own literatures. For example, the whole theory of a properly Western modernism now needs to be revised in the light of the experience of modernization in the third world. This ought to issue in a new period of cultural comparatism on a global scale that will replace, but have nothing in common with, what used to be called "comparative literature." It will henceforth need to include the media (and replace what used to be called "cultural imperialism"), and it needs to be conflictual, full of critical sympathy with the various nationalisms, attentive to religion and to language revolutions, suspicious of United Nations–type liberalism, and alert to the paradoxes that obtain when the "third world" also exists inside the "first world" in the form of minorities, ethnic groups, migrant workers, and the like (as this is the case in all three superpowers).

# Interview with Stuart Hall

**HALL:** *In "Postmodernism; or, The Cultural Logic of Late Capitalism," where you characterize what is now called postmodern culture, you assume a direct correspondence between capitalism and culture: "Bourgeois culture corresponded to the era of organized capitalism—what Lenin called 'imperialism.'" You suggest that we are now moving into a new epoch, in which "late capitalism" finds its correspondence in what people have designated as "postmodern culture." Is that still your position?*

**JAMESON:** The problem with talking about "bourgeois culture" is that one of the things one wants to posit about this epochal change is that the culture of the bourgeoisie has itself been destroyed by it. What we have now is a relatively anonymous systemic culture, in which it becomes as problematic to talk about ruling classes in the old way as it does about some of the other questions. It might still be useful to talk about those things, but one has to address all of the objections first.

When talking about postmodernism, it's more important to ask, what exactly were "classical modernism" and "high modernism"? I've found it useful to explore the idea that modernism was a response to a modernization in the West from, say, the mid- to late nineteenth century until the Second World War. It was a response to a modernization which was incomplete, and in which the modernized enclaves and forces themselves were still working against a background of older class situations, older forms of agriculture and, in some parts of Europe, even older aristocratic strata, some of which were not fully dissolved until the Second World War.

So the real difference between postmodernism and modernism is that

This interview first appeared as Stuart Hall and Fredric Jameson, "Clinging to the Wreckage: A Conversation with Stuart Hall," *Marxism Today* 34 (1990): 28–31. © Democratic Left. Reprinted with permission of the Democratic Left.

postmodernism is a situation of tendentially complete modernization in which those older remnants have been removed.

**HALL:** *Is one sign of what you call "tendentially complete modernization" the penetration of many of the elements previously associated with a rather exclusive "high modernism" into everyday life, into popular culture, into consumption?*

**JAMESON:** Absolutely. I would call it the plebianization of culture: the way in which much larger sections of the public now consume culture on a regular basis and live within culture in ways that they didn't have the occasion to do before. That's a crucial part of postmodernism, which underscores its ambiguity. One cannot object to the democratization of culture, but one must object to other features of it. Those mixed feelings have to be preserved in any analysis of the postmodern.

**HALL:** *You have talked about postmodernism as being more systemic. Can we still speak of this as a "class culture" in the old sense?*

**JAMESON:** It is really only a "class culture" in the older sense when one is looking at it from the outside, from the perspective of the non-West. Then I think the terms we used to use, like *cultural imperialism*, are absolutely relevant, and indeed *postmodernism* would be a synonym for that. It is essentially a North American culture which is exported and implanted by way of media technology and so forth. If you're looking at it from this other perspective, then it's very clearly a matter of domination at least, if not an immediate matter of class.

But from the inside that domination wouldn't be so visible, partly because what's systemic about it is not due to anybody's agency. We don't have a dominant class sitting up there and conspiring and imposing its culture on us any more. It's being imposed on them too. And obviously there's a certain way in which, for a lot of people, it's not unpleasant to have postmodernism imposed on you. It's a very elegant thing. One cannot think of it in terms of older notions of ideological control and domination.

**HALL:** *You've talked about modernism as a response to a particular restructuring, a reshaping of capital in the period of imperialism up to the Second World War. But it's hard to see postmodernism as a response, because that suggests critical distance, the ability to reflect back on and challenge. Mod-*

*ernism contested. It shocked, it scandalized, it challenged the taste of the Victorian and Edwardian bourgeoisie. Now postmodernism isn't doing that. It doesn't have that reflexive critical distance from what is going on in the economic and political system. It seems fully integrated into the system, part and parcel of it. Is that the case?*

**JAMESON:** That's absolutely true. Modernism, with its claims for the autonomy of art and its ideology of the genius and so forth, still reflected a situation in which there were certain entrepreneurial possibilities. Certain oppositional or critical cultural forms emerge only when the economy is not yet too standardized and there's still room for both individual entrepreneurs and the same kinds of agents on the level of culture.

That's much less the case now. This is a period in which there is a genuine collectivization of people's lives at either end of the economic and social spectrum: the great multinational corporations, on the one hand, and the collectivization of all the oppositional groups, on the other. So, for example, you no longer have that great North American notion of the "lonely rebel" who challenges society. There aren't any "lonely rebels" any more because they're all organized in some way or another. They have mailing lists, they have their societies of "lonely rebels." That itself makes a difference in the way cultural production is felt and in the relative anonymity and systematic quality of this way of being secreted by the economic, rather than being produced in opposition to it.

**HALL:** *I think there may be an American/non-American difference of emphasis here. You talk about these visible forms of collectivization and incorporation—the corporate character of postmodern culture. Whereas in Britain, perhaps because we're on the periphery of it, the transition feels slightly different. Of course, one can't ignore the fact that the whole economic and cultural system is much more organized, much more managed, much more regulated, much more rationalized. Everybody is plugged in, at some level, to those forms which only the corporate culture of late capitalism can produce.*

*But, paradoxically, this seems to have produced a new form of individualism. In terms of style, for instance, it seems that for the first time the ordinary "entrepreneurial individual" can make a difference. The corporations have to watch him/her very carefully indeed, because in a sense they are too large and cumbersome to catch the fluent rhythms of modern consumption styles. They have to respond quickly to what's going down on the streets.*

**JAMESON:** You're talking about music . . .

**HALL:** *Music and style and dress. Exactly where ordinary people, without necessarily knowing the name, live the postmodern. Maybe they don't have much sense of what it is in the system that is creating these openings, or how constrained they are. Undoubtedly what is experienced, and ideologically constructed, as freedom may not necessarily be freedom at all. But it does lead to a sense of difference. It's as if the era of mass production and mass culture has now yielded not standardization, but a proliferation of difference, of otherness. Corporations don't advertise to a mass public any more. It's now niche advertising—addressing the subtle differentiation between one consumer public and another, exploiting cultural fragmentation.*

*Obviously, you need to get to a certain level of massification before this is possible. This is difference after massification, rather than the old style of nineteenth-century individualism. But it is as much this return of individualism and difference which strikes people here about postmodernism as its collectivization, anonymity, and systemic quality.*

**JAMESON:** This is absolutely part of the changeover. But we must remember that massification, "Fordism," and the standardized products also went along with the individual rebel. That is what allowed revolt, as well as all of the other ideologies, such as authenticity and so forth, that we associate in a positive sense with the modern. What you describe is the way in which the economic system itself, in a post-Fordist way, has now become a machine for differentiation. In a way, North America was the place for this new moment at its purest, because there were fewer forces of tradition and resistance and less of a past to destroy.

There's also a linguistic problem with this concept of difference. The conceptualization of difference would not have been possible in situations of real difference. In an imperial system, where colonized peoples are really radically different from their metropolitan overlords, there's no great political merit in affirming those differences. The political, cultural concept of difference is paradoxically based on a conquest of a certain equality and identity among the social subgroups. It would not have been possible until the moment where there was less difference.

**HALL:** *Do you mean that the language of difference becomes much more common when we're all operating on the same plane, even if we only do so very unevenly and unequally? The balance of forces is not the same in the so-*

*called third world as it is in London or Paris or Bonn or New York. But these are no longer—if they ever were—separate worlds. They belong within the same increasingly global culture.*

**JAMESON:** Yes, although it's useful to separate the question of global difference from that of what goes on within a political entity like a nation-state, just for the purpose of keeping the problems separate. I've found it very interesting that in cultural life and in the university, postmodernism emerged virtually simultaneously with a whole new interest in what we used to call third world literatures, postcolonial literatures. There really is a fit between those things, which have to do with a certain kind of global standardization. Standardization, again, is both a good and a bad thing. And it makes me wonder how many illusions are present in the appeal to difference, even if the logic of the system is differentiation, when by producing difference it is producing a new form of standardization. Indeed, the whole logic of postmodernism is that: a new way of seeing identity as difference, which we wouldn't have been able to think or express very well in an older period.

**HALL:** *You said earlier that the cultural democratization which we associate with postmodernism is both positive and negative. Now you say the same thing about global standardization. But isn't this exactly the problem with "a postmodern politics": trying to guess whether its negatives outweigh its positives? You've got to take a wager on whether what is going on in the postmodern is simply a dominant system producing marked differentiation as part of its own logic of domination, or whether there really has been a shift, representing the power of the marginalized or subordinated cultures and people to make what you called, earlier, a real difference. If the system is producing this differentiation as part of its own logic, then the "logic of history" in a classical Marxist sense is still operating, while going through one of its many epochal changes. On the other hand, many people—as you know—read these changes as representing the suspension of the "logic of history"—as the end of the metanarrative of classical Marxism. Are we still in the same kind of game?*

**JAMESON:** Some of the problems that I'm having in talking about this may come from the notion of stages, which I'm anxious to keep. But I think the problems also have something to do with what we call the dialectic, and they were present in the way Marx described capital from the very beginning in *The Communist Manifesto*. It is both absolutely positive and absolutely negative, and to understand it, we ought to be able to think those two things together, or somehow speak them together in a single sentence. But we can't, so we keep waffling back and forth between describing the positive things and then remembering the negative ones. The politically positive aspect about what you've been describing is the fact that subgroups have been able to attain a certain collective existence that they didn't really have before. That clearly fits into a kind of cultural commodification on the part of the industries that now have a new submarket and produce new things for it. But the crucial thing would not be those badges of cultural difference; it would be the fact of collectivity.

**HALL:** *But don't those two things—cultural difference and social solidarity— play against one another? Look at feminism, which came forward in the name of some collective category—women—and of their collective experience of marginality and secondariness. But the women's movement has very rapidly been crosscut by differences between one feminine experience and another, one category of women and another.*

*Exactly the same thing has happened in relation to the diasporas. At one period in Britain, the term* black *unified them across their cultural differ- ences. But now the cultural differences begin to reemerge, and that makes black politics very complex. Our sense of agency on the Left has always de- pended on a sense of coming together: solidarity—not just the "lonely rebel" individual. But it's exactly that sense of totality, of collective action and soli- darity, which has been undermined by the new logic of "difference" which dominates the era of the postmodern.*

**JAMESON:** My feeling about politics, which may be an old-fashioned one, is that nothing finally happens without the reconstruction of a certain basic unity among groups. My own sense of this may be too pessimistic, but from the perspective of a politics of solidarity, culture would not be a substitute for politics. It would rather interfere with it. If the various subgroups invent powerful cultural symbols of their separateness, then it's much harder for them to get back together. I am more pessimistic about a purely cultural politics than I would obviously like to be.

**HALL:** *But isn't there a problem nowadays about identifying the common program around which those solidarities could be organized? What we've been describing is a space where a lot of active politics in society is going on; but there's a discrepancy or gap between the old political parties and their programs, which are lodged in an earlier political and cultural space.*

*Those programs don't reflect the life experience, the cultures, and the points of antagonism of the emerging social forces. And the social forces themselves are so divided and subdivided around different projects that it's not possible to see any single overarching program that could unite them. This is the problem of hegemony in the age of the postmodern. There's also a real suspicion, among these new social subjects, of submerging the things that mobilize and activate them by lodging them inside some grander program that will probably eventually submerge and forget all about them.*

JAMESON: Nobody could begin by inventing a whole program, but the first step in any solidarity between groups is the sense that, however different they are and however differently they are victimized, they all face a common situation dictated by what used to be called the ruling class. It's better not to call it the state anymore; I would say "the corporate" would be a good word for it, in the multinational and business sense, for one way or another the corporate is not a ruling class of the older type because of what's happened to individual agency. Yet how one begins to create an alliance of groups, by identifying the common enemy . . .

HALL: *The disappearance of a unified agency, like "the ruling class" or "the state," as the instrumentality of oppression presents its own difficulties. It requires us to produce a much richer picture of how that "corporate" force operates. There seems to have been a randomization of what it is that makes people victims, a collapse of any one enemy or any one source of power, a multiplication of the centers of power. The dispersal of what used to be called "the enemy" into a whole system leads to the difficulty of putting together any kind of common oppositional politics.*

JAMESON: The other great stumbling block is the fact that "the corporate" is now at one with culture, so that to identify this agent that doesn't seem to be there would really require passing through the mediation of culture itself. That for me really dramatizes what's at stake in this whole question of postmodernism and its critical analysis. Identifying the postmodern as a unitary logic is part of the process of trying to locate this agency, which seems invisible and fragmented somewhere within "the corporate." A politics that wanted to take on "the corporate" would, therefore, have to take on postmodernism itself and its corporate culture. That's a very complicated thing to do, and it's something which often strikes people as being puritanical or oversimplified because you then seem to be repudiating all of the postmodern as a form of decadence and ruling-class culture, when it's a much more ambivalent thing, with a whole lot of new things being created within it.

**HALL:** *I want to put all this in the context of what's happening in Eastern Europe. You may say that 1992 is a fulfillment of the system you're trying to describe. And presumably 1989 opens the way for everybody to be netted in that system. The second world will be netted; the third world is already netted; postmodern culture will be everywhere. There will be a new phase of the cultural globalization of capital.*

*That may be to come in Eastern Europe. But what is the explosion in Eastern Europe itself about? It has its own local, historical specificity and, within that history, there's something paradoxical about the fact that it is "democratization" which seems to have given it its most powerful impetus to change: an idea of democracy almost lost in the West. Democracy has been so assimilated to liberal democracy and liberal capitalism in the West that we find it hard to get very excited about it. It seems to keep things in place rather than change them very much. But in the East, they really got excited about democracy.*

*For the moment, the only way to describe the revolutions of 1989 is in terms of the democratization of "civil society" or some such terminology. So, both in postmodernism and in the explosions in Eastern Europe, some underlying tendency towards the "democratization of society" seems to be emerging. Have you had any thoughts about that in relation to the explosions of 1989?*

**JAMESON:** I hesitate to use the word *democratization* because it implies conquest that has not yet happened. It hasn't happened in the West either. Democracy must involve more than political consultation. There must be forms of economic democracy and popular control in other ways, some of them problematic, as with workers' self-management. That has not been achieved, so it's important to separate the democratization of culture from the achievement of real popular control. There are some permanent political dilemmas that don't vanish with the surface changes. Now in the East, I think it's very plausible to compare this to the revolution of 1848 in that it was not so much the economic that was at stake, but the national.

My other sense is that 1989 was really the result of the passage of the eastern countries into a whole new world system that has been becoming visible and organized in the past ten to fifteen years.[1] It is wrong to say that socialism was a failure. It was a success in those countries precisely as a modernization strategy. They wouldn't have this situation without near completion of that modernization process that was always the driving force of Leninism. One can have very different views as to whether that Leninist moment of modernization fulfills the spirit as Marxism in general. But a new stage wouldn't be taking place unless socialism, in other words, modernization, had been successful.

In those older circumstances of the Warsaw Pact, where a group of countries was essentially cushioned against the world financial market—against trade and so forth—questions about efficiency were most often political questions. But the minute that global capitalism sheds the older skin and organizes itself in a far more powerful and systemic global way, suddenly, these countries and their national plan and their modes of life, which functioned fairly well in the old system, are radically modified. Wanting to be part of the world market, suddenly they find that their factories and their currency are worthless. The dialectic of this is that they were swept away partly because of their own success and partly because they're now a component in a much vaster system with which those relatively old-fashioned forms of socialism or communism are just no match.

**HALL:** *The analysis that you offer, both of what's happening in the West, in late capitalism as you define it, and of the contradictory developments in Eastern Europe, is very challenging, putting together many puzzling elements in a new way. You respond to the postmodern in a very flexible, complex way. Yet underneath that is an absolutely unquestioned faith in the logic of classical Marxism. How do you keep these two things going simultaneously? Confidence in that particular grand narrative of history has undoubtedly been weakened by everything that we have been describing. The fact that so many things have turned out differently from how that logic was projected at some time in the past has led many people to say we just can't hold onto it any longer.*

*How do you manage to go on thinking new situations in a fruitful and novel way, while the underlying logic of your argument remains grounded in exactly the texts that were used to tell such a different story—the revolutionary nature of capitalism, its dialectical quality in producing its own negation, the proletariat, in* The Communist Manifesto, *and the* Grundrisse?

**JAMESON:** That's a question that's obviously hard to answer on the basis of individual belief, but my answer would have to reflect an absolute conviction that this is still capitalism in the classic sense. Postmodernism has this odd double standard where you're convinced that capitalism has triumphed: there's the market, on the one hand, and everybody's better off and everybody plays their own music, but on the other hand, we're also equally convinced that there's incredible misery in these societies, they're getting worse rather than better, people are not getting more prosperous. And we know both things are true and also that they are incompatible.

**HALL:** *The social fabric has disintegrated.*

**JAMESON:** Exactly, and the new global wealth and the new global immiseration are true simultaneously, but somehow we can't put them together. As a grand narrative, Marxism compensates for the fact that as biological individuals, our own life spans don't correspond to historical rhythms. Vaster historical movements are always astounding and unexpected, and yet from some large systemic perspective after the fact, seem plausible again from what we know about the way the history of capitalism works.

I'm convinced that this new postmodern global form of capitalism will now have a new class logic about it, but it has not yet completely emerged because labor has not yet reconstituted itself on a global scale, and so there is a crisis in what classes and class consciousness are. It's very clear that agency on the Left is not visible in its older forms, but the Marxist narrative assures us that some form of agency will reconstitute itself and that is the sense in which I still find myself committed to the Marxist logic.

NOTE

1. For an extended discussion of the collapse of socialism in Eastern Europe, see Fredric Jameson, "Conversations on the New World Order," in *After the Fall: The Failure of Communism and the Future of Socialism*, ed. Robin Blackburn (London: Verso, 1991), 255–68.

# Interview with Michael Speaks

**SPEAKS:** *You have previously suggested that with the modern it was the temporal that predominated the space-time configuration and that with the postmodern it is now space that predominates. Could you say something about this as it relates to contemporary architecture, especially in light of your own model of the postmodern, which differs significantly from most architectural ones?*

**JAMESON:** It is paradoxical to talk about the spatialization of the postmodern and then try to apply that specifically to architecture since clearly architecture was spatial all along. The idea was that in an older society, but one that's incompletely modernized—in which you have enclaves of different kinds of life, agricultural life, peasant life, and so forth—the temporal dynamics of that society, and of the modernism that it produces, will be much more striking. In effect, it is through the experience of time that the modern is apprehended. The temporality of high modernist architecture would be the way in which through an older city you arrive at something that stands for the future and that is radically disjointed from the older kind of city fabric. So this would explain the paradox of talking about one kind of architecture in a temporal way and the other in a more homogeneous, spatial way.

My idea on the postmodern was, first and foremost, that the aesthetics of this period and the forms it projects have to be seen in terms of a whole mode of production, and not merely as a kind of style: one that has to do with a more complete modernization and with the elimination of those older enclaves of historical difference that correspond to older kinds of agriculture

---

This interview first appeared as Michael Speaks, "Envelopes and Enclaves: The Space of Post-civil Society," *Assemblage*, 17 (1990): 30–37.

and older modes of life. As Henri Lefebvre puts it in *The Production of Space*, it is the urbanization of global reality: the tendential transformation of everything into something that one has to think of as urban. For example, we no longer have to do with agriculture but with agribusiness; in social terms, categories like those of the metropolis and the provinces no longer obtain: theirs is a kind of standardization of everything. In all senses, a new notion of homogeneous space seems to impose itself. The question that arises is thus not merely the stylistic one—although that's quite important—but how a specific monument or building makes itself felt in a homogeneous urban space. In Tokyo, for example, it is very hard to see how the city could be reorganized or rebuilt or turned back into a classical city of the type that seems to be presupposed by most urban projects; it is also hard to see how any specific building would ever stand out in this kind of fabric since it is a bewildering, infinite, endless series of built things, each of which is different from the next.[1] Some principle of perception then gets lost, and the very vocation to do a uniquely memorable building of some sort, it seems to me, would also be lost. And this is obviously a paradoxical prognosis in the light of architects as distinguished as Isozaki, as well as the "megastructures" of a Kenzo Tangai.

All this means that two kinds of ambition that were still present in the modern period or in the modern movement disappear into this random textuality. One has to do with the creation of the urban, beginning with Haussmann and on to Le Corbusier; the other has to do with the creation of the modernist building per se, Venturi's monumental "duck" as Venturi likes to call it. It would seem that in this new endless textual fabric neither of these things has any meaning anymore, and this is why, I suppose, one should think in terms rather of enclaves. That is, most of the interesting newer buildings that one might be tempted to call postmodern in one way or another (obviously that could mean almost anything) most of these projects seem to have turned around enclaves, such as museum complexes or college campuses; and, though not a third term between an isolated building and a planned city environment, they do offer provisional suspension of the problems that these both face now.

**SPEAKS:** *It seems your model of postmodernism and space displaces the space-versus-time debate that David Harvey refers to in* The Condition of Postmodernity. *That is, it eclipses the kind of modernist debate between, say, Wyndham Lewis and Henri Bergson.*

JAMESON: I think that's so. We have to keep using these two words—*time* and *space*—in any of these moments, but they change their relationship to each other. I think this could be made clear by insisting, for example, on the way in which MTV, and postmodern music generally, is spatial. I think if it's understood how this is really part of the way space itself is programmed, then in this period we have a new way of thinking about the relationship of time and space: rather than opposing one another as an ethical or metaphysical dualism, they tend to cannibalize each other and produce distended and monstrous kinds of symbioses.

SPEAKS: *What effect does this have on other nonspatial forms of cultural production: literature, for example?*

JAMESON: There now has to be a spatial dimension to the analysis of all of these things. It is, for instance, not indifferent that television is a home appliance, that you look at it in certain specific places alone; not indifferent that if literature is in crisis, this is, first and foremost, because of its spatial emplacement in a larger sense—and this is due not merely to the emergence of the monopolies of the great publishing companies but also to the crisis in libraries and book storage and the passage to information systems. So while you can sit and read a book in a certain contemplative isolation from all of this, it would seem that for us today any formal discussion of verbal forms needs to reflect that much more acute spatial situation in which their reception and production take place.

SPEAKS: *Recently, you linked the notion of architectural depthlessness to the philosophical and political problematic that you identify as the liquidation of what [G. W. F.] Hegel called civil society. This new spatial organization is marked most dramatically by the disappearance of the public/private distinction that you see presaged in the recent work of the architect Rem Koolhaas, in* Blade Runner, *and in the amorphous sprawl of Tokyo.*

JAMESON: What I have been struck with in the work of Koolhaas is the way it builds an enormous envelope for all kinds of unprogrammed but differentiated activities. If you follow Niklas Luhmann's idea that modernity is characterized by differentiation, and if you suppose that there are plateaus in the rhythm of this differentiation, as I do—in other words, that the differentiation of a postmodern global information society is going to be quite different from the differentiation of an older, "modern" society—then I think one can read one feature of Koolhaas's work as an exemplification of this. But the originality of Koolhaas (as theoretician and architect alike) is that his work does not simply glorify differentiation in the conventional pluralist ideological way: rather, he insists on the relationship between this randomness and freedom and the presence of some rigid, inhuman, nondifferential form that enables the differentiation of what goes on around it (in *Delirious New York*, within the building, the elevator, and within the urban context itself, the Manhattan grid). Koolhaas offers the picture of the imposition on the differential of a rigid, and if I may say so, contingent or meaningless structural form, a form that, like the elevator, has no internal meaning of its own, but whose function is to allow this improvisation and differentiation to go on outside of itself and around itself. Thus the free spaces are enabled by the rigidity of the framework. It is almost a political paradigm in the sense that the combination of formal requirements of a certain order without content permits all kinds of forms of freedom or disorder within the interstices.

I think that what's brilliant about Koolhaas's work is not only the obviously very striking nature of the buildings themselves but also the way in which the work offers an interesting paradigm for other levels of social life, not only for other arts but also the political or even the ethical, and the psychoanalytical. I don't mean that one should endorse this program and draw a politics or an ethics from the success of these buildings, but it is very interesting that they do project the combination of law and freedom that seems to be characteristic of the present time. In other words, as an ideal, this interesting combination is very different from the authoritarianism of an older corporate or planned society, whether that's conceived of from the Left or from the Right, and as it might be seen to be embodied in the International Style or in the work of Frank Lloyd Wright. But it is also very different from the fantasies of an anarchism that wants to dissolve all structures and create spaces for a free play that would reinvent its structures at every occasion or at every moment. I think Koolhaas's projects offer free play only on the condition of this rigid and meaningless internal structure, and so whatever else this is, it's a very striking solution to the contemporary intellectual problem that seems to be a reaction against an older authoritarianism and, nowadays, against an older anarchist libertarianism as well.

**SPEAKS:** *I know that you have recently visited and viewed some of the work of Arata Isozaki in Japan. Do Isozaki's buildings, or does Tokyo in general,* *presage a future-present towards which, as some commentators have suggested, the West is moving? Or does the work of Koolhaas, Isozaki, and Portman, for that matter, each form a kind of nodal point in an immanent force field that has sloughed off the old linear constraints?*

**JAMESON:** The first point to understand is that (and not only in my view, but as I understand it in Koolhaas's as well) one can't discuss either Europe or Japan without talking about the United States, which is the real form of the future: what Koolhaas has called in a striking phrase, "the culture of congestion," a "culture" that figures a very different way of living space and law and order than anything preconfigured in the older Europe or in Japan. What I think has to be understood about the Japanese city is that it requires enormous discipline on the part of its subjects to exist in this enormous agglomeration, and this obviously differentiates Japan very sharply from the United States. That is to say, these are inner-directed people with a very keen interiorized sense of control and convention. Thus if Tokyo represents some future, the Japanese character would, on the contrary, seem to represent some past that the other-directed, or consumerist, moment of the United States has left far behind, in terms of both the work ethic and the relationship to law and convention. So one can't immediately project all of Japan into our own future since it seems clear to me that we are not going back to "inner-directedness."[2] Now in the case of Europe, I would think what Koolhaas seems to be implying, and maybe one can distantly imply the same thing about Japan, is that the new Europe—in which all of these nation-states come together, unified not merely by currency and presumably in the future also by political institutions but as well by the increasing rapidity of communication, crossing over of borders, and so on—that this Europe will tendentially approach something like American congestion, both in the characterological nature of its citizens, who seem to feel freer when they cross a language border than they do within their mostly rather rigid internal social traditions, but also in the very mingling of all of these different national traditions, which will tend to break them down on the American model.

As for Japan, this is clearly less likely to happen, though people have muttered dire predictions about what a Japan would be like after this flood of consumerism and after the end of their "Protestant ethic," and potentially even after the end of the emperor system. So I would say that Koolhaas's work at least tries socially as well as spatially to address this kind of future. Isozaki is not at all like this; I wouldn't see him as a comparable figure. I am obviously not terribly well placed to judge Isozaki's role in Japan, except that he is a very eminent and remarkable artistic figure there, and surely one of the world's greatest architects as well. But the buildings I've seen of his that I find interesting are, in essence, extremely elegant enclave structures, such as the Mito Art Tower, in which the problems of congestion that Koolhaas deals with are not, as far as I can see, at issue. And, in fact, I guess I have not seen any buildings by Isozaki within Tokyo itself, so I don't know how his work addresses the problem of a future city like that, if indeed it does.

**SPEAKS:** *Given this new model of the space of post-civil society that you have been developing, could you draw a comparison between the kind of space you analyzed in the Bonaventure Hotel in Los Angeles and the space of these Koolhaas projects and buildings?*

**JAMESON:** Yes, I think that's an interesting comparison, and it's quite right to juxtapose these things and try to figure out their difference. I think the essence of what I am trying to get at by this end of civil society is clearly at issue here somehow. The point is that the hotel is still private property. We might enter it to mill around as a crowd, but we're still within the authority of private property. Therefore it's a strange kind of mixture—a private space used for some form of public deployment of the private. Now the crucial thing about the end of civil society is that what used to be public is reprivatized, what used to be spaces or places marked by government and therefore by the public somehow revert to faceless forms of private control. So that some new kind of thing comes into being that is neither the place of one's private life nor the monumentalization of collective powers. This may be related to (but I think it's somewhat different from) Hannah Arendt's notion that the public in our time was being reprivatized in the sense in which politics became personalized and people were more interested in the personalities of political figures than in their programs. Hers was a psychological diagnosis, whereas in my view the development has much more to do with mutations in the very juridical forms of property, so that new entities emerge that are not covered by the previous categories.

Now the crucial thing about Koolhaas, in particular, the project for the Zeebrugge Maritime Terminal, is that it is an interspace between all of these countries that are streaming in to merge into others. As the crossing point or arrival point for the Channel ferry boats, the terminal is therefore public in a new way, and yet somehow outside of the public spaces of any of the nation-states involved. It is as though Koolhaas, observing the new "culture of congestion" by way of the rapid mixture of these populations that are streaming through, somehow also offers a machine for producing this culture in a Europe that never knew it before. This somehow seems to me much more interesting in terms of future historical development, in terms of things that will happen in these categories of public or private, than the Bonaventure, which is a far more conventional building with its hotel police force and predictable categories of behavior. The Bonaventure could stand as a symptom of these developments in the strong sense; Koolhaas's work constitutes a strong formal and cultural reaction: an attempt both to register these developments and in some way to make a statement about them and potentially to appropriate them.

**SPEAKS:** *Earlier you mentioned that Koolhaas's projects, especially the Zeebrugge Maritime Terminal, could be considered as a kind of envelope. There is thus an inside and an outside. With Tokyo, it would seem that there is no inside and outside: there is an inside without an outside. But this could also be true of Koolhaas. Could Isozaki, as one expression of the Japanese scene, be described as a more global architect than Koolhaas? Given your suggestion about Koolhaas's projects as envelopes, it would seem so.*

**JAMESON:** It's very important to make clear that although we use the words for this business of inside and outside, what's novel about the new situation is that the opposition no longer maintains. That is, as you say quite rightly, it's an inside that has no outside, even though a word like *envelope* seems to suggest this. And that's why in a way the Zeebrugge terminal and all of Tokyo are comparable. These are macrocosms. They are definitely felt to be insides. The notion of an inside hasn't disappeared; it's been reinforced. But the other thing that this seems to imply—and indeed Koolhaas talks about this himself when he says that now, at this scale, the externals of the building are so far from anything that goes on, on the inside, as to render old-fashioned and meaningless attempts to correlate the two—is that this all has to be understood on the enormous scale of the urban totality, just as much as on that of the building.

Now, as I've said, I don't quite agree about Isozaki in that I think that the institution of the enclave, whether it's Disney or the Mito Art Tower, allows you to do some things that you cannot do in this absolute correspondence of macrocosms, whether it's the city as a whole or the Zeebrugge terminal. It seems to me that we are in another dimension and dealing with another genre: we shouldn't use the same word *architecture* to subsume both things because they are working at completely different levels. The outsides of Isozaki's buildings are very splendid expressions of the spirit of the insides, so we have a kind of different architectural dynamic there from what's going on in the others. The difference may be that Isozaki's work corresponds much more to the space that corporate society opens up for building: these enclaves are essentially the spaces of corporate contracts. Whereas when we talk about either the project for the Bibliothéque de France or the Zeebrugge Maritime Terminal, I think that we are no longer at the level of the corporate, but seemingly not at the level of the old-fashioned state either—for these two are not simply downtown state or city office buildings or monuments, but something else.

What interests me about your question is something that is not, I think, specific to architecture, but that I would call the dynamics of genre or generic criticism—the way in which the objective situation gives rise to specific genres as it blocks out others. I think that's at least a part of what is at stake here in the way in which the possibility of very different kinds of buildings and of building itself as an activity is given by the situation and by the structure of corporate global power.

**SPEAKS:** *One of the languages you have used to describe Koolhaas's recent work is that of "dirty realism."* [3] *As you note, you borrow this term from Liane Lefaivre's own borrowing of the term from Bill Buford's account of the American short story. Could you distinguish between Buford's, Lefaivre's, and your own use of this term, and distinguish these from critical regionalism, which also bears a strong relationship to all three?*

**JAMESON:** If one looks at the original text that Lefaivre quotes, which has to do with the newer American short story, one can see that there is, in fact, a very strong regionalist impulse in Buford's original description, and it amounts in his description of these writers to the spread of standardization to the suburbs and the countryside and the combination of the remains of an older nature with things we used to think of as urban. This isn't, I think, quite the resonance it has when transferred to architecture, and pretty clearly both Koolhaas and *Blade Runner* no longer have any of this regional spirit and thus would express the strong forms of some anonymous contemporary or future urbanization rather than the residual forms of a kind of combination of country and city that one might still get in parts of the formerly provincial United States. So there's been a slippage in the very use of this term. Now, I use *dirty realism* as part of a larger combination scheme that seems to make some sense in dealing with the varieties of recent architecture, which seemed more and more difficult to fit under the notion of the postmodern, if only because the temptation to think of the postmodern as a style is so strong (in the restricted sense in which one might think of Charles Moore or Michael Graves as the preeminent practitioners). This restricted style is only one of many recent forms of architectural production. It seems to me that what emerged was a sense that this was not (as apologists for postmodernity have often liked to say) a wide-open pluralism in which anything and everything goes, but rather a production itself internally limited by a certain number of problems as well as features.

This understood, perhaps one could then begin to map out what I have called the "constraints of the postmodern," that is, the way in which a system is nonetheless at work behind this recent architectural production. I've tried to do this by superimposing two axes along which it seems contemporary architecture continues to define itself against the older past of the high modern. One of these axes turns on the matter of totality versus its parts, elements, or constituent signifiers. The other one turns on the matter of the new and the repetitive, or innovation and replication, on the supreme value of the modern to produce a radically new art and a radically new space as opposed to the ways in which contemporary, postmodern work, in the larger sense of the word, has tended to revel in pastiche and the return of all kinds of older languages with which it can then play. These four terms (totality/parts, innovation/replication) give us a certain number of combinations that seem to me to make some sense. We haven't mentioned Eisenman yet, or so-called deconstructionism, which, insofar as it has a kind of deep aesthetic impulse towards an almost Mallarméan purity, still embodies a notion of innovation that is combined with a commitment to the permutation or combination of parts or layers or whatever.

One can thus see a more central or characteristic form of postmodernism as involving an abandonment of innovation, a consent to replication, and a return to all kinds of dead traditions and its combination with parts or elements or signifiers. This suggests that memory of past architecture that seems to float across the surface of the work of architects like Graves and Moore. Clearly, the strong combination here is the modernist ideal of innovation and totality. But then, in my view, *dirty realism*, Koolhaas, if you prefer, emerges as the term in which there is a certain consent to replication—at least the way in which the individual microcosm replicates the macrocosm—but, at the same time, there is a will towards totality, towards all-inclusiveness. And this form of "dirty realism," it seems to me, which wants to include all of this "culture of congestion" within itself, is a distinct form from the other three. Now, should one then go on talking about the postmodern in these terms. It's very clear from Koolhaas's own statements that he is quite willing to repudiate this term and this idea. On the other hand, if one is interested in all of this architectural production as a set of symptoms for the age and in finding out what is distinct, specific, and different about our own historical moment, then one has to, at least initially, put them all side by side and see how they correspond to some new and original situation that we all face.

**SPEAKS:** *In the 1988 MOMA exhibition, Koolhaas and OMA were included under the "deconstructivist" rubric. What does replication offer that the decon solution does not? It would seem to have something to do with architectural realism and representation.*

**JAMESON:** Yes, I think that comes back to the role that the term *totality* plays here. I'm not sure I'd be happy with using the term *realism* for any of this. But if we talk about mimesis, at least we can see some fundamental differences in the sense that *Learning from Las Vegas* involves the mimesis of a part of a total urban fabric, whereas Koolhaas's buildings seem to wish to stand as a mimesis of the whole macrocosm itself. I think that's why these buildings, as I suggested before, can carry certain kinds of political messages, or can include, if you like, political and social models, because they do have the ambition to grapple with the totality of the social itself.

**SPEAKS:** *At the end of your 1985 essay on Manfredo Tafuri's* Architecture and Utopia, *in which you reject Tafuri's pessimism and Venturi's giddiness, you suggest that perhaps there is something to be said for a properly Gramscian architecture. Is this still true today?*

**JAMESON:** Well, I guess the problem with Gramscian architecture today is that, at least in the way I was describing it, it implies that one can find spaces outside of the world system, and, in that sense, the paper architecture that you mentioned fatefully reflects both the attempt and the impossibility of doing this. That is, if it's only in imaginary space that one can project some alternative, then this says something about real space and real possibilities. Given the force of the world system today, it becomes harder and harder to imagine this alternative or utopian space concretely. The various enclaves that one can imagine (we spoke, for example, of the enormous power that the enclaves give to Isozaki's architecture) are part of the system, and in this they are corporate. It seems much harder today to imagine economic units being able to withdraw from this world system or to sustain an independence separate from it, and to this degree, this optimistic Gramscian strategy seems increasingly problematic. Another form it took was, of course, the notion of critical regionalism. I fear that while it is important to keep this alive as a value and a possibility, here, too, the very nature of the development of the world system has unexpectedly appropriated the region—since now the autonomous languages of separate cultures are themselves the very tourist mechanisms by which the world system reproduces itself and spreads its form of economic standardization. So it's unclear even now whether the fight for stylistic autonomy in these various regions is really a struggle about autonomy or, in fact, a kind of pluralism that the system itself, in its forms of postmodern marketing and international export, the tourist business, and so forth, can not only perfectly well accommodate but indeed do so with enthusiasm.

**SPEAKS:** *You remarked in a previous interview that your call for Gramscian architecture had less to with an architectural practice per se and more to do with, as you said, "recognizing the locus of a new reality and that the cultural politics by which it must be confronted is that of space." Does architecture play a role in developing the idea that politics is now spatial?*

**JAMESON:** Yes, I think that's right, but, paradoxically, it returns to Tafuri's own position, which is that you cannot have an ideological critique of buildings because the critiques are just what the system has to produce. Ideological critique operates on the level of the theory of the buildings and on the manifestos and on the constraints of these things in the realm of analysis and of thought and of programs. One very important new possibility that all of this has added to cultural and political criticism is that everything about the discussion of architecture itself is now political; and also that political discussion somehow seems quite impossible without reference to architecture, that is, to space generally, to the way the urban is organized, to the way geopolitics is organized. This is the new spatial dimension of things. So I guess one could say, going back to the very first question, that what is spatial about the postmodern is that theories about this current situation, whether they have to do with its culture or its politics, must now pass through the code of the spatial in order to match their object of analysis.

# NOTES

1. For fuller discussions of this problematic, see Fredric Jameson, *The Seeds of Time*, 145–59; Fredric Jameson, *The Cultural Turn*, 136–89. See also, Fredric Jameson, "Tadao Ando and the Enclosure of Modernism," *Architecture New York* 6 (1994): 28–33.

2. A term proposed by David Riesman in *The Lonely Crowd*.

3. See *The Seeds of Time*, 145–50.

# Interview with Horacio Machín

**MACHÍN:** *Taking into account the broad sense that you assign to the concept of postmodernism as an extensive cultural manifestation, what is its link to the concept of mode of production?*

**JAMESON:** The necessity of insisting upon the concept of mode of production and its connection with cultural concepts is that without it, we fall back upon either intellectual history or some form of anthropology, or of the history of culture and civilization. That is to say, there have been a series of changes in history, in the sciences, in artistic styles, but unless these are tied to a rigorous concept of transformation in the social structure, then what we have is simply a kind of typology where things happen without any particular logic, or a kind of anthropology or history of civilizations in which general categories like Western Civilization or Baroque are deployed. Both approaches seem to me to make for idealist history, and they don't represent the advances of modern historiography.

Finally, for me, a concept of postmodernism—seen as a rather intensive change, not simply cultural, but in terms of social practices and even economics—can't be appropriately constructed or explained unless it is somehow connected to modifications in the mode of production itself.

Now, the critical problem here is that we have various contradictory versions of these changes. I would say that these theories of something like the postmodern first became evident from the Right rather than the Left. The notion of the "end of ideology" from the 1950s, as it was proposed by liberal political scientists and the right wing, meant for them—in the period of Eisenhower—the end of Marxism as the principle ideology and

---

This interview first appeared in Spanish (translated by Santiago Colás) in *Nuevo texto crítico* 4:7 (1991): 3–18. Although it was conducted in English, it has never been published in that language. Unfortunately the original typescript of the English version could not be located, so it had to be retranslated back into English.

vision of change. But it also anticipated in some ways some characteristics of the postmodern, notably the way in which abstract thinking, ideology, and value, et cetera, have disappeared—into what Adorno denounced as positivism—that is to say, the eclipse of the transcendental characteristics of thought. So, these right-wing ideologues seem to have anticipated something of this development in a period in which it still didn't exist, but obviously they used it for their own political purposes.

Later, Daniel Bell elaborated upon all of this in a complete theory of what he called "postindustrial society," for he understood perfectly, as a former Trotskyist, that if one is going to talk about a change at the foundation of modes of thought and culture, it is idealistic to hypothesize it unless one postulates a theory of radical social change. But in this case, the radical social change was the end of capitalism itself and the emergence of some new thing he called postindustrial society—presumably based on a primacy of science and technology that would be driven by the technocrats and the scientists. Now, it seems to me that this is not the theory one wants either, but it certainly is the example that one has to follow. If, in other words, one wants to theorize intellectual and cultural change in modern society, then it is necessary to connect it in some way to a modification in the mode of production. Now, in more traditional Marxism there already existed the conception of two stages of capitalism: Marx himself developed one of them, although in effect, he was simply describing the tendencies of the system itself; and Lenin, in his pamphlet on imperialism, theorized a second moment, around the period of monopoly and the imperialist system of the 1890s, which he related to each other. One could say that, in fact, according to a classic Leninism, capitalism was restructured in this second moment.

After this, the Marxist tradition seems to have pronounced its own "end of history," and the Marxists have generally been unwilling to admit that there could be something like a third stage of capitalism because the second, according to Lenin, was presumed to be the "highest" and the last. It was disconcerting to have to produce a third. But after World War II, specifically with society's development of new cybernetic means of communication, and with the disintegration of the old imperialist system of nation-states laid in place during the Berlin Conference of 1885, and with decolonization everywhere, one is confronted with a new set of facts and features that need to be examined, an impression powerfully reinforced when we begin to see the changes in daily life and practices of the 1960s and 1970s. So all of these things suggest, then, that on one hand, a series of profound cultural modifications are taking place, and on the other hand, that it might be desirable to theorize perhaps a third moment of capitalism. Therefore, when people start to think in terms of naming the new cultural entity, and when the word *postmodernism* begins to come into currency, it seemed logical and acceptable to link it not to a new mode of production (because this is not socialism, it's not some new form of oriental despotism or federalism, it is still very much capitalism), but to a third stage of capitalism which is derived infrastructurally from the other two and yet superstructurally and culturally different from them.

Now this notion of stages—it's not mine, of course, but derived from Ernest Mandel's book *Late Capitalism*, which in some languages translates precisely as *The Third Stage of Capitalism*—can ultimately be traced back to the Marx of the *Grundrisse*. He there posits the need for capitalism to set boundaries it can then transcend and negate, and replace them with vaster ones. (The rate of profit falls, the exploitation of labor is no longer so productive, the market is saturated, and so forth.) But what happens in such a crisis of limits is that a new series of technological innovations is pressed into the service of an enlarged capitalism, and the process is able to begin all over again, so that each moment of capitalism can be identified by new productive technology, as well as by expansion. This would seem to be precisely what is happening when the national moment of capitalism described by Marx in the first stage expands on a global scale with classical imperialism and the system of the various metropolises and their colonial systems. At the end of World War II this system is exhausted, but a completely new technology emerges—according to Mandel, cybernetics, computer science, and atomic energy—which allows for the possibility of a complete restructuring of the earlier one and its enlargement into a much vaster and now even global scale of integration and economic organization. This is, then, what we might call the multinational stage. So it seems to me that this notion of the stages of capitalism is present in Marx, in the *Grundrisse*, and that it permits us to frame a hypothesis with respect to transformations in culture, understanding it in a broader sense, from the structure of the psyche, the practices of everyday life, the role of culture in society, to art forms, theories of philosophy, and so on.

So, those would be the connections I would like to make; and it seems that much of our postmodernity, the schizophrenic aspects of its temporality, the decentering of the subject, the enormous expansion of culture, the predominance of images in our new systems of information and publicity, et cetera—much of this can be tied to just such a notion of a third stage.

**MACHÍN:** *Postmodernism alludes to a new articulation between politics and culture, to a displacement of politics towards culture. Is this about a new form of Marxism or of post-Marxism?*

**JAMESON:** For me it seems that—whether or not it is a new form of Marxism (I don't think that Mandel was particularly unorthodox, and I don't think that I am either)—what is required is not necessarily a rewriting of all these new cultural phenomena in terms of the old categories, but rather recognition that those categories themselves were historical. There was a Marxism that corresponded to the classic period of the Second International. There was a Marxism that is now referred to as Western Marxism that corresponded to modernism and to the imperialist stage, and I think that now we need a Marxism for the new or third stage. But this seems to me perfectly consistent with Marx; Mandel shows that the third stage of capitalism is not a deviation from the original concept of capital that Marx offered in his incomplete version: rather, it is a purer stage of capitalism than what Marx described. So, I see part of the function of my work as an effort to show the way in which there is a much more profound correspondence between classical Marxist theory and the newer things happening today in our culture.

**MACHÍN:** *With respect to a possibly negative characterization, postmodernism as a cultural phenomenon also holds the possibility of a positive characterization: one of historic reconstruction. Or, if you prefer, a historical vision and dialectic that attempts to capture the present as history. What interest do you have in the possibility of this kind of periodization of a new stage, and how would this relate to the tracing of cognitive mapping?*

**JAMESON:** I don't think that it would be so much an issue of the end of history in the sense of Fukuyama as much as a reconstruction of history or a new kind of history that takes into account global urban planning and spatialization. I believe that this question is related to the first one since it highlights the importance of the notion of the mode of production. With the concept of mode of production, one retains a sense of historical change, but a nonlinear one: although, since you mentioned evolution, I think that one has to say that nowadays there is a revival of evolutionary thought, and a renewed study of Darwin, from Stephen Jay Gould and others (which might do for Darwin what Althusser tried to do for Marx, or Lacan for Freud), so that I'm not sure it would be appropriate to use Darwin as a scapegoat for this type of thought since it turns out that not even Darwin was "linear."

In any case, the notion of the mode of production continues to provide a vision of history. That is to say, it posits the possibility of the transformation of one mode of production into another, and that is the fundamental form of revolutionary change in history. Consequently, I think that when we talk about the end of history, what we are talking about is the difficulty many people have to imagine another social system beyond this one. The Utopian vision of things no longer works, whereas in the 1960s there was still a strong sense of alternative societies very different from the Soviet model. The irony is that the entire Left that rejected the Soviet model now finds itself, with the failure of the Soviet model, to be incapable of conceiving or imagining something beyond it.

Yet one can recover the possibility of trying to imagine new stages of history by thinking of this possibility of its absence as being itself a historical phenomenon. At the very least, then, the operative part of my theory of postmodernism lies in insisting upon the nature of this as a stage after which other stages can follow that are not necessarily socialism either. But if one thinks about this as a stage in progress, reaching its limits, experiencing crisis and contradictions, followed by a different structure, then I think that one retains a historical perspective. On the *grand récit* of J.-F. Lyotard, I don't think anymore—although I've also used the term—that Marx's series of modes of production are really a *récit* in a narrative sense. I think that the latter is a historical axiom and a series of abstract terms and a combination scheme, but narrative takes place either within each one or around the strange moment of transition between them.

And it has always seemed to me that just as in the Freudian vision there is always this unconscious narrative at work without your knowing it, in this or that primordial fantasy—so also on the level of history the most profound thing that we think without knowing it is perhaps precisely this mystery of transitions in general. It's very clear in the Foucault of *The Order of Things* where one has these cataclysmic ruptures conveyed in a geologic, seismological, and catastrophic language, as if the human mind, in some Kantian way, encounters something inconceivable in such systematic change. For if we necessarily think from within a system, it is hard to see how we can imagine another one. So this is a very profound mystery that is also examined in the Marxist tradition, in the so-called problem of transition, above all that from feudalism to capitalism. It's there that one

would want to think about Marxist notions of narrative and about historical narrative as such. I therefore see a theory of postmodernism, on the
contrary, as a way of reinventing a notion of history on a larger scale, rather
than surrender to postmodern theories about the end of history. We might
say it this way, that a theory of postmodernity need not be postmodern exactly: that is, at any rate, the distinction upon which I want to insist here.

MACHÍN: *In the context of the previous question, what role is played by the
notion of representation?*

JAMESON: Now, what it is crucial to say first about representation is that
the term can clearly mean many things. It can mean the possibility of thinking history finitely, and if we want to talk more about this—and I think we
will in another of your questions—then we should return to the question
of the Utopian impulse, which is indeed implicit in the representation of
history.

Then I see two other things in which the notion of representation is
crucial. One has to do with the reproduction of society through representations—that is to say, the issue of the society of the spectacle, or the society of
the image, or the communicational or informational society. Here, representation is significant in another sense in that, far from being impossible,
it is everywhere—we are drowning in representations. There is a tremendous comment that Hegel makes about thought: speaking about the beginnings of modern philosophy, he observes that the difference between us and
the Greeks is that while the Greeks didn't inherit abstraction, and therefore
had to conquer the abstract laboriously through empirical and perceptual
means, we moderns, on the contrary, are drowning in the abstract, and
because of this we need to rise from the abstract (as Marx puts it) in order
to reach the concrete—this would then be a dialectical way of treating the
abstract without returning to *pensée sauvage*.

We encounter something analogous in the realm of representation.
We are in effect drowning in images and representations. There are various ways to break away from representations. Baudrillard talks about one,
which Susan Sontag also endorses—focusing on the Chinese revolution as
she saw it in those days of the 1960s and 1970s, during the Cultural Revolution, and thinking about a revolutionary Puritanism—when she suggests
that one way of breaking away from images would be the famous remedy of
a diet cure of images, an ecology of images, reducing them, attempting to
make a world in which fewer ads or fewer images assaulted us. But it seems

to me that hers is a nostalgic and regressive approach. We need to go further than this and find a new way to live with images that is not what people had to envision fifty or seventy-five years ago, when society was much poorer in terms of images and representations.

So, one way of speaking about the postmodern would be as a new situation in which we have to adapt to the bombardment of images in ways that the modernists didn't need to confront, let alone the even older modernisms of a Kant or a Descartes.

Finally I would like to talk about representation precisely in terms of modernism and postmodernism, in a more narrow literary sense. It's crucial to make a distinction here: we've characterized the postmodern as a crisis in representation, but another look at modernism suggests modernism was also characterized by a profound crisis in representation. The similarities are sufficiently plausible to make us go beyond this explanation, and here is where I think that one has to link the notion of representation with the idea of totality. Because what we are talking about, I believe, when we use the term *representation* in its elevated, theoretical sense, is in effect the representation of totality. The realist period, in a period of national capitalism, and of relatively small cities and consequently less complexity, people were capable of having a vision of the way in which social order was organized. Indeed, in going back to precapitalism, one remembers Malinowski's famous question about their kinship system to a native of New Guinea. "Just a minute," the informant responded, "it's very complicated, let me show you," and he took out a stick and traced the complete system of kinship of his tribe on the sand of the beach. This is genuine cognitive mapping, producing an image of the totality of the social as it is linked to the very cosmos.

In the realist period, people continued thinking that they knew what a nation-state was, what a collectivity was, who the enemy was, who was on top and underneath in social classes, et cetera, and therefore that the issue of representation of a social totality was a problem that could be solved. But in the imperialist period the problem suddenly gets more complicated. This is the moment in which society extends beyond its national borders and the inside now includes parts of the outside like the colonies. In that moment, it seems to me, it's much more difficult for the subjects of an imperialist metropolis to understand these others that determine, and in a sense define, them. This is why I wanted to connect a theory of modernism, of classic modernism, with a theory of imperialism, because it seemed to me it is the break of imperialism that then explains the crucial characteristic of modernism that is the first crisis in the possibility of representing a social totality.[1]

The concept of such a crisis is then a useful interpreting tool for the modernist period because although the great modernists didn't understand that it couldn't be resolved, they tried to do so, resulting in projects like Joyce's *Ulysses*. The premise of all modernism is that language cannot express these things—that finally the human psyche is too complicated, you can't trace the map of society, you can't position yourself outside of an individual life and look down at totality from above—and yet this is exactly what Joyce tries to do. This is, then, a necessary failure, but it is a failure whose authenticity is guaranteed by the urgency of the impossible attempt to represent this totality. I believe there is already a beginning of this in Lukács's *Theory of the Novel*. But all the great modernist achievements, it seems—whether in music, architecture, and all the rest—revolve around this desperate attempt to skip over the impossibility of representation, and to represent everything in a way that would end in outright representation.

That is the connection between the crisis in representation of totality and the modern. Now, as I've said, this crisis is a desperate matter for the modernist artist, in which he invests all of his existence and passion. But what happens in the postmodern, and the lesson they have learned from the modernists, is precisely that, that the representation of totality is impossible. In that case, it's no longer necessary either, and I think that postmodern art doesn't even try to be monumental in this way; it can live with the impossibility of representation because the totality is out of sight for good; we don't need to represent it. So there is slackness in the postmodern that comes precisely from this abandonment of the effort to represent the social totality. Meanwhile, one has to be dialectical about this and say that the totality has itself changed. In the first or national period, you have a nation-state with one classic capital city. In the second (imperialist) period, there is a group of metropolitan centers, with their colonial systems, with their rivalries between themselves. But this is a series of constellations that can still be conceptualized. Now, suddenly all that has exploded—we have the entire postmodern globe that no longer has centers of power. Imagine trying to think about a multinational corporation alongside the British Empire. The British Empire continues to be a vast and monumental thing, somehow visible; while the multinational is like the core of your computer: it's everything, but one can't grasp it, in a representational way.

That also, then, explains the quantum leap from the problem of the representation of totality in the modern age, and also the reason for being of postmodern art, which for the most part, along with postmodern philosophy and the theory that drives it, has renounced the attempt to do this thing that is now understood as futile. One can talk about the great modern Hegelian and post-Hegelian attempts to construct a system, and I don't see how not to include Heidegger as the last of these along with Sartre and the existentialists; Adorno, in his aesthetic and philosophy is, then, the last ultimate modernist witness of the impossibility of the modern. It is not a matter of saying that the postmodern is bad; but rather that this is the period that we are in and that we have to work with, and that the new problems that we are confronting are not the same as those admirable dilemmas the modernists faced. Modernism was a very great thing; I think that it was a cultural moment as glorious as the Tang Dynasty, or the Athens of the sixth century, but it has disappeared, and it can't return.

MACHÍN: *Your conception of ideology introduces modifications with respect to more classic positions, and particularly with respect to the Althusserian, which is recognized as tributary. What gains does this achieve relative to the state of theoretical discourse, to the cognitive character of tracing "cognitive maps" and to social class?*

JAMESON: In the 1970s, for all kinds of reasons, people began to express their dissatisfaction with the concept of ideology, and they tried to think of new concepts that could be substituted for it. There were many proposals at the time—I don't think it's necessary to enumerate all of them. In effect, "practices" was a crucial one, "discourse analysis" another, and there were psychoanalytical versions of these things. Now it's clear why people became angry with and tired of the concept of ideology, the classic one—what Ernesto Laclau calls the reductionist side of class—being the idea that ideological analysis is simply a question of emphasizing a certain number of visions of the world, and then linking them with various social classes.

I have always thought—but I came to political and philosophical life in a later generation, and I started with people such as the Western Marxists and Sartre, who worried about complicating this notion of ideology—that ideology had to be linked to psychoanalysis. The problem of ideology wasn't only a question of abstract thought in the air that one linked to social class, but it had to do with very complicated mediations between these things. To do ideological analysis was always to postulate a problem, and not a solution; as soon as the question of ideological analysis was raised, you were obligated to invent a new model that would dramatize, in some new way, how a thought or cultural product was linked to social experience, to the history of the family, to the economy, and everything else. Obviously, if people think ideological analysis and the old concept of ideology are simply a group of fixed and unchanging categories, then it is not satisfactory. But, in my opinion, the most productive notion of ideology is the model that tries to connect questions of individual subjectivity with larger issues of the social and of group fantasy, as in Althusser.

His model is, without a doubt, not completely satisfactory, but it seems to me that it tries to put together a series of things that one would need to link in order for any theory of ideology to be satisfactory. I also have the feeling that the theorists who have abandoned the word *ideology* for something else always end up losing sight of the bigger connections, and the theories and analyses that have followed this cource, many of them very exciting (like the work of [Pierre] Bourdieu, for example) have, in my opinion, failed in that final function of the classical concept which was to convey a model.

Having said this, I think that we then have to add something else. It's implicit in my theory of postmodernism that the nature of culture itself, its own location in social life, has been modified. The culture of the nineteenth century was a relatively limited part of social life. Today culture is virtually omnipresent, and this means that the very function of cultural production will be different in the two periods. The place of abstraction, of opinion and abstract values in this society is radically different from what it was in the nineteenth century. In the nineteenth century, the new regimes—like the Third Republic in France—still required the legitimation of the ideologists; it was called the "republic of professors" precisely because the positivists, the philosophers, and sociologists were called upon to invent the theory of a new secular state, that is, to give it a crown of philosophical and ideological value and assure its legitimization by means of philosophy.

Our own society no longer needs legitimization of this type. Abstraction is no longer called upon to fulfill this task. Our philosophers no longer have that function, which means that the role of abstract thought itself, the function of abstract thought in this society, is different and, I am tempted to say, very reduced. Many of the things that Adorno said about positivism continue to be relevant in a much-modified sense for our society. What makes our society function, then? What makes it legitimate? It seems to me that it's not philosophical justification or ideological justification in that abstract sense; nor could it be simply the material fact that it fulfills, because it doesn't fulfill many people in this world, or even in this society.

Because of this, there has to be a third thing that continues being ideology, but an ideological mechanism of another type; some have argued that it's simply consumption itself. It is indeed the fact of the ideology of consumption as a practice which assures this society. There would be other ways of talking about the basic ideologies of our society, but it's clear that if you see the principal ideological mechanism, the mechanism of legitimization as consumption, and the vision of consumption as practice, that is very different than talking about the values of the bourgeoisie—liberty, equality, fraternity. And in that moment, therefore, ideological analysis has to be restructured in order to accommodate the forms of ideology that are, in effect, revealed in social practices and in space itself.

Many of the new theories that replace ideology, or that attempt to replace the old concept of ideology, try to resolve this and therefore highlight the postmodern change of classic ideology to new types that adapt to practice, to daily life, to consumption, to images. And there has to be a modification in the role of philosophy itself. We know what some of these changes are because the philosophers have told us: we no longer have a concept of the truth; we don't want a system; and so on. There are a series of ways in which contemporary philosophy has become textual and doesn't want to create a system of the type that endured, no doubt, from Descartes to the existentialists. None of the contemporary philosophers do that. Therefore I propose to call what happens now not philosophy, but rather, theory; and even then I don't like the word *theory* because it still implies a way of thinking, when that thinking has in effect turned into a way of writing.

For that reason I want to call this new thing that has replaced philosophy "theoretical discourse." This is meant to imply a certain type of writing that is very difficult to make concrete. And it implies a situation like the following: truth no longer exists, but error does. Therefore in your writing as a philosopher, you can no longer express the truth—and in effect, expression doesn't exist anymore as a category—but what you can do is denounce error. So the work of theoretical discourse is, in effect, to write sentences that don't affirm philosophical positions in a positive nature and are also in a constant battle to denounce, intercept, deconstruct forms of error or fallacies. And those are very complicated ways of writing because, obviously, they never work. You may not want a position or a system, but it is as if it ends up organizing itself around you, so that there come to be philosophers whose entire philosophy is constructed upon not having a system, but whose key terms nonetheless suggest one.

The slogans for today are "antifoundationalism" and "antiessentialism."

Everything seems to come down to this, that you don't want to have fundamental principles, you don't want to have ultimate presuppositions, you don't want to have a system or truth, and therefore your thinking becomes a textualization, a process of writing. Except that the text congeals into a game of positions, and your own name is stuck to the thing like a brand; it becomes a system despite yourself. So these are necessary failures in contemporary philosophy, in the contemporary system, and in effect I believe that Derrida himself expressed the impossible, tragic aspect of this a long time ago (I don't know if he still thinks this) when he said that we cannot, today, invent new forms of thinking and new concepts because we are inside the system in which we are surrounded by traditional concepts, and in which conceptuality has disintegrated. But they are all we have; and we can't invent new words and a new language; what we have to do is continue using those "under erasure" until the entire system itself is transformed, and then, in that moment, fresh conceptual languages and new forms of philosophical truth and creativity will again become possible.

This idea seems to me consistent with Marxism, namely, that the dominant thought inside a certain mode of production will be the hegemonic point of view of the class that governs, and that new things finally come to pass and bear fruit only when there is a transformation in the system. What is now ambiguous is that for many people, this new stage of capitalism seems to be a wholly new system. So, many people think that postmodernism gives one the possibility of new thought in new ways, which is something that I will discuss. But it seems to me that the debate on the postmodern, about that postmodern philosophy that was previously called poststructuralism, and that now I call theoretical discourse, should start there; and it is in that sense that theory is a cultural expression of postmodernism, as much as other types of cultural phenomena.

Certain elements of poststructuralism have been profoundly contestatory, usefully negative, political in local and restricted ways; of course deconstruction can operate in that way in many places—as can Foucault, with his emphasis on one's own local politics. And then clearly there are political aims and emphases throughout a range of contemporary theoretical discourses. But I think that very few of them are capable of anticipating the transformation of the system entirely. And to the degree to which my politics include that, then at that point I must think that these contemporary philosophies are no longer politically productive and that one's task, as an intellectual, is to think about how systematic change would be conceivable in a period where it seems that no one sees it as being possible any longer.

That strikes me as a loftier mission for philosophy and theory than the mission of local forms of resistance.

On the other hand, obviously resistance must also continue. This is the point, both about philosophy and local politics, that I tried to make here—that nobody is talking about abandoning every form of struggle and local resistance. But the force of those resistances tends to be undermined when people are faced with a Nietzschean eternal return, a permanent struggle that never leads anywhere. While it often seems that these struggles do ideally project a vision of total change, it is not empirically present in them, but it has an allegorical relationship with their content. I have been impressed by the way that this has occurred in some North American political attempts. The late Michael Harrington, for example, traveled tirelessly throughout the whole country, giving at least two hundred speeches a year, talking about socialism and the necessity for systemic change. So there has to be activity on both levels—the empirical and the systemic—in order for there to be an authentic politics.

I don't believe that people really think politically if they have surrendered to the idea that the system can't change in its overall dimensions, and that they can only attempt to modify the parts that they don't like.

The question of social classes, the question about cognitive mapping, is that we are in a situation where the world is so complicated, and the capillaries of social power are so small, that it becomes very difficult for people to orient themselves as class subjects within this totality. I don't think for a minute that classes in and of themselves have disappeared. If you want proof that this is still capitalism and not postindustrial society, it's that the multinational companies and all the other businesses still aim for profit and profitability. New forms of organization haven't emerged, with new and different means and ends. Besides that, it's not important to me how much production has disappeared from the United States; things continue to be produced elsewhere, they are produced by producers, and because of that there needs to be a system of dichotomous classes, provided that one always remembers the famous distinction between "classes in themselves" and "classes for themselves." It seems very clear that there remain classes in themselves, class positions, in this type of society.

On the other hand, the people that occupy these class positions are not necessarily conscious of themselves in terms of class, and there was clearly a crisis in the "classes for themselves" that accompanied the classic workers' unions and the classic forms of industrial production. When Marx talked about proletarianization, he talked about salaried work; and this is a global development and a tendency implicit in globalization. But the forms of class consciousness that correspond to the new global division of labor, and the new global situation, have not yet emerged because they are too new. Because of this, what cognitive mapping tries to do as a form of class consciousness is dual, it is epistemological as well as cultural, critical as well as Utopian.

Epistemologically, one has in the first place to stress all the difficulties that we have in seeing our class position in this enormous global reality, and one has to verify the difficulties of such consciousness for all the other social subjects around us. It seems that a sociology based upon this notion would want to explore that—to see how various social subjects imagine and trace their worlds, what they omit, what they can't see. If they believe, for example, that the working classes have disappeared and that there are only middle classes today, to what type of map does this correspond? And what are the causes that determine such limits? So, there is an empirical investigation to be undertaken as to how, in fact, we continue to make imperfect images of the world for ourselves in a situation in which the Cold War seems over; or at least in which people imagine that revolutionary movements have ceased to exist, and therefore they have to adjust their vision of the world in other ways.

On the other hand, if it's true that all these subjects continue being class subjects, then behind all those images—that can focus on nonclassist visions of things, which can take the form of nationalisms and neonationalisms, or the form of the various populisms or of religious fundamentalism—behind these things, the fact remains of the classes in themselves. So perhaps it would also be possible to detect the possibility of class consciousness within those other forms of consciousness. That class consciousness would then be the Utopian element in these other maps of the world; and it seems that there is something—for intellectuals—something active and political in the process of not trying only to see what images of the world are reflected by our culture and our social visions but also in some sense to try to think about what other possibilities and radical alternatives they carry within themselves unconsciously.

And here we return to the other question about whether postmodernism can be political, if it's completely complicit with the system of multinational media. I believe that one of the healthy things about art today is that perhaps people are, again, a little more willing to tolerate certain new didactic elements in art that were anathema for modernism. So, I think that it's not impossible to imagine ways in which a postmodern art could teach people about the structure of the world. Hans Haacke, for instance, talks about the homeopathy of today's art, suggesting that if this is a culture of images, and we are sick of images, then there also exists a homeopathic strategy that consists in absorbing the toxin deliberately, as an aesthetic.

What he then tries to do, for example, is to take the museum in which he is exhibiting and turn it inside out—the museums themselves become part of the work of art. So when the Guggenheim commissions a work from him, included within the resultant work turns out to be a list of the owners and donors of the Guggenheim, and what those people were personally and institutionally involved in and responsible for: the war in Vietnam, for example. And suddenly this small speck that was a work of art within an institutional structure swallows the institution and can be used as a lesson about the entire multinational institution in the world today. So, I believe that there is an entirely new range of possibilities for political art that could in a sense be didactic. And these are related in a more profound way to the spatiality of the postmodern.

And we are also in space in the sense of the spatiality of the image, of television, including, I would say, music—you could think that rock is very important in the postmodern, and I agree—but it's a spatial music, that is to say, music is transmitted through a thing inside your ears, or it's installed in a club and orchestrated by light, or on the music channel MTV, it is captured by the narrative space of video. Thus it seems that even music passes under the aegis of space. The victim of all of this is language and the language arts, together with traditional philosophy. Language has suffered the destiny of primary objective manipulation by a system of standardized means. Consequently, the art of language and what it can do has become a good deal less significant. This is the sense in which, from a narrow cultural point of view, space is important. Now, clearly, the notion of cognitive mapping wasn't an accident, because from a wider political perspective, the fact of global space is now determining in a way that it never was in the imperialist period. For England, to have had the Suez Canal and the connection to India was always crucially and strategically important, but other parts of the world were no longer so important from that older perspective. But a new and simultaneous geopolitics is being born that is at one with the postmodern system, of the multinational system, and that fixes the agenda for both culture and political theory, so that it's not an accident that one of the best contemporary geographers, David Harvey, has come to write one of the principal books about postmodernism, having come to understand that the postmodern phenomenon is his topic. That is to say, postmodernism is profoundly geographical in a way that wasn't obviously the case for earlier modes of production.

**MACHÍN:** *Perry Anderson, in his characterization of the model of Western Marxism, argues that the aesthetic has always been a laboratory of social theory. What is your opinion with respect to this, and to the relationship between aesthetics and politics?*

**JAMESON:** I think that Anderson's commentary is a timely one because it seems to me to have been the case—Lukács is the one that really confirms this—that much of Marx and the dialectic itself can be seen as a product of [Friedrich] Schiller's aesthetics. This is true in a certain Marxist tradition that reaches Lukács himself and, after him, includes [Walter] Benjamin; Sartre in another way; Adorno also; and so on with others. But it may no longer be so pertinent once the classic aesthetic has disappeared: it's clear that if you don't have an aesthetic, then you aren't going to have the same kind of laboratory in which to work, or from which to emerge. So I would want to restrict the historical relevance to that period and ask what the newer laboratories are to be.

NOTE

1. See Fredric Jameson, "Modernism and Imperialism," in *Nationalism, Colonialism, and Literature*, by Terry Eagleton, Jameson, Edward W. Said (Minneapolis: University of Minnesota Press, 1990), 43–66.

# Interview with Sara Danius and Stefan Jonsson

**DANIUS:** *When Jacques Derrida lectured at Duke University a couple of weeks ago, he presented fragments from his latest book* Spectres de Marx *which, among other things, appears to be both a defense of Marxism and a critical rereading of Marx's writings.[1] He said that "Marxism is indispensable and insufficient." Do you agree?*

**JAMESON:** I don't mind endorsing that statement. I think what he means is that the Marxism that has existed so far is insufficient because we're in a new period and much of it has to be adapted to new realities. You see, I think of Marxism as a problematic, and therefore I don't think that the various solutions that people also sometimes identify with Marxism as an ideology are necessarily binding. Marxism consists in acknowledging, recognizing, or being committed to a certain problematic, and that problematic includes notions of contradiction, commodification, and so forth. I would rewrite Derrida's remark as suggesting that we need the problematic of Marxism today more than ever in confronting late capitalism, but we have to invent new solutions to some of its problems.

The problem with new solutions, however, is that if you shift languages, you often lose the problem itself. This has happened several times in the history of Marxism: for example when Gramsci, under the threat of censorship, out of concern that the prison authorities were reading his manuscripts, used a systematic series of euphemisms for Marxist problems. Marxism was called "the philosophy of praxis." Ideology was called "hegemony." Then a later Gramscianism developed after the war, in which suddenly "hegemony" replaces the older Marxist themes and sails off as a theory in its own right. Thereby it lost, I think, some of those connections to the earlier

---

This interview was recorded at Duke University in October 1993. It first appeared in Swedish in *Res Publica* 24 (1993). It has not been previously published in English.

problems that it still had in Gramsci's mind. Another example: in the 1960s, there was a systematic attempt to replace the notion of "ideology" with notions like that of "practice." But there, too, once you lose the problematic that ideology was invented to solve, once you embrace "the theory of practice," then you suddenly cease to ask yourself certain basic questions that "the theory of ideology" still kept alive. How far you can innovate is a very tricky business. That's why I come back to notions of what I call transcoding. One has to keep translating these things back and forth; one has to invent a new language, and then every so often translate it back into the older one in order to see how far we've come, what difference in perceptions or focus the new concept gives us, to what degree it still connects up to the older problems, and so on. But if one invents a new language—it is like inventing a new religion. At what point does the new religion cease to be connected to the older one and declare its independence? That's the problem with Marxism and its offshoots. If I hear Derrida right, he's saying that we have to keep our affiliation to the old "religion" but invent new versions of it for the contemporary, or rather postcontemporary, period.

**DANIUS:** *You said earlier that you perceive Derrida's talk as a statement, a forceful and courageous statement.*

**JAMESON:** You have to remember that in France the intellectuals in the 1960s were 95 percent Marxists. Today 89 percent, let's say, are anti-Marxist. On the French scene, Derrida's project is very provocative, as will be Deleuze's forthcoming book *Grandeur de Marx.*[2] They are very basic challenges to a whole new anti-Marxist, neocapitalist orthodoxy among French intellectuals. It will be very interesting to see what reactions this gets. Derrida himself seemed rather sanguine about it. He seemed to feel that a lot of people he knew were dissatisfied. A good deal of the media and the intelligentsia in France are committed to certain kinds of anticommunist, antisocialist, and anti-Marxist positions for which a statement like this ought to be unsatisfactory. Here of course, it doesn't matter so much because there wasn't the same kind of Marxism, and therefore not the same kind of obligatory Marxism on the part of the intellectuals.

**DANIUS:** *At the same time there's a cliché about Derrida and deconstruction as being altogether apolitical.*

**JAMESON:** Yes, but I never thought that was true. One knew that Derrida had, via Althusser, associations with French Marxism and communism that were much closer than those of many other poststructuralists. If you look at some of the earlier interviews in *Positions*, for example, they spell out the whole political context and the political presuppositions that Derrida brought to deconstruction. When his work was removed from a fundamentally Marxist and political context and exported across the water to a fundamentally non-Marxist and nonpolitical context, the things that Derrida took for granted in many of his own formulations and expressions simply evaporated.

But again, this involves a global mapping, if you like, and differences in national situation. It would be interesting to see who comes out for *Spectres de Marx* in Germany, especially the new Germany. It doesn't seem to me at all implausible that someone like Habermas would do that. I think Habermas is very keenly aware of what is lost in this transition to global capitalism. I'm not predicting anything, but there will certainly be German versions.

**DANIUS:** *Your own more systematic interest in the Marxist tradition of cultural and literary criticism comes to the fore with* Marxism and Form. *To look back on your intellectual career, what made you write* Marxism and Form?

**JAMESON:** I was a student in the Eisenhower era, and the years of McCarthyism. The image that even liberals had of Marxism at that time was crude and relatively unphilosophical. The idea that most people had of any kind of Marxist literary criticism or cultural criticism was a very stark caricature. I was formed by contemporary French thought at that period, for example, the Marxist elements of Sartre. Roland Barthes's *Writing Degree Zero*—I think it was published when I was in college—was also very important to me. I therefore understood Marxism and the possibilities of Marxist literary criticism in a different way from the way I think most Americans did. At that time, as I've said, the French intelligentsia was essentially Marxist in orientation. Actually, my first influence, or the first example I ever had of a Marxist criticism, was not Sartre but Henri Lefebvre's book on Pascal. And since I had an association with Lefebvre later on, that always struck me as interesting and fitting.

I also studied in Germany. This was in the late 1950s, and West Germany of course was very far from having any Marxist intellectual movements in that period. Nonetheless, in Germany there were two monuments to Marxism. One was the Frankfurt School, which had just come back to West Germany. The other was Lukács, whose writings were published in East Germany. So I knew there was a range of Marxist criticism in German that was also very far from these caricatures.

The whole ambition of *Marxist and Form* was to make available in English some of those traditions, and to make it more difficult for people to entertain these clichés and caricatural ideas of what Marxism was on the cultural level, particularly since we all have come to realize in recent years that the great and interesting developments of twentieth-century Marxism have been in the realm of the superstructure—culture, theory of ideology, and so forth. I don't know whether we actually accomplished this, because frankly, some people still have the same caricatural and idiotic notions of Marxism today. But at least that was the point of the book, and that's why it ranged over French—Sartrean—and German elements. My other book of that period, *The Prison-House of Language*, was originally conceived as part of *Marxism and Form*. That's where I deal with Althusser and more recent French structuralist thought, which also have a connection to Marxism; for example, Lévi-Strauss has a declaration of faith in Marxism at the beginning of his autobiography, *Tristes Tropiques*. I separated out structuralist thought, however, and that's why the French side of *Marxism and Form* may seem a little bit truncated.

**DANIUS:** *It's ten years between your Sartre study and* Marxism and Form. *The historical materialist interest isn't really pronounced in* Sartre: Origins of a Style. *Was there a slow shift in your intellectual orientation during these years?*

**JAMESON:** No, I don't think so at all. I think I always thought in these ways. But the framework of the Sartre study, which was a dissertation and focused on style, was designed to explore formal aspects in Sartre's work that people hadn't noticed. On the whole, he was seen as a rather trendy or slogan-oriented philosopher. I never really did a Marxist analysis of Sartre himself. I played at doing that at various moments. I think the sociological analysis of philosophy is very rudimentary in comparison to the sociological or historical materialist approach to literature, and I know very few good examples. Bourdieu's book on Heidegger is one, and Sartre's own analysis of philosophy is of course another. But then I wasn't equipped to do that, and I think that's why the Sartre book seems relatively ungrounded sociologically in comparison to later books of mine. I had already begun to read the Frankfurt School when I wrote the book, however, and I wouldn't say there was any fundamental change in my positions, although I'm sure they got complicated and acquired a wider range of theoretical references later on. And then, it's not just people who change, it's also history itself that changed between 1959, when I finished *Sartre*, and 1969, when I was finishing *Marxism and Form*.

**JONSSON:** *Then you published your book on Wyndham Lewis,* Fables of Aggression, *and after that* The Political Unconscious, *which in many ways is a highly theoretical work. A central category of this book is the "political unconscious," which refers to an aesthetic or cognitive agency that fabricates symbolic resolutions of historical and social contradictions. At the same time, this is a category—or notion, concept, or word—that remains undefined and floating. What has happened to this concept in you later work? And was it a philosophical concept or more of a metaphor?*

**JAMESON:** One could argue that *The Political Unconscious* is not a theoretical but a methodological book. It's a book about interpretation, and it tries to defend and illustrate a kind of depth interpretation, or hermeneutics. The idea of the political unconscious is a symbol for that process. I'm not endorsing some ontological idea that there is a personal unconscious, on the one hand, and a collective or political one, on the other. We have derived from Freud's notion of the unconscious a very basic form of interpretation which he lays out in *The Interpretation of Dreams*—the interpretation of the symptom. That has always been for me a fundamental model of the interpretive process, and it is one of the great influences on me. This model was enriched and modified by Lévi-Strauss's structuralist interpretation, which I have always found interesting, although some of it is more questionable. To adopt the Freudian slogan of an unconscious is by way of a gesture indicating the relationship between ideological analysis of literary or narrative texts and Freud's analysis of dreams, because I would like to keep that connection. Now, I think there might be several reasons for why I don't practice this so much anymore. When *The Political Unconscious* was thought through and composed, none of us had a very clear idea of the thing we now call postmodernism. We were not really aware of the magnitude of that cultural break that had already taken place, and which only gradually was being discovered.

The Political Unconscious was written especially with an eye to modernist or realist texts. In the postmodern area, the notion of an unconscious, along with the notion of a hermeneutic or interpretation, has fallen into discredit; one could use an even stronger word than that. Foucault has a very powerful attack on the notion of hermeneutics in the first volume of The History of Sexuality. His stance is characteristic of a lot of postmodern intellectual positions: that hermeneutics is somehow intellectually unjustified, that there is no unconscious in that ontological sense, and so forth. Now, I take that seriously, but as an intellectual symptom. That is, it seems to me that if everyone thinks this, then the thought has a certain symptomatic importance, and I take it to mean that postmodern texts really do not function in the same way as earlier ones and do not offer themselves to interpretation in the same way. I think this also has something to do with the relative retreat of literature as the fundamental art form of postmodernism. My interpretive proposals essentially have to do with literary works and with the kinds of interpretation that they demand, but I would still argue that the method I'm suggesting remains absolutely valid. It's essentially a symptomal method, to use that kind of neologism the Althusserians like. It wants to see literature as symptom, not only in the content but in the form itself. It wants to read the formal structures of the various, especially modernist, innovations as so many signs and symptoms that can lead us back to transformations in the social raw material. So there's a way in which this ties on to theories of literary production that were current in the 1970s, but it adds in the problem of the raw material, which I think none of those theories really did (except for Macherey). I continue to think that if literary texts no longer offer themselves to interpretation today in the same way, it seems possible that mass cultural texts do, and I have done a number of interpretations of mass cultural texts that I think are very much in the spirit of the literary analyses of The Political Unconscious. So I see why you would think I have moved away from this term and idea, but it's really more of a readjustment to differences in the cultural situation that have happened since then.

**JONSSON:** *So it is only in certain historical moments that cultural artifacts have a political unconscious?*

**JAMESON:** To be sure, yes. I think that in precapitalist society, for example, formulaic texts, and texts that work in very fixed forms and genres clearly aren't interpretable in the same way at all.

**DANIUS:** *Is there a link between your idea of "cognitive mapping" and the need for it, and the fact that in the postmodern period texts do not seem to have a "political unconscious"?*

**JAMESON:** The program for "cognitive mapping" has more to do with cultural politics and with what one would want to suggest that the artists themselves do. That's a more active cultural-political idea. The notion of the "political unconscious" is more interpretive and retrospective; it has more to do with analyzing texts of the past than [with] projecting ones for the future.

**JONSSON:** *But both concepts would, in some Lukácsian sense, be about trying to think the totality?*

**JAMESON:** First of all, they're both epistemological ideas. The political unconscious implies that certain kinds of knowledge about society are encoded in literary texts and in their forms. The analysis I propose is designed to make it possible to recover some of that knowledge. The notion of cognitive mapping insists much more strongly on the way in which art itself functions as a mode of knowledge, a mode of knowledge of the totality. Obviously, both ideas do that, but in different ways. I think one has to remember that concepts of totality have acquired a very special meaning today when capitalism is a genuinely global functioning system in a way it was not in the imperialist period, or earlier. Therefore today the concept of totality has a much more concrete meaning.

**DANIUS:** *In your work, the notion of narrative is closely related to that of the "political unconscious." In* The Political Unconscious *you say something like, "using the shorthand of philosophical idealism, I take narrative to be the central instance or function of the human mind." There appears to be a conflict between this belief in what seems to be an almost Kantian or transcendental category—narrative—and the historical materialist presupposition that all human experience is mediated by history.*

**JAMESON:** I'm glad you quoted the matter about "shorthand" because I'm using this ontological or Kantian language as a way of making this point very quickly. I don't believe in a human nature, and therefore don't believe that the mind has a given structure, or that this narrative instance is part of the mind's structure. Part of the importance of the insistence on narrative—it's obviously not just mine, it's been present since the beginning of the structuralist period—is, at least in the United States, a reaction to the emphasis in literary criticism on lyric, and the way in which even the modern novel is understood to be non-narrative and essentially lyric, and the way in which therefore both lyric poetry and certain kinds of poetic language are placed at the center of what became an aesthetic of modernism as an ideology. My argument is a reaction against this; it wants to replace this centrality of poetic language with the notion of narrative as such, and with a different conception of form. It's a conception of form that has to both involve process and, at the outer limit, history, since historiography is essentially telling yourself a story of events and organizing events in narrative terms.

I'm also influenced by a book by Arthur Danto on history and narrative, in which he tries to show that all historiography, even statistical history and so forth, can always be rewritten in narrative form, and that its basic categories, such as causality, are fundamental tropes or forms by which we understand human events and realities. This shorthand means to imply all of those things, and hopefully would take us in a direction of history and historical narrative rather than in the direction of static Kantian categories. Even when one deals with the importance of space in contemporary or postmodern thought, this is a very different emphasis from Kant's notion that space and time are these empty, immutable categories, or rather preconditions, for thought. I think the contemporary idea is that there are various kinds of historical space and apprehensions of space, just as each mode of production has had its own conception of and experience of time. So one cannot address the issue in these general terms. But I meant it to be provocative, and I guess it has been!

JONSSON: *What happens with the notion of narrative in postmodernism? Clearly, the notion of "cognitive mapping" and narrative are related, although you use the notion of narrative much less in your later writings than in, for example,* The Political Unconscious. *Sometimes, however, narrative is foregrounded as a key category that you use to analyze the way in which cultural spaces in the periphery of the world system still provide a possibility to grasp the totality and the processes of capitalism as such in certain kinds of narrative form.*

JAMESON: Well, that's because narrative often takes refuge in either non-hegemonic spaces or subcultural areas. So there is a great deal of narrative going on in the contemporary world, but it seems to me that when litera-ture becomes conscious of its postmodern vocation, it tends to have the form of sheer textual production. That is to say, the narrative categories disintegrate, and one has to do with a microscopic notion of change from sentence to sentence, and that tends to interest me less than the larger, older categories of narrative. I also think that there is a postmodernity which entails a basic change, at least in the center, of the ways in which narrative is produced. On the other hand, there is also a recrudescence of nonliterary storytelling, so narrative is very much present in our culture, but I think it's no longer so strongly identified with literature itself. This is why in the center literature is enfeebled as a form of cultural production, although not necessarily in the periphery.

The other thing one should say about narrative is that it becomes in-creasingly difficult to construct a narrative which does justice to what we were calling "cognitive mapping," which does justice to the situation of in-dividuals in ever more horrendously complex social matrices which end up being global. Narrative seems supremely able to deal with the way in which the truth of individual life was constructed by smaller environments. In the nineteenth-century novel, the narrative apparatus became much more complex in order to deal with the truth of individual experience in a na-tional setting, and of course even more so in imperialist settings. But in the global perspective of late capitalism, there's a real crisis in this older nar-rative machinery. The places from which one ought to have expected a real development of a global kind of narrativity are the ones in which narrative has been in crisis, that is to say, the center, whereas in the periphery, certain kinds of narrative reactions to this seem possible, because they're not at the center of the multinational complexity.

JONSSON: *Why does narrative, as you said, take refuge in nonhegemonic spaces or subcultural areas? Why would narrative be more "vital" or even "true" in such areas? It could be argued that in contemporary Western lit-erature, there is a kind of return to narrative and storytelling. What is the difference?*

JAMESON: Maybe I could illustrate it best not so much for postmodernity as for modernity, and then we could extrapolate to postmodernity. If mo-dernity emerges essentially in the first world, in the 1880s, in the moment of global imperialism and of the setting up of the first imperial systems and the dividing up of Africa and so forth, then that is strictly contemporaneous with modernism and its emergence in symbolism. The point is this: In the center there is a separation, a gap, between knowledge and lived truth; and in the center, which develops these very complex, subtle, and responsive instruments of representation, there is a very keen sense of how to represent what's happening in the psyche. But the center does not have to know about the periphery, and therefore the center thinks it can tell those stories without reference to the structure of imperialism as a whole, that is, it tends to omit the parts of the story that result from the way in which the first world derives its wealth and its privileges from the third world.[3] Epistemologically, its mode of expression is incomplete. It need not know about the third world, whereas the third world obviously cannot *not* know about the first world. The third world *has* to know. The periphery must be aware at every moment that everything that happens to it is somehow determined by absent forces elsewhere. You know the famous saying, "When the United States sneezes, Brazil gets pneumonia." That's an argument one could already make for the modernist period, and it's even more valid for the postmodern.

Your question about the reemergence of narrative and storytelling in the West actually has more to do with a different kind of phenomenon, namely, the conflation of high art and mass culture. In mass culture, the storytelling impulse is fundamental, and narratives never disappear out of mass culture. They come back in the form of parody and pastiche in postmodern narratives. So the fragments of narrativity are now far more omnipresent in what used to be high culture in postmodernism than was the case in the modernist period. On the other hand, one also has to say that the periphery is much more sophisticated too. The information revolution means that in fact the third world knows even more about the first world than it used to, and that the third world is also in the first world, in the cities, and so forth. These relationships have obviously been modified, but I think the formula might still be useful and valid.

**JONSSON:** *Would that also account for the impression that many people have today, that the most powerful and vital literary stories are being told by writers that occupy the border between center and periphery, or have access to, or experience of, two or more cultures? I think of writers such as Nadine Gordimer, Salman Rushdie, V. S. Naipaul, Toni Morrison, and Derek Walcott.*

**JAMESON:** Yes, absolutely. There are several reasons for that. One is that they deal with social material that has not been named yet, whereas white first-world male writers have behind them a history of other white male novels that go back several hundred years. A great deal more of their normal daily experience has already been expressed in literature and found its form than is the case for other social selves. That's one thing. Another reason is indicated by the classic dogmatic prejudice of a certain kind of vulgar Marxism: that capitalism is anti-aesthetic. Now, we can see that this not only expresses anti-intellectualism in certain first world countries, at least in the United States. But, in addition, it designates the exhaustion of culture in the first world, and the need for the first world constantly to cannibalize fresh sources of cultural production. Hence the vogue of black language in the United States. Black language is still alive, and it is constantly reinventing itself. The white cultural power structure cannibalizes that, draws on it, co-opts it, if you like, and reinvigorates itself. This is now going on in the world at large; if you look at music, for example, the way in which black music, South African, or Latin American music is being used in the first world. It's probably wrong to call it completely exploitative. The argument has to be more complicated today. Paul Simon's *Graceland* is not only plagiarism, cultural theft, or whatever, it's also a form of cultural diffusion which is comparable, if you like, in mass culture to what the Romantics did for world culture in the early nineteenth century. It's a complicated matter that has many positive features, but it also signals the exhaustion of the capacity of first world societies to produce their own culture. This is even more strikingly true in Europe and Japan, which are both, I believe, dead culturally. They are great museums of the great classical culture that they have both preserved. But the Europe of today, this pan-European culture that people try to patch back together, is just a parody of what existed in the 1920s and 1930s, the culture of Eliot, Rilke, and Valéry. It doesn't exist anymore; what exists is a simulacrum. As for Japan, and according to the Japanese themselves, it is very much in that same situation. And if the United States is not, this is because of the role of the minorities. American hegemonic culture has until now been much more permeable to this presence of minorities than Europe or, especially, Japan, although with the new immigrant voices in Europe the situation seems to be changing.

JONSSON: *When you mention "dead cultures," "vital cultures," and "cultures being vitalized by minorities," what do you mean by the word* culture?

JAMESON: I mean that aesthetic production spills over into daily life and organizes or reorganizes it. In the modern period, the great modernist paintings and modernist architecture gradually began to lend a style to modern daily life. Today, Europe and Japan are drawing on North American mass culture and are essentially colonized by it. It's very sad, and I speak as a Europhile and an anti-American.[4]

**DANIUS:** *The attempt to create or name a pan-European culture could also be understood as a reaction to being on the threshold of postmodernity and postmodernism.*

**JAMESON:** Yes, as ways of resisting what is essentially American cultural imperialism. Unfortunately, so far what is oppositional to Hollywood and US TV productions are the museums full of masterpieces. I suspect that if and when other areas recover economically, there will be whole new impulses. Eastern Europe and Russia have enormous reserves of cultural energy, and so does Latin America. The three Chinas are already producing enormous amounts of culture and will have a profound impact on everything we're thinking, from film and music to fashion.

**DANIUS:** *You said earlier that it is only in certain historical periods that literary texts have a "political unconscious." In* The Geopolitical Aesthetic, *you talk about a "geopolitical unconscious," and you've moved into what we call the periphery and into mass culture, more specifically film. What is the difference between your earlier notion of the political unconscious and the idea of a geopolitical one?*

**JAMESON:** One way to describe these differences would be to say that *The Political Unconscious* dealt with the national culture, the culture of the nation-state, and the ways in which the collective imaginary of the nation-state registered—both concealed and expressed—its class dynamics. When you come into the postmodern period, it seems that much of what we think of in terms of class dynamics is still present, but now it's projected onto a global map, so to speak. It is no longer a national working class, or its fractions, or the consciousness of a national bourgeoisie that's in question, but rather essentially imaginary representations of the United States versus Japan as an adversary in industrial production, or worries in the United States about cheap labor from Mexico, cheap labor in Latin America and China. The unconscious fantasies that were constructed around the national situation have been projected onto an international space, in which they wear again the masks and the trappings of national identities and foreign cultures. These fantasies are, to be sure, very often simply disguises for new class fantasies on a global scale.

**DANIUS:** *So in a sense, it is only by moving into the "margins" of the world system that we get a more encompassing, "total" map that includes the center as well, and this on the logic of some Hegelian master-slave dialectic?*

**JAMESON:** Right. At the same time, we're talking about this in very simplified ways. The fantasies themselves probably are very complicated. The center becomes a character: America versus terrorists, who are generally Arabs or Iranians, or Muslims generally; America versus the Somalis, who want to blow us up or shoot our soldiers and so forth. In that version of the fantasy, America is a simplified character/actant, whereas in other ones, all of these things would be America's own minorities that would be part of a fantasy of the outside world. The fantasies about foreign rivalry are used to integrate internal minorities and make them into a single national unity.

**JONSSON:** *Gayatri Spivak once said a similar thing about the Gulf War: it's precisely because you have female soldiers fighting in the American army that the US appears as a country of liberty as against the patriarchal Iraq, where women walk behind veils.*

**JAMESON:** Yes, that's very important and very clearly the case. You have any number of movies, videos, or television programs in which the American team includes a black man, a woman, or a Chicano. A more complicated formal game is at work here.

**DANIUS:** *I would like to ask you about the notion of reification, which is central to your theory of postmodernism and many of your analyses of both high cultural and mass cultural phenomena. You repeatedly insist that today's culture, at least in the West, is completely immersed in the commodifying process. We consume consumption, we fetishize the commodity. Yet to say that commodification is everywhere is in a sense to say that it is nowhere. Now, of systemic accounts of a certain cultural period or episteme you have said that the cultural critic wins by way of his total, interlocking system, and the reader gives in to a sense of pessimism and powerlessness, and this is something you yourself want to avoid. In regard to Foucault's account of the Panopticon in* Discipline and Punish, *you have written that "if the system* *were as tendentially totalizing as he said it was, then all social revolts, let alone 'revolutionary' impulses, . . . would in reality be a function of its immanent dynamic." You add that "the point is that systems, even total systems, change." One could say that with your emphasis on reification and commodification as analytical tools and codes with which to describe the logic of contemporary culture, you end up with something that is close to a "total" description of the fate of culture and the entire Lebenswelt in late capitalist society. My question is: If, as you also insist, the task of the critic is to produce concepts with which to think reality—the world system, late capitalism, the "nature" of postmodernism—then why not invent or produce concepts that enable us to perceive emergent tendencies, emergent changes, even emergent cultures even in Western culture? In other words, it's partly a consequence of the theory itself, since it centers on the notion of commodity fetishism, that we have now reached an age where, to paraphrase Adorno and Horkheimer, "the fully commodified earth radiates disaster triumphant."*

JAMESON: Well, that's very much the discourse of a certain kind of postmodernism—that a new cultural pluralism is possible, that new forms of resistance are emerging, that those are organized around the new social movements, around race, class, gender, and so forth. I don't think one needs to invent these concepts; they are everywhere. There are really two separate issues in what you said. As for the issue of the total system, the models of total systems built by Foucault and others left out a very fundamental notion, an innovation of the dialectic, that is, contradiction. Therefore they tended to give an illusion of absolute stasis setting itself in place—think, for example, of Foucault's nightmare picture at the end of *Discipline and Punish*. But if a system is contradictory, as Marx thought capitalism was, then it increases its power, but at the same time undermines itself. It's producing resistance, but it is also "digging its own grave." To put history back into a description of a total system means, first and foremost, to show how it is contradictory, and how these contradictions tend to unravel what the system builds. In capitalism so far this has mainly taken the form of crisis, and taken the form of the realization that even crisis is not the right word for it. Crisis implies that normally there is a steady state but every so often there is a crisis, whereas in fact capitalism is a permanent crisis. I think everybody is able to think the idea that late capitalism is a permanent crisis: there's structural unemployment, increasing poverty, environmental disaster, and so on. Then on the other hand, they see that late capitalism is also a moment of enormous social pluralism, new opportunities and all these cultural openings that we spoke of. The dialectical move would be to see those things together. I think that's why the notion of postmodernity is difficult. It's difficult to do it right, because one has to see both at once: permanent crisis and *also* new kinds of social emancipation. It's on this that I base my objection to total systems, and I think it would have to lead us back into the economic in order to put contradiction back into the system.

As for reification, I guess what's being said is what a few global economists have begun to discover, namely, that consumption today is also an ideology. Consumerism is a style, and there's an ideology of consumption and consumerism, which really organize people's lives. Obviously, commodities have always been around, even in noncapitalist societies, and commodity fetishism must have been there in the nineteenth century for Marx to have spoken about it. This level of consumerism—which some people have tried to underscore, for example, Guy Debord, with his notion of the society of the spectacle—that consumption now is a matter of image-production, something which Baudrillard also tried to theorize in the notion of the simulacrum: this seems to be a moment in which a new momentum of consumption, its omnipresence, gets dialectically transformed from quantity into quality. We reach another level of this process which is perhaps more extreme than anything that people have known before. It has to do with the saturation of people's lifeworlds by these now disposable commodities, including the way in which nature itself gets transformed. If you use all these products on your grass, your lawn, your trees, and so forth, then little by little everything in nature becomes a commodity. This entails a qualitative leap in the role of commodities in people's lives and the way in which images enter the unconscious and colonize the unconscious as well. And, of course, mass culture is a colonization of the unconscious or of what the German idealists called the realm of aesthetic freedom. So the reason I insist on the language of commodification is to emphasize this quantum leap. To be sure, there are enclaves which are poor in consumption—poor in all senses of the word—and then there are peripheries which are relatively less saturated than we are, and it's in those places that we find some more heightened awareness of what consumption means. Since we are in it up to our ears, it's much harder for us to have historically original notions about how different this is, unless we have sympathy with these areas in which commodification has not yet been completely implanted.

What one wants to add to that picture of the nightmare—or paradise— of total consumption is its own set of contradictions. The New Left in the 1960s always tried to insist on the idea that consumption was an explosive force. They argued that if you encourage people's desires to consume, you reach a point where the system cannot possibly satisfy those desires, and at that point the system itself explodes. It has in effect produced demands and forces that cannot be contained any longer. That seems not to have been true for the 1960s; that is, it seems to have been premature. But it doesn't seem to me quite so implausible for some future society in which only 30 percent, or maybe even only 10 percent, of the population is employed, a society in which you have a sort of standard dole or annual salary for the unemployed. But in a society which is formed by the habits and the culture of consumerism, such demands could present very serious challenges to the system, and there may be other ways in which consumption is itself progressive.

So all I'm trying to argue in the things I've said about reification, fetishization, commodification, or consumption is not that we need new models, but that we have to go back to the old models, complexify them, and see whether we cannot develop them further. I thought that Derrida's presentation of the "specters of Marx" contained a lot of fresh perspectives on commodity fetishism and on new ways of dealing with this problem. The problematic is set by the notion of the commodity. But we are far from having exhausted this problematic. Today, given an omnipresent culture of consumption, and given that consumerism is the fundamental ideology that the United States and the multinationals export to the world—the *fundamental* form of cultural imperialism in the West—this is the space for theory and intellectual work, as well as for politics. Obviously, such work is closely linked to the analysis of cultural forms because these ideologies are now conveyed in the forms of culture.

**DANIUS:** *You are increasingly interested in cultural production in the so-called third world, where capital is more intermittent. Can this be understood as—at least partially—a way of trying to show how "even total systems change," a way of pointing to differences within the system?*

**JAMESON:** Yes, its purpose is in a sense to compare achieved forms of commodification and reification to incompletely commodified spaces. At any rate, one needs those spaces, and as I said, sympathy with those spaces, in order to return to this one and not be completely submerged in it. Because otherwise, it's rather difficult to verify the proposition that commodification is "tendentially complete," for in that case how would you ever be aware of it? The dialectic of consumption and noncommodification is very interesting and important process.

**JONSSON:** *It seems clear that you can study these things theoretically, as a cultural critic, that's pretty obvious. On the other hand, as a politician, or as a political theorist, how would one go about even thinking of an alternative to consumerism today? Almost all intellectuals say, "well, consumerism is here to stay, there's not much to do about it, it's after all pretty pleasant, and it's impossible to think a world without it because that would entail a complete remodeling of the world, a planned economy with fixed prices and the like."*

**JAMESON:** Well, we might end up in some *new* kind of planned economy. Some of this is the hangover of the end of communism and the Reagan period and the general discouragement of intellectuals about new possibilities. It's pretty clear that intellectuals can't invent this kind of cultural politics all by themselves unless there are vital mass political movements going on.

I think the question should first be posed in terms of postmodern political culture, that is to say: in the light of what we have discussed, are political postmodernisms possible? What would a culture be like that uses the image against the image? What would a culture be like that uses a commodity form against a commodity form? In recent video production, a lot of artists are using the video image against the video image—Martha Rosler is one example. Another example would be Barbara Kruger, who also uses the image against the image. There are a great many painters who are working in the same vein, Hans Haacke, for example, and among younger artists surely even more. There's a lot of experimentation, and the first task of intellectuals is to look at that and provide some kind of analytic support for that production. The other important phenomenon to explore is that didactic art is far more possible in postmodernism than in modernism, where the didactic was absolutely repudiated. Postmodern cultural and artistic production can apparently accommodate didactic and pedagogic functions, functions that I have called "cognitive mapping," trying to analyze the system and show it in works of art. Among the things that would be explored in that production of art would be what some of us have tried to analyze as the cultural commodification of the period. So I think there are modest tasks possible for criticism and theory.

But we're also working out of certain kinds of national situations, and the most important thing for us as first world intellectuals is to be open to the experience of both intellectuals and artists and people generally in other parts of the world. We have to cannibalize their possibilities of experience in the absence of our own, in much the same way as Paul Simon has to cannibalize South African music. And again, I don't think it is necessarily a bad thing to draw on the things that they're able to do that we may not be able to do right now. By doing that we make our own network of contacts with intellectuals in other countries, and we create something like that International of Left intellectuals that Derrida calls for. We will then maybe have a new global Left intelligentsia which might be a kind of answer to the networks of business internationals that obviously have existed in reality for a number of years, and also to the emergent international relations of labor movements which are so important for the future.

**DANIUS:** *In* The Political Unconscious, *you stress that the business of the cultural critic is in some sense to make whole again, although the ultimate whole has to remain absent. The process of making whole has to proceed by way of both sameness and difference, by way of both connecting and separating. The notion of semi-autonomy is vital in this book. In your book* Postmodernism, or, The Cultural Logic of Late Capitalism, *however, the transcoding process, as analytical tool, is much less evident, and the architecture of that book is also different. The introduction and the conclusion function as an umbrella, an overarching frame, and within this frame we get particular analyses of particular works, texts or phenomena, and yet these chapters have extremely general titles, such as "Culture," "Ideology," "Architecture," "Sentences," et cetera. What is the relation between the part and the whole? What is your view on mediation in the postmodern?*

**JAMESON:** It's very interesting what you're saying. There's a continuity between *The Political Unconscious* and *Postmodernism*, to be sure, but I think that in my work on postmodernism notions of mediation are replaced and redeveloped as the notion of allegory. It seems to me that it is allegory that is the dominant operative concept in the postmodernism book. It is as allegory that the universal and the particular in postmodernity are understood to be related to each other. Allegory is then seen as a kind of parasitic form that undermines itself and is multiple. This kind of allegorical structure is, I think, quite different from the old notion of a one-to-one relation, for example in Bunyan's *Pilgrim's Progress*; for one thing it excludes personification.

When a system wishes to do away with its universal elements, so that it can't be recognized as a system, and when you come upon particulars in that system that would allow you to deduce the universal, or to make connections to the universal again, those connections, I think, always have to be made allegorically, as in my reading of the Gehry House, for instance.

**DANIUS:** *There's an obvious likeness to Adorno's idea that the distance between part and whole must not be closed, that the detail or the part cannot and must not be reconciled, and that this tension must be preserved in the analytical process.*

**JAMESON:** Right. But allegory also means *imperfect* representation or the failure of representation. If you have the notion of the symbol, then you think that you can imagine a particular and a universal that combine in some perfect way and give a successful and full representation. Allegory means that it's always necessarily a failure; it always breaks down. There is an impulse to join these two, but finally the particular is being linked to a universal that does not exist, but on the other hand, the particular itself has no existence without the universal. So allegory is a much more self-undermining form in this period than anything in the modern period, which of course also knew the crisis of representation but which thought that it could build these vast architectonic things that, like Joyce's *Ulysses*, unite the part and the whole. I have attempted to keep this process open, all the while knowing that the process can't be a successfully completed one.

**JONSSON:** *So any account of the cultural production in late capitalism would have to operate with the notion of allegory?*

**JAMESON:** Yes, I think so. I think that all of cultural production today has to somehow obscurely acknowledge this problem. One of the things I try to do in this new book, *The Geopolitical Aesthetic*, is to show that all of those allegorical mediations are present in mass culture. Anybody who tries to think about the process is bound to be involved in this problem of the allegorical, the dilemma of the allegorical, although one doesn't need to be reflexively aware that this is an issue. To think about the possibilities of representation today is automatically to raise this issue. Insofar as that is also a central issue in the modern period and in modernism, people today may have a false sense of the continuities between the two periods. Anybody who is aware of problems of representation today is essentially talking about allegory. There were a number of people in the modern who already anticipated the problem as it presents itself to us, Walter Benjamin, for example. I think one can go back to certain modernist works and see much more substantial anticipations of these issues back then, because despite discontinuities there are also continuities, and there's a way in which the structure of capital in general is allegorical. But we are talking about a very unique and intensified version of that today. I would say that, for example, Deleuze's works certainly turn on this, although *allegory* is not a word he uses. I think the economists also have to confront this, except that they don't use the same language that we do, and perhaps they wouldn't even be grateful to us if we explained to them that the problem they are dealing with is allegory!

NOTES

1. For an extended commentary on this text, see Fredric Jameson, "Marx's Purloined Letter," *New Left Review* 209 (1995): 86–120.

2. Alas, Deleuze never completed it.

3. For a fuller discussion of this point, See Fredric Jameson, "Modernism and Imperialism," in *Nationalism, Colonialism, and Literature*, by Terry Eagleton, Jameson, Edward W. Said (Minneapolis: University of Minnesota Press, 1990), 43–66.

4. For fuller discussions of these points, see Fredric Jameson, "Globalization and Political Strategy," *New Left Review* 2 4 (2000): 49–68; Fredric Jameson, "Notes on Globalization as a Philosophical Issue," in *The Cultures of Globalization*, ed. Jameson and Masao Miyoshi (Durham, NC: Duke University Press, 1998), 54–77.

# Interview with Xudong Zhang

**ZHANG:** *My first question concerns the overall outlook of your theoretical language and the constitution of your methodology. It is a common view that you combined Marxism and structuralism—not structuralism per se but the general emphasis on language and textuality since the so-called linguistic turn—to make these things indispensable to one another in your critical practice. Is this picture misleading? Could you explain the way in which these dimensions become intertwined in the development of theory in general and in your own interventions in particular?*

**JAMESON:** Several things have to be said. First of all, what we have called structuralism or theory in the largest sense, ranging from psychoanalysis to linguistics and everything else, not as a precise term but as a general historical term, emerged within the Marxist problematic. If we limit ourselves to France, the dominant French thought right after the Second World War was, of course, existentialism. But it very quickly became existential Marxism. And that was the point at which structuralism as a problematic began to emerge. I do not mean the structuralist position—particularly that language is the ultimate determining instance—but the question as to the relationship of language to other social levels emerges from the Marxist framework, which did not yet have an answer for it. I would say in general that you could probably show that all the specific themes of poststructuralism emerged from the Marxist problematic, which was at that point attempting to arrive at a more refined notion of culture and ideology.

I also want to add something else: The other important influence I have

---

This interview was conducted at the 1995 MLA convention in Chicago. It first appeared as Xudong Zhang, "Marxism and the Historicity of Theory: An Interview with Fredric Jameson," *New Literary History* 29:3 (1998): 353–83. © The University of Virginia. Reprinted with permission of The Johns Hopkins University Press.

been interested in lately is that of Brecht, because Brecht's appear-ance at the Théâtre des Nations in Paris in 1954 was really a very decisive event. Brecht was not normally thought of as a philosopher or theoretician. But his dialectic also set an agenda that would turn out to be poststructuralism—something in particular to be called antihumanism. In Brecht you have the simultaneous attack on the bourgeois classical tradition that Lukács, for example, defended, as well as on the socialist humanist tradition of which Lukács was obviously also a proponent. Then this antihumanism was further developed by people like Althusser—Althusser wrote something on Brecht incidentally, so there was a direct connection. So the point I want to make is that you can certainly read various poststructuralist texts outside their history for their immediate truth value, but if you want to put them in context to see how the problematic was developed, then you have to look at the larger Marxist framework. In a country like France after the war, an overwhelming percentage of the intellectuals thought they were Marxist. At any rate, at least they found the Marxist problematic—class struggle, modes of production, how to connect base and superstructure, what the nature of ideology is, what representation is—essential to their programs.

Another thing to be said about this first point is that it also explains why, surprisingly for some, we get this intervention of Derrida, in his book *Spectres of Marx*.[1] It is because, I think, now that France has de-Marxified, and many fewer intellectuals consider themselves Marxist, the great theoreticians—this is true for Deleuze, too, although, unfortunately, he did not have time to write his Marx book, but it is also true for others—understand more acutely how their own framework built on the Marxist problematic (again I do not want to say Marxism). And I think what Derrida was trying to rescue there is a multiple thing: he is making commentaries on certain texts of Marx, he is making a political intervention in a situation in which there seem to be no radical alternatives. But I think he is also trying historically to save that base of Marxism from which he himself in an idiosyncratic way emerged.

As to the problem of what the relationship is in specific cases, I believe this has to do with the nature of theory itself. Theory emerging after the end of great philosophical systems, in a kind of market environment, has tended to become a set of name brands. If that seems too frivolous to say, then we can say that theory exists as named theories, as specific idiolects or private languages. The whole point of the philosophical system is to take a mass of ideas in the air of all kinds and give them a single coherent language, a unified conceptuality and set of terms and categories. In that sense, the end of philosophy means that no one thinks such coherence is possible any more. This means that we have to speak all these theoretical languages all at the same time. There really is no way to synthesize them into a master language, nor is there even a desire to do so. I think this situation then creates some of the appearances you are alluding to; it looks for one minute that we are talking about Marxist language, but suddenly you begin to sound like a Jakobsonian structuralist, or a Lévi-Straussian, or a Lacanian, and so forth. I am often accused of eclecticism in this respect, but I think we have to think about it in terms of language. It is as though we could say certain things sharply only in French, but what you can say sharply in German is less clear in French; you can say certain things in Chinese, but they don't exactly work in French, and vice versa, and so on and so forth. So the ideal would be switching languages depending on the problems you are addressing, but obviously that is also next to impossible. That is why I believe there are far closer connections between the various Marxist problems and some of those poststructural languages with which at first glance you do not see any relationship.

I guess it is very difficult to pursue these discussions without some reconstruction of the historical development. I would like to hope that when I explain some of these complex issues for myself that this can also serve as an introduction to some of the more primary theoretical philosophical questions. But I have to keep the names there. If I just speak of these problems without the names, it would look as though I am claiming the ideas for myself. That is not the case.

ZHANG: *The common perception is that you are both "French" and "German": the French side being poststructuralist, and the German side dialectical—the Frankfurt School, and so on. Now you are saying that the "French" aspect is not purely linguistic or "theoretical" but also part of the Marxist problematic.*

JAMESON: That is right. It is an accident of my own background that I am fluent in both French and German, and that I had contact with both national traditions as a student. I always found it as understandable as it is strange and deplorable when people take sides for the French against the German or for the German against the French. On the other hand, as I said before, I do not think syntheses are desirable. I also think that to borrow back and forth is not very successful. I am thinking in particular of the moment in the 1970s when Adorno became better known in France. Then the so-called anti-identity side of Adorno—a German theme, so to speak—became enlisted in French poststructuralism's attack on Marxism. That does violence to Adorno's thought. But how you dialogue between positions is very complicated. You may recall the attempts of Habermas to talk to Foucault, or of Foucault to talk to Chomsky. Except on basic political and cultural matters, a simple dialogue between these languages is not possible. I am Eurocentric to the degree that I believe that the French and the German are the two great philosophical-theoretical traditions. I happen to have been formed in that atmosphere in which Anglo-American thought—empiricism and common language philosophy and Wittgenstein and logical positivism—was really in some sense an obstacle for me. All those philosophical positions seemed to me to constitute a "resistance to theory," as Paul de Man puts it. Therefore it is often objected that I am not sufficiently hospitable to these things, even though they have included interesting thoughts, beginning with Peirce in the Anglo-American tradition. But my basic frames of reference remain French and German.

ZHANG: *A brief interruption: It is very helpful for you to point out the historical moment and situation in which your theoretical interventions emerged. Bearing in mind the readership outside the West, there is still a tendency to read any positions in terms of a division among conservatism, liberalism, and radicalism. Would you like to say something about the relationship between Marxism and liberalism—the latter being both an intellectual tradition and a cold war ideology—in postwar Europe and America?*

JAMESON: Well, I think whatever Soviet communism was, the liberal position in the West since the end of the war was very largely defined as social democracy, that is, as anticommunism and as anti-Marxism. Therefore, for many of us, this liberalism discredited itself. Now there is a revival of certain kinds of liberalism which is relatively less tainted because they do not have to be anticommunist any more, whatever their deeper political commitments. But I think that one must understand that most of us expected nothing productive from that essentially cold war liberalism, which essentially colored Anglo-American philosophy.

ZHANG: *You understand by asking this question I am curious not so much about the structural relationship between Marxism and liberalism but about*

*the habit for many to see things in terms of a position taking between radical-
ism, liberalism, and conservatism.*

**JAMESON:** I understand that. It is a matter of existential politics. But it
would be best to begin with the philosophical questions themselves and
only later to decide if these are liberal positions, radical positions, or conservative positions, because all these poststructuralist themes and problems can be inflected in a number of directions. While it is essential that
at the end of the line political judgments be made, I think the problem
initially should be analyzed and discussed in terms of their inherent, immanent conceptuality. The same would be true for works of art. I have always stood for political, social, and historical readings of works of art, but
I certainly do not think that you start that way. You start with aesthetics,
purely aesthetic problems, and then, at the term of these analyses, you end
up in the political. People have said about Brecht that, for example, whenever in Brecht you started with aesthetics, by the time you came to the end,
you came to politics; and whenever you started with politics, at the end you
came to aesthetics. I think that is a much more desirable rhythm for these
analyses. But that of course makes my positions sometimes very ambiguous for people, because they want a political message right away, whereas I
am interested in going through the problems or the aesthetic form in order
eventually to get to a political judgment.

**ZHANG:** *A particular figure to mention here might be Heidegger. What is
Heidegger's role in the constitution of philosophical-theoretical operations,
both in Marxism historically and in your own case?*

**JAMESON:** It depends on the national situations. I studied in Germany in
the early 1950s. Heidegger had not been allowed to teach again until 1951. The
Germany I knew was intellectually Heideggerian. The Frankfurt School's
influence came only much later. Meanwhile, in France, he had French disciples. The French soldiers who captured him in the woods around Freiburg
gave him a cigarette and then asked for his autograph. Nonetheless, the
penetration of Heidegger in France after the war was much slower. Later,
we would have to mention Derrida, who clearly placed a certain Heidegger
on the agenda. But this was not the Heidegger that the Germans knew, not
the ontological Heidegger. Rather, this was the destruction-of-metaphysics
Heidegger, who played a different role. To think of Derrida as a Heideggerian is a very odd thing, because he certainly does not take ontological

positions of the Heideggerian type. He is not interested in ontology. For him, that is the more deplorable side of Heidegger. But Heidegger is essential to the operation of deconstruction because of the historical problems—essentially problems in the history of philosophy—which were also posed by him. So it is very complicated. I think Heidegger is now gone in Germany, a country now massively, almost completely, dominated intellectually by Habermas. Of course there are now American Heideggerians, and this is a thriving industry. New manuscripts are still coming out. My own formation is Sartrean; therefore there was a lot of Heidegger I did not need, because Sartre's version was selective and to my mind more "advanced" (in the way it posed the problem of the other, for example, or in the originality of its relationship to psychoanalysis).

I would like to add, though, that I think there is a part of Heidegger which is very consistent with Marxism. This is the so-called pragmatic Heidegger: the Heidegger of the tool, of work and production. This is the phenomenology of daily life, which for all kinds of historical and philosophical reasons was never part of Marxism. It is an empty framework or square in the whole Marxist problematic that was not developed. Indeed, the Althusserians, for example, thought that the notion of everyday life was ideological. So the pragmatic side of Heidegger becomes very attractive as a basis for the Marxian notion of praxis. Some of that was also present in Sartre in a different form. Sometimes in Heidegger's *Sein und Zeit* [*Being and Time*] that whole analysis of *Dasein* as active first and contemplative or epistemological only later on seems to me to be very useable within a Marxist framework.

**ZHANG:** *How do you describe the presence of Heidegger in your own language? Or, is there any?*

**JAMESON:** When I studied in Germany I read some of Heidegger fairly intensively, although I was much more interested in *Sein und Zeit*, the so-called existential Heidegger, than the later, "ontological Heidegger." I have always admitted that I found Heidegger's ontology very attractive, provided that it is understood to be a Utopian one rather than a description. I think this is the problem of all phenomenology, by the way. It is a Utopia rather than a description of our alienation, of what we actually live. But then there is a big problem in Heidegger, which is the whole notion of modernity and technology. It seems to me that this problem does not achieve a philosophical solution in Heidegger. It marks a problem he never adequately solved. The famous *Ge-stell* was so enigmatic that I do not think that anybody has really cracked that nut and found a concept there, let alone a translation. I think it is a place Heidegger wishes desperately to think. Obviously the postmodern framework, and this new technology of cybernetics, makes it more urgent to try to think this in different ways, which to be sure Heidegger could never have encountered. So I guess I could say that at various moments of my life I have been a Heidegger fellow traveler! But I cannot say that this was the strongest influence on my own work, except for this notion of activity, production, praxis, and so forth.

ZHANG: *So the perceived Heideggerian moment in your work, when you use terms such as* Being *and* deconcealment, *should be understood in Utopian terms.*

JAMESON: Yes, exactly. There they can serve as a very dramatic way to mark the space of Utopia. But it is not the only language I would use. And of course ontology has its disadvantages. From a Utopian perspective, a "being" is essentially the individual human being and the being of Nature, so the social is evacuated from those later things, along with the future, in ways that are less than useful for us.

ZHANG: *Recently there seems to be some interest in figuring out your career or intellectual development, which for many remains miraculous in some senses. For instance, in the preface to your* Geopolitial Aesthetics, *Colin Mac-Cabe describes your career in a very interesting way. He says that you spent more than two decades working out your theoretical premises "patiently"; and, once that was achieved, it was replaced by a "riot of cultural analyses." He describes it in a way in which yours seems to be a very deliberate self-design and personal strategy.*

JAMESON: I was very gratified by Colin's essay, which I think is one of the few that has really given an overall picture of my work. I do suspect that Colin wishes to downplay its more specifically Marxist side and political elements. I wouldn't necessarily tell the story that way myself, although I can see that the story he tells has a certain persuasiveness. I would not myself start like that. I would say that between methodological questions there are always tensions which open onto larger philosophical problems. Ultimately, this goes to the base and superstructure problem if you like, that is to say, how you link culture and consciousness to the context or to the situation. It is the tension between those dimensions that set the terms for the reading of any individual text. So when one talks about the "riot of cultural analyses," the same thing can be said about my literary work. That is, there is a tension between a whole methodological-philosophical side of things and the reading of the individual, literary text, just as much as between that and the reading of any specific mass-cultural text. So the problem is not one of passing from a general canonical or literary set of preoccupations into some more mass-cultural, cultural studies environment. I seem to have written more on films and mass-cultural things in the past few years. But actually I have several very long literary analyses that have not been published. I think the two kinds of texts demand very different approaches, which I would not necessarily want to combine. But the real problem, the real alternation here is between the general and the particular, between specific readings and the more general theoretical approach. I am not sure that I would say that first I took care of my theoretical problems and then I moved on to those specific analyses. In this new global capitalism, in this age of postmodernity, the older theories that one invoked for the earlier world of modernity must now also be rethought. I consider that the theoretical and speculative task, and it is by no means finished and done with, allowing one simply to do readings. Rather, it is also an ongoing one, which surely demands further elaboration.

ZHANG: *What is implied here, other than a career design, might be something like this: conceptually, you can still for a moment concentrate on your theoretical-philosophical infrastructure, so to speak. Then that infrastructure can serve as a sort of inner drive and mode of thinking, which motivate and navigate your journey through a fragmented terrain.*

JAMESON: The notion in *The Political Unconscious* of the three levels of context, the three frameworks—historical, political, economic—in which one can focus a concrete context implies that you could work on an immediate social-historical level (then you might be talking about the whole rollback of the welfare state). You could also talk in the larger context, the class dynamics, which are slower and include the history of classes, their memory of their struggles and their defeats. Then, finally, you can talk on this most abstract and totalizing level of the mode of production. So, already, in that notion of the three levels, there was implicit the sense that the context was not only the here and now politically but could be approached in somewhat longer time frames. I use there, maybe without saying so,

Braudel's idea of multiple temporalities and longer or shorter *durées*. I do not often write in terms of specific political struggles, partly because works of art take somewhat longer to write and to put together anyway. It is only in mass culture that you get a more immediate kind of response. But there is a time lag involved even in those most ephemeral cultural statements. I certainly admire the people whose task is immediate cultural and political commentary. I am not sure I am best qualified to do that kind of work, particularly because my formation is not in American Studies but in other languages and national cultures.

I also want to add a rather different kind of remark about what Lukács has meant to me. One of the things that Lukács taught, and one of the most valuable, I think, is that the form of work of art—and I would include the form of mass-cultural product—is a privileged place in which one can observe social conditioning and thus the social situation. And sometimes form is the place where one can best observe that concrete social context more adequately than in the flow of daily events and immediate historical happenings. I guess I would resist the idea that I start with aesthetics, then I look around for some historical context, and then put them together, even though Marxist analysis has often been understood in those terms. And there is a truth in this, because we are attempting to look at the aesthetic and extra- or nonaesthetic simultaneously. That often makes for a slippage between these two realms. I think the clumsier Marxist analyses do tend to take this form of a break in the essay in which, first, you put all the social facts, and then, you turn to the work and talk about form and ideology (or vice versa). That in principle ought to make writing Marxist analyses interesting, because there is a fundamental formal problem in writing such essays that demands to be solved; there are no ready-made solutions in advance. But I think what Lukács meant to me is that ideally, one should somehow get to the content through the forms.

To that I would add something else. The difference between Lukács and this humanism that Brecht attributed to him in its negative sense is that Lukács always talked about achieved form, successful form. It seems to me rather that we have to look at failures of form, the impossibility of certain kinds of representation in a certain context, the flaws, limits, obstacles, which become the clue to the social truth or social meaning, and not so much canonical achievement in that old Lukácsian sense.

**ZHANG:** *When you say that, do you have in mind the mass cultural products or the avant-garde "work of art"?*

**JAMESON:** What makes the matter of determinate representational failure interesting is that it happens to both. I think the most interesting way to look at mass-cultural debates is precisely through just these failures grasped as formal failures and formal impossibilities. Of course, we can also talk about failures, formal flaws, and constraints in so-called high literature. That would be the point, I think, in which what is to me a more adequate kind of cultural studies would not feel obliged to choose between literature and the canon, on the one hand, and television and pop music, on the other. It seems to me that these are dialectically parts of a nonunified field ("two halves that don't add up," Adorno called it). The most interesting comments on both sides are made by those who are, like people hesitating between France and Germany, committed to both rather than to taking sides for one or the other: as though one were elitist, and the other populist. I understand why that is done. Sometimes I feel that way myself. But I do not think that is ultimately a very productive attitude.

**ZHANG:** *I think your readers would understand very well that both the social-political and the aesthetic-theoretical are constant in your critical intervention. And that is one of the most persuasive aspects of your work. But I am wondering if the "theoretical moment" in your career can be seen as a moment of intensification, a process of encoding in which you acquired not only a style or philosophical form but also power; subjectivity, some kind of organizing principle, which now enables you to engage the field at a different level, given that your position is perceived as a privileged one, meaning that when everybody gets stuck in a schizophrenic world, you still maintain a certain kind of coherence, continuity, and energy, the politics of which is not determined only by your immediate social-cultural location. Does that have to do with the "decades" of theoretical mortification, so to speak?*

**JAMESON:** There, too, we have to make a historical remark. The theoretical books [*Marxism and Form* and *The Prison-House of Language*] which precede the later textual analyses (in McCabe's view) were written at a time when neither of these two traditions [the French and the German critical traditions] were very well known in the Anglo-American world. So my task was partly to introduce and popularize these things. But then with translation, with wider dissemination and the greater theoretical sophistication that the American intellectuals began to acquire in the 1970s and 1980s, that particular kind of project was no longer necessary.

The second point is that for me the practical readings have only been interesting insofar as they contain a theoretical development. That is why this connection between theory and interpretation has always been very close. It is an odd fact, a strange paradox, that just because you are excited about an object does not mean that you are qualified to write well about it. One would think that one would always have something to say if you are interested. There are great cultural journalists whom I very much admire and whose gift is to respond immediately to all their situations and objects. But for me, the works that I have felt empowered to write about are always ones that allowed me to focus on a specific theoretical problem. I think the reverse is also true. That is, even though sometimes it does not seem that way, the theoretical problems that interested me are the ones that ultimately had a connection to interpretations of specific texts. There is a whole range of philosophical problems that do not interest me at all because they do not bear on this. That may also have something to do with this connection you are talking about.

As for the motive for the speculations on postmodernism and post-modernity, I would say that before the 1980s, historical contexts seemed more clear and stable than they began to be in the 1980s and 1990s. When I began to think about these things, at least what I described as postmodern suddenly seemed to be connected up with some very basic structural changes in infrastructure, in the economic, in globalization, and so forth. That then again gave me a coherent framework to look at all these things as manifestations of the larger cultural logic or experience of the period.

ZHANG: *But this framework of periodization is basically a Marxist one.*

JAMESON: Yes, of course. I consider this essentially a Marxist periodization. I have colleagues and comrades who feel that acknowledging the postmodern amounts to giving in to the most frivolous tastes generated by capitalism. But I think of the notion of periodization in terms, first, of realism, the relatively limited national framework of capitalism; then, of imperialism, this larger global—not yet global in our sense, but larger, worldwide—expansion of capitalism; and finally, of a new globalized capitalism. I think these are stages in the evolution of capital, and their conception is profoundly Marxist. That is why I am often pleased when people try with some embarrassment to avoid terms like *late capitalism*, because that shows that they understand that such terms are at base political ones and imply political positions. There is then the accusation that I do not think enough in terms of class. That may be so for certain kinds of things. But I believe that class, class dynamics, and class struggles are always present. Only to-day they take very complicated forms. There is no clear-cut working-class ideology. There is no clear-cut ruling-class ideology either. It is a more complicated game. I would not want to say that Marx was an economic determinist, but for me the important historical, original, unsurpassable thing about Marx and Marxism is that it requires you somehow to include the economic. It requires you to work back in such a way that you finally touch economic structures. If you limit yourself only to class, that can very rapidly turn into political considerations, considerations of power; then it begins to lose its connections to the economic structure. That is why I often felt hesitation about the emphasis on power coming out of Foucault and others today, which I think sometimes is a little too easy. For me, the theory of the postmodern stage is an economic theory. If you do it right, you have to end up talking about capitalism. Therefore, the coherence of my work comes from the stage we are in. The Marxist component comes from the ultimately economic dynamic of the stage.

**ZHANG:** *In that particular sense, Marxism becomes a philosophy, or does it?*

**JAMESON:** No. This is the value of Derrida's latest work [*Spectres of Marx*], which reminds us insistently that Marxism is not an ontology, and should be neither an ontology nor a philosophy. I agree with that. What is very peculiar about both Marx and Freud is that they are this thing which in the Marxist tradition is called a unity of theory and practice. That means that there is not a philosophical system of Marxism that you can write down; rather, there are some very important philosophical implications and speculations, which offer the construction of something like the presuppositions of a Marxist philosophy, such as we find, for example, in Lukács's *History and Class Consciousness*. I have even just now perversely suggested that Heidegger's *Sein und Zeit* could be seen as having elements of a properly Marxist philosophy. But there are many other attempts. The deplorable mistake of the so-called Eastern, orthodox, or Soviet Marxism was the idea that you could have a full philosophical picture of the world called dialectical materialism that could be written down the way the old philosophical treatises were written down. You start with matter and move on to mind and society in an orderly fashion. I am very resistant to that notion. I can see why in loose terms one can still talk about various Marxist philosophies. But I would not want to think Marxism is a philosophy in that sense.

Now the other thing people sometimes do with this word is to say not that Marxism is a philosophical system, but, even worse, that it is that rather different thing: a philosophy of history. That objection demands a different reply. There is certainly an ambition to think history in Marxism, and I am very interested in the so-called philosophy of history—it seems to me that those are some of the most exciting texts we have, which range from bourgeois philosophies of history to Ibn Khaldun or St. Augustine or Thucydides. I must feel generally that it is not quite right to call Marxism a philosophy of history in that sense either. But that is a different matter from Marxism being a philosophical system.

ZHANG: *You invented a now widely circulated term—*metacommentary*—to indicate a certain mode of cultural-intellectual production and intervention. The ground cleared by this notion is, in your case, and probably in the way this notion functions, reserved for Marxism. In that respect Marxism does not seem to be just another brand name in the market, at least not for those who write along that line. For others in the field, it seems that you can always draw from a historical and theoretical source, from which they would rather disengage, but which allows you somehow to place yourself beyond the field.*

JAMESON: You could say that in several ways. You could say that in terms of these theoretical discourses and, despite everything I have said about the various theoretical discourses, there is a Marxist theoretical position that is more privileged than others. But today there are a number of different Marxist theoretical discourses, so one cannot really say that exactly. Is it, then, the survival of that older philosophical foundation which is for contemporary antifoundationalists suspicious? That would be so if Marxism altogether were a philosophy in their sense. I do not consider that accusation to be entirely accurate either. I would also want to say that there are probably people practicing metacommentary who do not know that what they are doing is Marxism. One does not have to be conscious of this intellectual commitment to have a Marxist view of the world. After all, Marxism has really suffused all the disciplines to the point where it is omnipresent and active without any longer being a separate field or specialization.

As for the idea that I have some secret truth that nobody else has, well, the whole point of the public sphere is that you make your own interpretation, and then people take it or leave it; they find it plausible or not plausible. The real problem is that a lot of the interpretations made today do not push things far enough and are thus not really in the running. Or else they are not aware of themselves as ideologies. I do think that there are Marxist ideologies, that we are all ideological in our specific situations—national, personal, psychoanalytical, and so forth—which determine deep ideological and classical commitments we are not always aware of, and this is true of Marxism as well. All the great Marxist thinkers, including Marx, came out of specific personal, class, and national situations. What they have produced, alongside what Marxism calls "science," are a number of Marxist ideologies. I try to be interested in a range of those and move back and forth (between some of them). I am not sure how to describe my own personal view of Marxism, and am not particularly interested in turning it into another brand-name ideology.

**ZHANG:** *Does the view that Marxism has a certain power over other theoretical discourses have to do with its internal unity, its interest in "grand narratives" and "totality"?*

**JAMESON:** Let me try to answer that question by going back to the notion of theory being an idiolect or private language. My feeling is that if you are going to address a range of people formed in different disciplines, you have to be able to translate these things and speak their language up to a certain point, even if you seek to undermine or criticize it. What I would like to propose is that this sort of belief or philosophy that people think they see unifying my work is, rather, a translation mechanism. I would like to defend the idea that Marxism is a far more subtle and supple mode of translating between these languages than most of the other systems. It is true that the great universal systems—Catholicism, for instance—had that capacity once. There was great power in the way in which certain kinds of Catholic theologians, the Jesuits, for example, were able to pass from one philosophical language to another. Marxism is the only secular version of this capacity I know today. I do not think structural linguistics or semiotics has that ambition, (nor) was it successful; and there remains to be analyzed from a historical point of view the connection of the various semiotics with existentialism and Marxism. It is a very interesting historical story. But I think Marxism remains the only one of these translation techniques or machines that can encompass all these things.

If you want to say that this is a privileged thought mode, then it is because of this mediatory function, not because of some mythic idea of the "truth"! It is because you mediate between these various theoretical codes far more comprehensibly than anything these codes themselves allow. Žižek now wants to tell us that Lacanism is just such a translating code, or better, one that includes the dialectic and Marxism. I have always been fascinated with Lacan, and I am certainly willing to toy with that idea, for which Žižek makes a persuasive case. The notion of mediation between these codes is the crucial one, not the truth power of one code or philosophy—like Marxism—over the other. Reality takes care of truth; the codes are our business.

ZHANG: *The purported "power" of Marxism, at least in the case of your work, might also have to do with the notion of productivity, with the way you absorb things and mediate between them theoretically. Many people might not have the opportunity, or interest, or energy, to encompass such an enormous space.*

JAMESON: Well, I suppose people tend to develop certain passions through their work, and once they have achieved the formal expression of these passions, they feel relatively exhausted. Maybe that gives a different way for coming at this question. That is to say, my relationship with Marxism is not so much in terms of belief or truth but rather interest. Politics is, after all, the most interesting thing in life. It seems to me that it is politics and political commitment that gives one some perpetual drive to confront new problems. Many people on the Left have become fatigued now at the end of Soviet communism because they do not know where that politics is going, and they turn back to invest in local "nontheoretical" issues. Whereas for me the question of what capitalism is, what alternatives to it are possible, remains a burning issue.

Things look very different now than they did twenty years ago, so I have a continuing interest in retheorizing these things. I hope I do not come to a period where I am not interested in any of these problems any more. But that can happen to people. But I prefer to put it in terms of a kind of interest which drives one, rather than any preconceived notion of political engagement, because those vary and you are not always in a political situation where action is possible, where you know what the stakes are, and so forth, particularly at this time. The interest in connecting culture to the economic situation has for me been a constant, even though both of these things change and, the very nature and structure of that relationship changes.

ZHANG: *Does that translating, mediating mechanism enclose a coding system in itself and generate its own theoretical formulations?*

**JAMESON:** It is a coding system, all right, but I think it is also a problematic. I think one could look at a whole range of work I have done in terms of the central problematic that I continue to feel to be significant. If it is a matter of dialogue with other theories, then we have a range of new theories today, from gender theory to postcolonialism, which demand theoretical engagement.

**ZHANG:** *The reason why I am so persistent in getting an answer for that is this: for a Chinese reader looking at the world through the prism shaped to a considerable degree by "Western culture," "Western scholarship," or "Western theory," any understanding of his or her own sociohistorical situation must be at the same time an understanding of the mechanism of that medium or that factor. In pursuing the historical truth, some kind of methodological "truth" tends to be dehistoricized to accommodate the need for figuring out what is going on in the structure of the Western cultural-intellectual world. In that sense, your work—and probably the works of "Western Marxism" in general—has been a preferred site because, for one thing, it seems to allow people to absorb things while maintaining a comprehensive critical subject position.*

**JAMESON:** This then becomes for me the problem of the dissemination of my own work in other national situations. I do believe in the primacy of the situation, and I also think it is very foolish to say that nations have disappeared. I think that there is today certainly much more give-and-take between intellectual communities. But it seems to me that intellectuals are anchored in their specific national situations. That would give one two ways of looking at this. One would be that the United States is the most advanced, but also the most brutal, form of contemporary capitalism. An American at this stage has a unique position as opposed to, let's say, Europeans—not to mention Chinese. I noticed in Germany, on my last visit, that there are a range of intellectual issues (about mass culture, for example) that Germans do not have to pose, or at least not yet. My perhaps chauvinistic view is that Americans are obliged to confront more of these things than most other national intellectuals, no matter how attractive one may find the intellectual climates somewhere else. That would be one thing.

The other thing is that I always conceive my work in a polemic way. Besides these theoretical investigations of culture and its mechanisms that you mentioned, as a Marxist one also has to confront other intellectual ideologies. Therefore I think that while, I am sure, in China today and in the Pacific Rim in general, a whole variety of different ideological positions are being developed, there is a way in which I have had to confront a whole range of these things here that may be rather different from what, let's say, a Chinese intellectual would have to face in the People's Republic or Hong Kong or Taiwan. The enemies may be different; the ideologies might in some cases be more developed, in some cases less. That gives everyone's work a kind of situational specificity.

We all have this nostalgia for the ideal form of the intellectual and the life of the intellectual, whose historical realization, for many people, is France. There can still be a kind of nostalgia for the role of the French intellectual, although that is in serious crisis right now. But that may account for what is peculiar about my own work. Because in the pluralism in the United States that accompanied the emergence of theory in the literary, aesthetic, and cultural field—something that has tended to be rather characteristic of the United States—there has often resulted a kind of small-group reaction in which you decide to work within a certain theory and avoid confronting other positions. Whereas I have felt, for better or worse—and sometimes I do it well and maybe sometimes not so well—that I really need to confront all of those other positions somehow. If you want to call it Marxism or the dialectic, when one does that by absorbing the languages from inside, showing their limits and so forth, then that may be a special feature of Marxism, as opposed to some of those other literary or cultural ideologies or philosophies.

ZHANG: *Besides the ideal form of intellectual life and cultural activity, people, especially people in the non-Western societies, I suppose, are looking for an ideal form of representation or narrative, a mode of thinking as a way to organize your private and collective experiences, which might otherwise be utterly fragile and fragmented. Marxism seems also to promise some possibilities in these areas.*

JAMESON: Absolutely. I think that is the whole point of the narrative of postmodernity, and its relationship to late capitalism. Whatever is going on in the other parts of the world, in the Pacific Rim, for example, it seems to me that everyone in one way or another is caught in this force field of late capitalism (automation, structural unemployment, finance capital, globalization, and so on). That then, it seems to me, is the organizing dynamic. One does not necessarily solve this fragmented reality in existential terms. One does not map that out or represent it by turning it from fragments into something unified. One theorizes the fragmentary and symptomal interrelationship.

It seems to me that this framework—and for me it is a historical framework—is the one in which one best does that and best provides a coherent narrative even if it is a narrative that explains incoherence. This is what I think we have to do today. Then we can come back to some of the things we have talked about, formal failure, for example. It is a mistake to imagine that because there have been great and successful representational moments in the past, we have to struggle to make a new one now. It can often be the emphasis on the impossibility of representation that gives the clue and organizes things. I think my global narrative does both these things better than the other ones I know of, the narrative of liberalism, of the market, or the various political narratives, of freedom and democracy, or of law and order, of belief and value, and so forth.

ZHANG: *So the narrative of contemporary experiences does not necessarily provide a haven for renewed forms of interiority or unity, subjectivity, nostalgia, and collectivity. But all these things still seem to play a role, culturally as well as politically, in many situations.*

JAMESON: Yes. And if one goes on to use that kind of terminology, one can produce other formulations. If coherence is narrative, then—this is a Lukácsian question for me—what do you do when you are faced with stubbornly, intransigently non- or antinarrative materials? Well, if you think about them dialectically, those get turned into narrative too, but not of the old type.

ZHANG: *For readers in many places—China, for example—there still seems to be a die-hard habit to think that once you achieve a narrative, you are "closer" to the truth; and in order to achieve that narrative, you have to have a strong subjectivity.*

JAMESON: One has to say that coherence comes from the world, not from the Self. It is not by doing something to the Self, acquiring belief and convictions, that you can make the world coherent. It is the world, capitalism, that produces both coherence and incoherence. Therefore that is what one must focus on, and not on subjective resources of various kinds. Of course one has to invent a certain relationship to the Self in order to get rid of it.

ZHANG: *This is not to say that languages or narratives do not "create" or invent new spaces and subject positions—in the field of literary and cultural*

*studies in China, as well as in China Studies in the United States, for ex-*
*ample, new spaces and positions seem to be produced by different theoretical*
*discourses.*

**JAMESON:** But I do not know how we can produce these new things by an effort of the will. "The owl of Minerva flies at dusk." That means that what one has to be alert to is the emergence of this new being-in-the-world. But that does not necessarily mean that by noticing it, articulating it, you can bring it further into being and you can have an effect on the world. I am not sure that individuals can produce the new out of themselves, even though they must always be vigilantly alert to it.

Another question is what to do with theory today. A complicated answer, a Hegelian answer, to that is: what we often observe in the dialectic or opposition between subject and object is that the subject is part of the object; the subject is being produced by the object. I would say the same thing about theory: that theory did not just come from nowhere, and then people liked these disembodied abstractions, took them over, and did awful things with them. Theory came out of the situation. Theory is an integral product of this whole new late capitalist situation. So it is itself a newly emerging content and then, as an objective reality of the world, it undergoes its own autonomous development and reacts back on reality, makes changes in thought, in the university system, in the role of the intellectuals, in the production of culture, and so forth.

If one sees theory merely as just something subjectively willful over against this objective cultural, historical, and social reality that we know, then one is not thinking about theory historically. Theory is part of that historical situation. Therefore the emergence of theory itself becomes a crucial cultural and historical question to be looked at. And I think this is being done more today than in the early period when all theory was new. But there are reasons why theory came into being; why, if you associate theory with poststructuralism, structuralism itself emerged. That was a many-leveled social and cultural event. It was not a whim or some subjective thing, given that even technology itself, very much including communication technology, is also part of the social reality.

On the other hand, there has been this awful, indeed catastrophic, tendency in Marxism to say that the New we want is the preconceived formula, which you the artist must now produce. In terms of the owl of Minerva figure, artists are a registering apparatus for the new reality. You cannot predict in advance what they are going to do. Whenever you spot the emergence of something new, then that, for us intellectuals, becomes our object of study, and we can try to do something with that *Novum*. When it fails to emerge, then we go on as before. I think with theoretical production, it is not dissimilar. Just as the work of art is a registering apparatus, so is theory, and so was philosophy when it was still alive.

**ZHANG:** *Does Marxism, being a more self-conscious registering apparatus, propose a new solution beyond the realm of instrumental reason, beyond the enclosure of "human desire and social engineering" as liberalism has seen it?*

**JAMESON:** Marxism is not a recipe. There are certainly forms of Marxism that do not do that well at all. I think, for example, just as a personal opinion, that the language of rationality is not very helpful. In German there are two words for rationality: *Verstand* and *Vernunft*. The limited or instrumental rationality you are talking about is *Verstand*. The dialectical view that could encompass thought itself as part of the world is this larger thing called *Vernunft*. I do not know if we can reach that right now: it is a very complex dialectical relationship of consciousness to the world. But the most crucial thing we can speak of in terms of art, perception, theory, and so on, is a certain technique of getting away from the Self and allowing the Self to become this registering apparatus, to pick up these things. I would not want to judge whether things are "rational" too quickly. The things themselves simply are; they exist in the world, they are real phenomena, therefore they have their historical origin and their ultimate explanation. But I do not think that the language of rationality or irrationality is a very effective way for evaluating them.

In the French 1970s, *desire* became a buzzword, not so much in Deleuze himself as in the people inspired by him. All these things seem to me to go back to some attempt to find a single-shot explanation for things, to find the ultimate motive: power, economics, desire, the irrational, and so on. That is humanism. That is an attempt to make a theory of human nature. Whereas the emphasis on the situation means that the world has a logic and rhythms of development that are mostly very mysterious to all of us individually or nationally. But that situation is what we need to look at. Then the language of ultimate motivations or ultimate drives becomes less helpful.

**ZHANG:** *Being a product of modernity, Marxism tends to secularize and demystify. But isn't Marxism also proposing its own notion of authenticity and totality?*

JAMESON: The first topic one wants to mention is religion. I have been rereading Kojève's lectures on Hegel. He makes the point that Hegel is a radically atheist philosopher, but not an antireligious one. Because for him religions as such were existent, real social phenomena. They do mystify social phenomena, but it is not (Hegel thought) by ignoring these phenomena, by treating them as delusion or sheer error or superstition (in the Enlightenment fashion), that one gets all the way through them and comes out the other side. I think that contemporary religion is very interesting. For example, there are all kinds of reasons why Islamic fundamentalism has been able today, in the absence of socialism, to stand as this fundamental alternative to the American way of life. Yet I suspect that the new religious movements are of a rather different type than the great, older, all-encompassing religions of older modes of production.

Coming back to Europe, the more specific question is that the moment of the Utopian is crucial. We are talking about the dialectic of ideology and Utopia. Demystification is always valuable, even when it is done by people who have no social vision. It is obviously always useful and always painful—it does not work unless it is painful—to demystify the illusions that we all have all the time, in our own individual heads and those floating through society. Marxism was certainly a very powerful form of demystification, and can always still be one in as much as the economic is what bourgeois people least want to think about, and class is something they would always rather ignore. There is always a job for a more specifically Marxist form of demystification of all those attitudes. But unless that demystification is linked to the vision or the attempt to envision an alternate society altogether, unless there is a Utopian component or drive which is linked to the drive to demystify, then it seems to me that the most productive possibilities of demystification are not achieved. Rather than say that Marxism has another, semireligious agenda alongside of demystification, it seems to be that one must see the two drives as linked.

But I think there is a difference between, let's say, most of the things we consider to be religious in this historical moment and in this daily life and the Utopian ethos of the future, which you can call a kind of religion if you like, but which is also essentially political. Maybe those little Heideggerian moments in my work try violently or forcefully to reinject that Utopian thing alongside the other deconstructive, demystifying operations. My feeling is that it is only that larger, Marxian Utopian drive that can compete with various religious impulses. Is the market Utopian? Well, to be sure, in some intellectual ways, but I think that is not a Utopia that is really available for very many people on this planet now.

I also want to say that I greatly respect liberation theology and its equivalents in the other great religions. There are reasons why it has been a more effective way of motivating social politics in some countries than certain forms of Marxism. But I would prefer the terminology of the Utopian. Then you have to remember the whole tradition of vulgar Marxism and Stalinism and their relationships to various different religious movements. That is a sorry history which has left its mark. So that for many people Marxism is this narrowly defined Enlightenment rationality which excludes religion and even the Utopian. I do not happen to see it that way at all. And indeed, some great Marxist philosophers have made the connections: Ernst Bloch is the most obvious reference, but there are others.

ZHANG: *But you refuse to think of Utopia in terms of humanism, is that right?*

JAMESON: Well, the meaning of those words slips and slides. I think the narrower target of Althusserianism, and of Brecht, the attack on the Soviet idea of the great bourgeois tradition, or indeed on bourgeois thought itself, is something rather different. At least in the West, humanism is organized around notions of the coherence of the individual, the value of the autonomy of the individual experiences. The whole movement of poststructuralism against the autonomous subject is a critique of the philosophical reflexes of just such a humanist individualism and forces us to re-envision the ideology of what is called collectivity, community, and so on. But now, of course, there is what is called communitarianism, which is a relatively more right-wing humanism of collectivity, and also deserves to be criticized in perhaps a very different fashion.

ZHANG: *You have explained the socio-political nature of Marxism. But in China, Marxism—to be precise, Western Marxism—is viewed, first of all, as an aesthetic protest against the reification and vulgarization of mass society and, by implication, of "totalitarian" society too. The moment and the way in which Western Marxism was introduced into China in the 1980s—one example is Liu Xiaofeng's* Poeticized Philosophy *(1986), in which people like Adorno and Marcuse were discussed side by side with Schelling, Hölderlin, Heidegger, and so on—made it a more "poetic" and therefore a more appealing mode of thinking than other competing theoretical discourses from the contemporary West. How would you characterize the "poetic"—if not "existential"—aspect of Marxism?*

**JAMESON:** There has certainly been a strong, interesting attempt to reposition Schelling as a source of a certain Marxism, in the work of Manfred Frank and of Žižek, for example. I think the effort involves the construction of Utopian features of Marxism. That is, it is an attempt to escape from the narrowly economic stuff and precisely to extend Marxism to an existential or poetic vision of how the world could be felt and how human beings could live in it. To that degree, it is greatly to be valued.

But again, one has to look at the influences of such kinds of poetic Marxism as you call it; one must look at the influences historically, at its moment of emergence. Certainly there was a reason in the American 1960s for the resonance that Marcuse's work took on. His theories become political, but in some broader sense. That is, one does politics on a number of levels—some are immediately economic, like the strikes in France a few years ago. But one crucial kind of politics is the vision of an alternative. There were reasons why people needed to develop this Utopian vision, why it becomes politically important in a specific national situation, where it has its own specific political, social, and historical function. I think that one has constantly to replace these things in their historical context and see what their ideological functions were.

It seems to me that this kind of metaphysical vision is often very important. But that does not mean that is the only kind of thinking or analysis or politics one has to do. In a situation in which life seems reduced to rationalization, technology, and market realities, it becomes a very important priority to reassert the other Utopian features of what the transformation of the world will mean.

**ZHANG:** *So far, it seems to me, you have been focusing on the objective side of Marxism defined by its relationship to the situation. How about the active, to avoid the term* subjective, *side of this powerful mechanism for mapping something out, for narrative presentations? I guess this points to the question of the dialectic.*

**JAMESON:** The question of the dialectic is very complicated. There have been Marxisms—Althusser's, for example—that thought we should get rid of this idea altogether, partly because it was too idealistic, or perhaps too complicated to explain. I think that, first, there are a number of forms that the dialectic can take. It seems abusive, except in a philosophy seminar, to speak of *the* dialectic.

Also, I think the dialectic has never been fully realized. That is, there is this massive corpus of Hegelian writings, and also Marx's equally massive but much more fragmentary writings. I would prefer to see the dialectic in a Utopian way as a thought mode of the future, rather than as something that once existed in the 1820s in Berlin or the 1870s in London. I think that would be simpler and more useable ways of talking about the dialectic. I see maybe three of those that interest me right now. One would be an emphasis on the logic of the situation, rather than the logic of the individual consciousness or reified substances like society. The emphasis on the logic of the situation, the constant changeability of the situation, its primacy and the way in which it allows certain things to be possible and others not: that would lead to a kind of thinking that I would call dialectical.

Then, there is the matter of the so-called philosophy or dialectic of history. There, too, the dialectic is a kind of constant, undermining or demystifying of various historical narratives already in place, including some of the Marxist ones, like the inevitability of socialism. It would not be an elimination of causality because I think that narrative and causality go together, and that narrative logic is causal logic. But the dialectic would certainly involve an undermining of the received forms of narrative and historical causality. Because if you look at Marx's *Eighteenth Brumaire of Louis Bonaparte*, you do not see syntheses in any simple form. Instead, you see a bewildering number of new and more complex social and historical causalities correcting those simpler ways in which people tell themselves stories about history.

The third feature is an emphasis on contradiction. If one insists on that, then one is always dialectical whether one knows it or not, whether one has a philosophical approach or not. It seems we all have an existential stake in not seeing contradictions. We would like things to be stable, we would like to think that time was this habit of presence that has played its role in contemporary theory. We would like to think that we are unified subjects, and that the problems we face are representational and thus relatively easy to think through. If at every moment in which we represent something to ourselves in a unified way we try to undo that and see the contradictions and multiplicities behind that particular experience, then we are thinking dialectically.

There are obviously many more pragmatic ways of describing how the dialectic operates in terms of the way we think of the concrete situation, in terms of the way we think of history, and in terms of the way we think of reality.

ZHANG: *The way you describe the operation of the dialectic, especially the entanglement between things that themselves become the form of thinking, reminds me of Benjamin's allegorical mapping of the Parisian space (which is itself reminiscent of Marx's* Eighteenth Brumaire). *What is the relationship between the dialectic and allegory? For Adorno, the Benjaminian mode was "undialectical."*

JAMESON: I guess one should make some proposals. First of all, a lot of people have described the dialectic by asserting that the dialectic is a method rather than a system. In one sense I agree and have sometimes said so myself. But it is also very misleading, because when you say method, you think that all you have to do is learn some recipe: something you could learn, and use over and over again, remaining in the truth. The dialectic is not a method in that sense yet, even though there is something of the spirit of a method in it.

Now, as to allegory, I think that is something else: a mode of representation. The reason why allegory is important is that even though we talk about holding to the situation in its historical changeability, trying to break through old narratives of change and seeing fresh ones and perceiving contradictions, none of these targets were really objects to begin with. Therefore there is the second problem of how you would describe those phenomena, how you model your consciousness of them if they are not really things. That is where allegory comes in. Because it reminds us that even if we believe in the situation, the situation is not a realistic thing for us to make a simple representation of; even if we believe in narrative, the perception of sheer relationality is also not so easy. Saying that the world has a narrative structure does not mean that you can tell a simple story about it, or that there are representational techniques for translating realities into stories. Insisting on contradiction does not mean that anybody ever saw one, or that it would be easy to make a picture of whatever it is. So the insistence on allegory is an insistence on the difficulty, or even impossibility, of the representation of these deeper and essentially relational realities. I hesitate to say impossibility not because it is not so—I do think that it is impossible to represent these things—but because the minute you say that, then you feed into some other ideologies about silence, ultimate unknowability, the chaos of the world, unrepresentability, indeterminacy, and so forth in all kinds of undesirable ways. In short, theoretical defeatism. Allegory happens when you know you cannot represent something but you also cannot not do it.

ZHANG: *But doesn't your own notion of "cognitive mapping," using the metaphor of one trying to figure out his or her situation and become orientated in the urban space, provide a bridge between the two realms of the dialectic and the allegorical?*

JAMESON: I have not thought about it that way, but it is an interesting formulation.

ZHANG: *In your view, dialectical thinking cannot be a purely "intellectual" or speculative operation; it is a constant struggle, which involves economics, politics, personal history. . . .*

JAMESON: And your own ideologies. No, I agree. The mark of some successful dialectic is shock, surprise, and the undermining of preconceived notions. You can glimpse the truth or the Real, but then your own ideologies seep back—your own illusions of the world, your own wish fulfillments—and then you are out of truth again. There psychoanalysis offers a good analogy, teaching that the moment of truth is this fitful, fleeting, and painful thing, a contact you necessarily keep losing all the time and only fitfully regain.

That is another reason why it is wrong to think of the dialectic as a philosophy. Because presumably in a philosophy you can write down your truth once you have found it. Hegel thought he was doing that (or at least pretended to think so). Capitalism is a much more complicated thing than ontology. Marx knows that you cannot see Capital as such. His book then was a very interesting—as he says—literary experiment, a *Darstellung*: how you put this together in some form in order to gain a glimpse of the real; for if the dialectic is as I have described it, it cannot be a systematic philosophy of a representational kind.

ZHANG: *For many Chinese readers, "cultural criticism" is primarily a Jamesonian notion, first brought to them by your visit in 1985. Now "cultural studies" has started to gain currency in parts of academia in China, Taiwan, and Hong Kong. What are the relationship and difference between them?*

JAMESON: I think the best way to begin is to say that, taken narrowly, in the United States, cultural studies is a new discipline. It is a new place that younger scholars have opened in order to investigate a whole range of what we used to call mass-cultural phenomena, all the way from music to television, from gender to forms of power, ethnicity, and so forth; and it has been a very important opening, allowing intellectuals to grapple more intensely with new forms of everyday life that have emerged in so-called postmodernity.

For other countries—and again the national situation plays a role—cultural studies seems to be something rather different in terms of cultural history, including the literary phenomena, the past, the social movement, and so on. There is often a certain tension or shock when Americans meet their counterparts in other countries, including Britain, where, of course, cultural studies first evolved in the Birmingham School. I tend to think that the Americans have been much less historical in what we were willing to include of the past, except for certain specific areas, as for example in Women's Studies, where history is obviously essential. This polemic between literature and mass culture, between the old-fashioned aestheticians and the newfangled cultural studies people has left a deep scar on the project itself. There are obvious reasons for that, and some of them are to be found in the structure of the academy, while others are to be found in the class structure of the United States, where literature is marked as elitist, and mass culture as populist.

My notion of cultural studies would be larger than the one of the younger American intellectuals. But that does not mean that I would in any way wish to depreciate the interest and value of what they are doing. I just think it is very American. The specificities and the exceptionality of American culture is that Americans think that they are in the universal; that somehow we are the end of history; there are no other realities than this one, or other realities are culturally determined—what the French do, what the Chinese do—but the United States is the true and universally human. Therefore, they need not take a historical perspective on this; maybe they do not even need to take a class perspective on this form of scholarship. They do not need to see themselves in terms of their own situation. Yet while it is certainly true that America's culture *is* late capitalism in some generalizable sense, we prefer not to take a critical distance from it and see ourselves as relatively parochial in some of our attitudes to ourselves and to the rest of the not yet late capitalist world.

When you read *Cultural Studies*, the collection of essays edited by Lawrence Grossberg, Cary Nelson, and Paula Treichler on which I wrote a long article, you see that the foreigners, particularly the Australians, are quite amazed by this American parochialism which does not see itself that way, which thinks of itself as instantly universal.[2] I guess I am anti-American enough, too, to wish for a little more dialectical self-consciousness about the project, a little more positioning of ourselves in the specificities of our situation. It is late capitalism, but it is an American late capitalism. It is not the way the Europeans operate, it is not the way the Japanese operate. I think the absence of that self-critical reflexivity limits the scope of the work of American cultural studies; that is to say, it blocks the connection of the analysis of the specific object with theory. I have to feel that it is a drawback. The point of doing these analyses is not only to do them for their own sake—although they are very interesting and should be thought through—but also to connect them with the theoretical problematic.

**ZHANG:** *The appearances of these works are very theoretical.*

**JAMESON:** Right. But much of theory today has, along with the attacks on theory, become antitheoretical, or at least has drawn back from the ambitions of theory. I have to put this in a Marxist framework and in a Marxist perspective, as this whole interview has shown.

**ZHANG:** *In that particular article of yours on* Cultural Studies, *published by* Social Text, *you said that academic politics is the only politics of the cultural studies people. What do you really mean by that?*

**JAMESON:** I do not want to be misunderstood on that. Because many of these modes of analysis come out of ethnic groups; they come out of group experiences. So I will have to add that American academic politics is so enlarged that social tensions are included in it, as one sees in the debates on affirmative action in California. That is a way of specifying it, not a way of reducing it in some antiacademic sense. To a certain degree, these issues can be also identified as identity politics, but in the academic world, those are also struggles for recognition. If you struggle to have a Chicano studies program, or an Afro-American Studies program, or a Women's Studies program, or other programs which are being rolled back nowadays, then you are expressing a more general social politics in terms of the framework of the academy itself. E. P. Thompson used to deplore this, saying that the old Left intellectuals were gone, and now these are just people in the academic world, fighting over academic theories. But academia has changed, too, in particular in the United States, and today the academic itself is not a purely academic issue.

**ZHANG:** *Yesterday, as you know, you were mentioned by someone at the conference as a "red Kant." Reading the first pages of the concluding chapter of your postmodernism book, interestingly, one notices something you have said which is kind of Kantian. You say that there are three levels of things which we may have an interest in separating: the level of taste, or judgment (at which you admit you like many things about postmodernism—food, music, video, and so on), the level of analysis, and finally the level of evaluation.*

**JAMESON:** No, I think that it ties in with things we were talking about earlier, namely, the ways of getting rid of the Self so that one could experience cultural, social, and other realities more aesthetically or directly. That is to say, it seems to me that the level of taste is the one at which we surprise, within ourselves, our attractions to certain kinds of cultural phenomena. Suddenly, cyberpunk appears, and we understand something new and important is going on here. Generally we also like these new things; I suppose the experience could also be negative, but I do not think one often does good work on things one dislikes. So the moment of taste is this moment of surprising new perceptions and of realizing new needs within yourself. Then the moment of analysis is one in which one looks at the way it functions: what is it that is new that has emerged, why it emerged, what the conditions of possibility are of this new thing, why cyberpunk comes into American cultural life at this particular time, for example. That would be the level that I would call analysis. That is trying to determine the shape of the novel, its relationship both to ourselves and to our situations and contexts. Then the level of evaluation is the one in which a historical perspective is going to evolve. That may not be possible for immediate things, but may be possible later on to decide if cyberpunk is an expression of late capitalism, for example, or a resistance to it. Or a replication or a critique.

I guess one could artificially divide up this process of perception or thinking in that way. But I am not at all wedded to formulations like that. I tend to think that you are probably right that it could be sucked back into more traditional and even Kantian modes of aesthetics, into something that obviously ought to be avoided.

**ZHANG:** *But wouldn't it also be interesting to see that as a juxtaposition of a kind of Kantian differentiation with the contemporary multiplicity of one's positions?*

**JAMESON:** If it were Kantian, then the difference would lie in the Western and postmodern emphasis on history. In other words, I would never want to do an evaluation on some eternal or timeless thing, but only in terms of historical change. Maybe that makes a Kantian system impossible.

**ZHANG:** *Geopolitically, the shift from philosophy to theory, and then maybe from theory to critical analysis of contemporary culture, is paralleled with the shift of power or productivity from Europe to North America. How would you describe this process and also your own role in that?*

**JAMESON:** That is the kind of self-knowledge one is probably least comfortable with. I think that, as you know, we Americans have been, in terms of theory, a kind of transmission belt. For example, French theory first came through England to the United States; it was transmitted by Verso, by Ben Brewster's translation of Althusser; and so forth. So England then served as a kind of transmission, at least for us. I think that we may be serving some of that function for China. So that the excitement we had in the 1970s in discovering all those things, now you get in a more concentrated form because it is delivered all at once.

I know there are positions that hold that there is a new division of theory and practice. The third world does the practice and produces the text, and the first world delivers the theory and thinks about it. But we increasingly have a lot of very specific forms of theory that come from the other parts of the world, Indian Subaltern Studies being the most notable one where that is happening right now. I also think there is a kind of situational, vested interest in the United States of not knowing what it is doing, and therefore of not becoming the center of theoretical production as you would think of the center of industrial production moving from England to the United States or something like that.

But on the other hand, I am sure that this must also be considered in economic terms. After all it *is* American culture that is now the principal export of late capitalism all over the world.[3] Therefore the theory of that culture would necessarily follow it. One can always distinguish between this imperial export of culture and those theories themselves. For good or ill, this has to reflect a world in which the production of the United States, namely, entertainment and culture, is dominant. I am against guilt trips and self-denunciations, so I feel temperamentally that we should not always be beating our chest and lamenting the fact that we should not be exporting our own theories and that we are sorry to be cultural imperialists. I think there are things to analyze in the United States that we have a privileged viewpoint on. If we think about our work as political and cultural intellectuals, we have certain kinds of important critical tasks to fulfill that cannot be really done on the outside.

ZHANG: *If late capitalism is the organizing dynamic, then one would expect a global united front of critical, political intellectuals taking shape. So far, however, that does not seem to be the case. Besides the gap between the Western and non-Western societies, various national, regional, and local politics seem to prevent one from thinking in a truly cosmopolitan fashion. How do you address that? Do you think such a united front possible, or even desirable?*

JAMESON: Well, it isn't surprising that just as a global labor movement has not yet come into being, so also there is as yet no genuinely international association of intellectuals. Nonetheless, it would be surprising if the technology that allowed businesses and financial centers to speed up their contacts with each other, and in particular their exchanges and transactions, were not seized upon by intellectual networks as well. Indeed, I think this is happening already, and there is a far greater awareness of movements and intellectual activities in other countries today everywhere around the world than there was in the modern or the imperialist period.

Along with this we have of course the appearance of something like transnational literary works and writers and intellectual figures. Surely, people like Derrida or Salman Rushdie live and work on a level of international exchange which may include various national contacts but which is distinct from all of them. This would seem to correspond to some new form of what used to be called "World Literature," which was conventionally understood to include those classics that appealed to a variety of national audiences out beyond the immediate national context. I think, however, that that was not exactly what the expression *world literature* meant when Goethe, among others, pioneered it. If one examines the few fragmentary texts he left on this subject, one begins to realize that he had in mind the fact of intellectual networks themselves and the coming into existence of new modes of intellectual and theoretical interrelationship, particularly as those were emphasized by the great journals, *The Edinburgh Review, La Revue des deux mondes*, along with the preeminent national newspapers, all of which he himself read in Weimar. It was this new communicational access to national modes of intellectual exchange that seemed to Goethe historically original and for which he coined this expression *Weltliteratur*, which no longer seems quite appropriate in the new global context. I believe that something of this sort on a far vaster scale is coming into existence today, but that we need to take special precautions to encourage its development. As with literature itself, it does not mean producing ideas that are immediately universal and can thus spring out of the national context and be available to everyone. It means mediation and passing through each of the national contexts. It means, in effect, that when we talk to intellectuals in other national situations, the home intellectual and the intellectual abroad are themselves merely the medium for the contact between national situations, or as we used to call them, national cultures.

We must pass through those situations in order to understand any of the intellectual or aesthetic events that take place in the other situation. What transpires, then, is a genuine comparativism of intellectual activity and not simply the decontextualization of that activity and its immediate ascension into the absolute, in some vacuous sense of the universally human. This obviously imposes on us enormous efforts of knowledge and sympathy. It also imposes problems of inequality and noncomparability. It causes us to devise exceedingly complicated equations in which the foreign prestige value of certain kinds of objects or items has to be reckoned back into the equation in advance. On the other hand, it seems to me to promise an enormously rich work of detail in linking Left perspectives around the globe. This is the area in which it seems to me that, despite the momentary political or social pessimism, despite the seeming immobilization of what can be done in the world of collective praxis, there is today an enormous and very rich field for intellectual activity on the Left which can keep us busy and productive for some time.

**ZHANG:** *Thank you very much for your time.*

NOTES

1. See "Marx's Purloined Letter," *New Left Review* 209 (1995): 86–120; "Interview with Sara Danius and Stefan Jonsson," this volume.

2. See "On 'Cultural Studies,'" *Social Text* 34 (1993): 17–52.

3. See "Globalization and Political Strategy," *New Left Review* 2 4 (2000): 49–68; "Notes on Globalization as a Philosophical Issue," in *The Cultures of Globalization,* ed. Fredric Jameson and Masao Miyoshi (1998), 54–77.

# Interview with Srinivas Aravamudan and Ranjana Khanna

*We would like to begin with a question about the particular Marxist theorists you are in dialogue with over your career. It has been frequently noted that the framework you occupy is broadly within the Western Marxist tradition, and especially the Franco-German one. Sartre, Lukács, Adorno, Brecht, Marcuse, Bloch, and Benjamin are obviously very important for you. Althusser seems to be an important intermediate figure, who you engage deeply although less sympathetically than the others just mentioned. However, when it comes to so-called cultural Marxists such as Gramsci, or Raymond Williams, would it be fair to say that these are less interesting to you, especially as some of their concepts have led to what has been called postmarxism? And, to what extent would you agree with characterizations of your approach as that of a full-fledged Hegelian? Also, are there Russian, Chinese, and third world Marxist theorists who have added significantly to your conceptual apparatus?*

**JAMESON:** I don't generally think of myself as a "Western Marxist," a term proposed by Perry Anderson in 1973; perhaps I'm more of an economic fundamentalist than that. In any case the idea was to characterize the non-card-carrying communists or Trotskyists (with the exception of the founding father, Lukács himself) and to show what happened when the overtly party-political was left out of the scheme of things. I would say that Western Marxism is characterized by three distinctive features: (1) the inclusion of psychoanalysis; (2) the suspicion directed towards Engels, who essentially transformed Marx's work into a philosophy and even a metaphysics, so-called dialectical materialism (something which also explains their Viconian hostility to science and the dialectic of nature); (3) and the predominant emphasis placed on culture and ideology. (On the strength of that great and neglected figure Karl Korsch, one might add in "historicism" for some of these people, and in any case the return from dialectical materialism to historical materialism implies some such general shift). I do endorse all these things, but feel it is important to prevent any modern Marxism from slipping into purely cultural critique or this or that psychoanalytic worldview; and so I have always insisted that these emphases were not only perfectly compatible with a certain orthodoxy in economic matters but indeed that they had to be accompanied with an insistence on the omnipresence of class struggle, and on the dynamics of capital itself, in constant if uneven or intermittent expansion and clearly enough always driven by the need to lower labor costs, to maximize profits, and to respond to competition. These features are perhaps once again, in full globalization, more evident and inescapable than they sometimes were in the Cold War and in the deceptive mists of various social-democratic movements and governments. So I always felt even at an early age, that Marx was right, and even though my first experience of Marxism as a creative movement came from the spirit of France in the 1950s, and in particular from the example of Sartre. At the end of that decade, the Cuban Revolution then proved to me that Marxism was alive and well as a collective movement and a culturally productive force. But I did read a good deal of Lukács when I studied in Berlin in the mid-1950s (and also a good deal of Brecht); and as for the Frankfurt School, they were always on the horizon too, as superb practitioners of the dialectic. Am I a Hegelian? I am certainly a fellow traveler of the Hegelian dialectic, but probably not any full-fledged Hegelian in the philosophical sense—some of those still do exist today!

As for Williams and Gramsci, what holds me back a little is what is so admirable in both of them, namely, the commitment to the concrete situation in which they worked and struggled. But it is precisely the primacy of the English or Welsh and the Italian or Sicilian situation that makes these theorists less useful for theorists in the superstate. I would also wish to warn against the tendency of such heretical or at least oppositional Marxisms to become fully fledged and autonomous systems in their own right. Thus I cannot follow Williams's critique of the base-superstructure distinction: the latter is for me not some orthodox solution, but the name for an interpretive problem which is always with us. Nor can I follow my great friend Wolfgang Fritz Haug in promoting "hegemony" as some new and original Marxian idea which might lead us on into a specifically Gramscian philosophy. In that sense, I'm also not particularly representative of anything called the New Left, I suppose.

**ARAVAMUDAN:** *So just to follow up, wouldn't Gramsci's major contribution or influence to Subaltern Studies coming from the South Asian context be one situation where Gramsci has indeed traveled to very different contexts?*

**JAMESON:** Well, I feel that Gramsci meant the idea of subalternity to apply in the framework of the working-class condition as a whole in Italy, not just Sicily but also the North, and to designate habits of the working class which both involved obedience and respect, but also lack of sufficient culture and political awareness, which the working-class movement was there to overcome. Whereas it seems to me that in India subalternity was really meant to designate the peasantry as opposed to the working class and that the discoveries that Ranajit Guha and others made had to do with the dynamics of peasant revolt and a political awareness that was specific to a peasant movement, as opposed to that of industrial workers. So I am not sure whether anything more than the term was transferred. Now I would say the same for *hegemony* in the uses that Ernesto Laclau and Chantal Mouffe make of it. The term was originally Lenin's, as they point out, but I don't think they mean exactly the kind of politics that Gramsci had in mind. Their work is very interesting, but maybe its appeal to Gramsci as an authority is not an altogether faithful one.

**KHANNA:** *I want to ask you something more specific about Sartre and your relation to Sartre. You wrote in 1985, in a piece called "Sartre after Sartre," that "regrettably but inevitably Sartre has become the name for an archival specialization in its own right." I wonder if you could reflect on the way in which your own work has been shaped today through an engagement with Sartre, and also where you see Sartre's future. It seems as if there has been a little bit of a comeback of a certain Sartrean mode of thinking in the current interest in Alain Badiou, or do you see that as being more about a resurgence of interest in Maoism—or do you see the two as related? There also has been some focus on Sartrean existentialism in a certain postcolonial interest in Fanon too—and that has been embodied itself as a resistance to the way in which he has been read as overly Lacanian (Henry Louis Gates Jr., for example, commented on how after Homi Bhabha's reading, Fanon became something of a black Lacan). So given your own interest in both Lacan and Sartre, do you think it is unwise to pit them against each other in that way? And do you see a future for work shaped through an engagement with Sartre and the kind of profound voluntarism that is there in Sartre's work in the cur-*

*rent world, or is the disjuncture between the current situations and potential human action just too profound at the moment? Or would Sartreanism today manifest itself differently from that kind of voluntarism?*

JAMESON: Yes, what I meant by Sartre entering the archives, so to speak, or the domain of specialization, is that already in the 1960s the structuralists had mounted a very extensive campaign against Sartrean existentialism which had been at that point the really single most overarching thinking and philosophical trend in postwar France; and they did this very thoroughly in a variety of ways that I think were not all incorrect. That is to say, they took issue with Sartre's Cartesianism, the emphasis on the individual consciousness, and they wanted to place a good deal more emphasis on those larger structures—linguistic, social, and other—that the individual conscious is embedded in. They also wanted to move away from phenomenological ideas of experience to other kinds of structural notions and I think in a very welcome way to turn us back to the economic or the unconscious and nonexperiential structures of that kind. That's where Althusser would fit in as well as Lacan. Later on there were the feminist attacks on and critiques of Sartre which I have always found distressingly and unnecessarily moralizing, and also singularly misplaced—the idea of Sartre as a sexist seems to me to be grotesque—but that certainly also had a profound impact. Now, in my opinion the afterlife of Sartre lies in what you could call constructivism. It's in the social and historical construction of the subject and the psyche that Sartre's legacy is very much alive, even though almost completely unacknowledged. Another place that was never really part of the original Sartrean or existential movement because it came too late, but which remains to be fully explored, is the *Critique of Dialectical Reason*, which has all kinds of stimulating new ideas about group formation and dynamics. It is certainly not a fully fledged philosophical or even political system, and there's a lot one might want to criticize in the politics it seems to project, which is essentially a small group politics, a guerilla politics; yet that Sartre very much remains to be explored, and it's interesting that when Deleuze does finally mention or footnote Sartre—I think there's only two references in his mature work (*Anti-Oedipus*)—it's to the *Critique* that he refers, since it obviously has something to say about war machines and face-to-face groups. I do actually still hold to the Sartrean analysis of consciousness and freedom, but this kind of existentialism has not been a part of people's philosophical concerns in recent years; and we have to remember how much of all that, including the earlier politics and the seeming voluntarism on decisionism, had to do with extreme situations as such. Those were classically the occupation and the French resistance in World War II, as well as in the national liberation movements. I am not sure that since then people in the West have had to confront those kinds of situations. In that sense Sartrean heroism has tended mainly to find its exemplars abroad in the various media and cold war protagonists like the dissidents. So there are reasons why the existential Sartre has not found a lot of application. I would say that the really original part of Sartre's philosophy had to do with his discovery of the Other, and this is an originality which is prolonged in the form of group activity as you find it in the *Critique*. I don't think anybody really gets over reading the section on the Look in *Being and Nothingness*, an idea that owes nothing whatsoever to Heidegger. Heidegger really has no satisfactory concept of the encounter with the Other. And this is really not even Hegel's master and slave, although that's a distant ancestor via Kojève. It is out of this that Fanon comes, because Fanonian violence is very much a part of this relationship to the Other as it is retranscribed in the Hegelian master-slave situation. But it offers an outcome to the master-slave dialectic (so-called redemptive violence) which is not in Hegel and not really even in Sartre in that form. Early Lacan is also very strongly influenced by Sartre. Anybody who reads the first five seminars, I suppose, maybe even the first nine or ten, cannot but be struck by that omnipresent existential or Sartrean problematic. To think that Lacan is profoundly hostile to Sartre is a historical misreading. Now as for Sartre today, who knows? I don't see any interest in Sartre's political writing, even though he was a great pamphleteer, and this was marvelous rhetoric and strong language.

ARAVAMUDAN: *Even though you took considerable effort to separate your descriptive diagnosis of postmodernism from any kind of celebratory political impulse, the rich and detailed analyses of the phenomena have confused several of your readers. I think you have remarked somewhere that it helps a lot to like something when you analyze it, and it does come across in your analyses of postmodernism that there is considerable aesthetic enjoyment to be had through at least thinking about it.[1] Also, while you describe postmodernism as "the cultural logic of late capitalism," to some, this sometimes seems indistinguishable from Americanism.*

JAMESON: I do think that to make analyses—I would probably prefer to say ideological analyses in general—the most productive position is from within: so that it is really as an ideological analysis of yourself and your own tastes and what your own contemporary needs are that one stages the thorough analysis, and not in the form of those hostile and denunciatory analyses that the Marxist political and cultural tradition used to make. Ideological analysis is certainly not irrelevant even today, but I think it involves a different kind of polemic and identifies different kinds of targets. So in that sense I did write from within an appreciation of postmodernity, so to speak, and I think that has to reflect our own situation within this zeitgeist or period style. The latter is not something that we can remove ourselves from either mentally or physically, which is to say that it's harder and harder to go out in the countryside and start a commune, or like the Amish secede from postmodern society and do something wholly unrelated to society at large, to late capitalism. Meanwhile in the outside world, most of that outside world has also been modernized and even postmodernized; so it's not so easy to find a country in which the same phenomena are not going on. This is therefore also the problem of critical distance, which normally meant some form of metaphorical or real distance from the thing: getting outside of it, seeing it from the outside. This cultural dominant one has to see from the inside, so it certainly complicates the cultural and political problem of judgment and/or "opposition" and "critique." As far as Americanism is concerned, yes, of course I think that this is the first really global style developed by America: for all kinds of reasons, having to do with the commercial centrality of culture in the United States; the fact that in a way we invented a mass culture which is not popular culture and not kitsch but which is both an industry and a whole new cultural style; and also because of this influence that we have as the global superpower and the exporter of all of these cultural practices. Yet I think one has to continue to try to make a distinction between this logic of capitalism as a global system at this moment and its uniquely American variant. There is again a dialectic of the universal and the particular here, the way it already existed for Marx when he dealt with the first full-blown classical forms of capital which were English. Yes, you have to take into account the cultural specificity of that moment of capital and explain why England was the privileged place for it to develop, but one has to nonetheless separate these two things out. There were very good reasons why Europe was very slow to become postmodern, so to speak, although we shouldn't exclude their catching up. Japan has traditionally been a happy hunting ground for new forms of the postmodern, and that certainly makes sense, but Japan is not the superpower and is not currently able to export culture and cultural styles and practices in the same way as the US.

**KHANNA:** *Given what you have just said, I am wondering if you can say a little bit about what you see as the potentials and problems that arise from the inevitable location of yourself and your own kind of critique and the form of postmodernism that has emerged in the US for your conception of the global. You have received, I guess, some criticism for your sense that alternative futures will emerge from the global South rather than the North, and I am wondering whether you think that new internationalisms could be adequately formulated in the US, or indeed from any one location. Or is an internationalism not the way to be thinking at all?*

**JAMESON:** Well, I think one should maybe, for purposes of the discussion, purposes of clarity, distinguish between the political and the cultural; and at that point we can indeed invoke Raymond Williams and talk about the residual and the emergent. I think that residual cultures are always necessarily resistant to new forms of capitalist development and that many of those cultures are found in countries that have a traditional peasantry and are able to preserve older modes of production including the cultural ones. So certainly where those traditions have been preserved—and I think that they are under threat almost everywhere in the world—there is certainly a cultural resistance to the process of postmodernization. I wish I could think that we could go back to any of those older cultures, but I suppose I have to think that anything of a Utopian nature that is to emerge from late capitalism is rather going to have to go forward and acknowledge and appropriate the dynamics of the information society rather than returning to simpler, pastoral forms. Now I have never thought that the United States was in a good place to pioneer anything truly emergent, including politics. If there's a sustained antiglobalization movement, it will certainly come out of both young people in the United States and out of the problems of the weaknesses of the labor unions, and the need to react against this whole process. But that movement has to be international, and I suspect that it's other countries, other kinds of populations, who will take the lead in that, for which we [in the US] are very poorly placed in all kinds of ways. The center is the worst place for any alternatives to emerge: the idea that nowadays some new positive politics will come out of the United States has seemed unlikely since the abandonment of the rainbow coalition.

**KHANNA:** *Well, following up from a couple of things that you said, we wanted to ask about the different modes of production existing simultaneously in globalization, and the way in which we can understand these in* *terms of a singular modernity. I wonder what that means for analysis of the fact that, for example, more women than ever are now employed in forms of industrialized labor, particularly, of course, women in the third world. So even if there is a singular modernity, aren't there multiple forms of labor and multiple modes of understanding value and the human? You seem to suggest that the differences put forward in notions of alternative modernity or vernacular modernities et cetera are cultural analyses, and they seem to be somewhat limited in your analysis, then, because the only real alternative as you see it could be about an alternative to the existing forward movement of capital. But these differences, the outsourcing of industrialized labor et cetera, seem to present difference in terms of labor, value, et cetera. So, is difference really only cultural difference? Isn't the cultural difference that is frequently analyzed also about a differential relation to capital?*

JAMESON: Well, I guess I do take a somewhat bleak view of this. I certainly had in mind the idea that the celebration of cultural difference was not really enough to create an alternative society, and also that the example of the United States has shown that postmodernity cannot only very handily absorb those kinds of cultural differences, but that they tend to be turned into a uniquely American cultural strategy which I would call Disneyfication. This is to say that in full modernity or postmodernity—or classical or late capitalism—the insistence on cultural uniqueness, national specificities, and social tradition tends to turn those into commodities as well and to market them the way Disney markets this whole variety of simulated American styles that was his genius to have invented. And I think that Disneyfication in that sense is part of globalization and postmodernity. When you can think of the early twentieth century in China, for example, you have real traditionalists who dress in a certain way, have a certain kind of life mode, for whom Confucian texts are central, and these are people who wish to exclude the West so far as that is possible. Then against them you have the modernizers. Now that's a classical kind of struggle in a great many countries, indeed, in most countries that have had a long civilization and that capitalism has only recently penetrated and colonized; but I don't think there are traditionalists like that around anymore. And even the current Islamic movement is scarcely anticapitalist; I would also have to wonder about the authenticity of its traditional religion as well, but maybe we'll get to that later on. So I think that in the very logic of capital development there comes a moment when the residual elements of a traditional national culture become commodities. Now what the theory of alternate modernities suggests is that in another nation-state, in another culture, in another national situation, there would be alternate ways to Disneyfy and that you could package your product in culturally specific ways so that the very shape of Disneyland would be Brazilian, or Indian, or Chinese. But I'm afraid I think that the process would be the same, and I also tend to think that emphasis on this idea is generally a diversion from the political as such. Now we've already talked about the gap between the universal and the specific: any form of capitalist development would have to take a specific and concrete form and would therefore naturally take on the characteristics of the country that it's emerging in. So it doesn't mean that all over the world late capitalism will look like American late capitalism, and this is why also American late capitalism is not the universal form of capitalism; it is just yet another specification or exemplification. But that doesn't really change the problem, and it doesn't seem to me that the notion of alternate modernities makes a useful contribution to the kinds of political and economic problems that we face under globalization, which involve the transnational communities, reintroduction of the profit motive, or let's say destruction of the welfare state, and so on. Those are all happening on the economic front, whatever distinctive forms and histories they take in each of the countries involved.

**KHANNA:** *I am particularly interested in the way in which we understand the gender division of labor. I do have a later question that relates to this as well, but it does seem as if there are so many women in forms of industrialized labor at the moment, precisely not in the US and precisely in the third world, and it does seem as if there is a marked difference in the ways in which the movement of capital is affecting women and men. And I'm wondering if you have any thoughts on that question of sexual difference, if you like, when it comes to these questions of a singular modernity?*

**JAMESON:** Well, it has been said that in the new informational production of the future with automation and computers and the like, the American working class will be largely made up of third world women, while the people with their hands on the levers of control in the sense of the old-fashioned proletariat will be the repairmen who can alone go around and service this technology which is apparently down 20 percent of the time anyway. So that's one way of looking at it; and I would also say that in the United States the corollary to this increased use of women in the marginal jobs is the structural unemployment of men, particularly young black men.

All of those things go together, and a new working-class politics has to address the very specific features not only of women's oppression in general but of the specific forms of women's oppression in specific nation-states and eventually the whole cultural position of women in these various situations. So that would, I think, be part of any national organizational or political movement. Add to that then the matter of the family and social reproduction and housework. Those remain questions that maybe were less visible in the classical period because there were fewer women in the workplace, but they're now all part of the essentially economic and political fully as much as they are of the cultural.

**ARAVAMUDAN:** *I think you've already partly addressed this when you were talking about the relation between the universal and the particular, but I do want to go ahead with this question because there is still an aspect of it that I would like you to address. In a recent article, your friend Harry Harootunian has expressed misgivings about the manner in which postmodernism, for you, has increasingly become too much of a spatialization. You have suggested that while modernism tended to be linked with something like incomplete modernization, postmodernism is linked to something like full modernization, and perhaps at some point it seems to indicate something like an establishment of an even ground that heralds the end of temporality. Indeed, you have that essay "The End of Temporality" in* Critical Inquiry. *But doesn't capitalism need to generate unevenness for strategic advantage, and are you not also overstating the case for full modernization, given the vast differentials in the world today when it comes to modernization itself?*

**JAMESON:** I was evoking tendencies, always a tricky matter. But what I particularly wanted to mark by those outrageous formulations was what you could also talk about in terms of changes in the nature of the psychic subject and in social existential experience and the like. Now, unevenness is certainly present, but now—and this is the reason for dealing with them in the framework of the world market—now these unevennesses are spread all over the world, and there is a relatively greater kind of homogenization of experience in the United States. There will always be many different ways of talking about such developments, but the spatial seems to me the most useful. The split between province and metropolis in the US has, for example, disappeared. The idea that with the standardization of the media we're at the center everywhere in the United States is another kind of spatialization. My idea was that the slogan of space was a way into this phenomenon and that it opened all kinds of new possibilities and new descriptions, new problems. I think that it's obvious that we're all still living in time, so one doesn't really need to insist on that, but since so much of the temporal language had already been in use to whatever effect in an older period, it seemed as though we needed something of a shift in vocabulary, and I felt that the lexicon of space might be more suggestive of the change. Some of these spatial connotations are not particularly metaphorical. Instantaneous communication, the virtual simultaneity of transactions on the market and so forth—this really takes place in a new kind of spatial simultaneity. But I'm not interested in defending the individual figures of this description. It does seem to me, though, that when people say postmodernism is over, postmodernity is over, it all ended on 9/11 and so forth, this betrays a complete misunderstanding of what the term means: that a certain postmodern style and architecture has long since been replaced by other things in no way means that this whole new economic structure of postmodernity, with which I equate globalization, has changed. I don't see that the rise in anti-American movements of the type that express themselves in the Twin Towers attack makes for a change in the situation either. Probably much that is deployed by al-Qaeda is really postmodern, although this does introduce new objects of interrogation such as postmodern conflict, postmodern struggle, postmodern warfare, which would need to be worked out.

**ARAVAMUDAN:** *Let me make sure I understand you correctly on this topic, then. You are saying that to some extent the shift to space is partly in order not so much to replace time but to add a sort of perspective that hasn't really been used for effective analysis. In a sense, you would just add that the spatial perspective that comes through something like postmodernism to temporality. I'm just kind of curious what your response would be to someone like Ernst Bloch who was suspicious of any kind of spatialization and wanted to insist on temporality on those kinds of temporal metaphors as crucial for any notion of change or revolution.*

**JAMESON:** The one feature of this—and this is where it gets a little more dialectical, I think—is that what was emerging in the social sciences and elsewhere in theory was essentially a new emphasis on space and a new exploration of spatial methods of analysis. It's not an accident that those things have been emerging, because they find in postmodernity itself a fitting object of study: they're called up by the very logic of the thing. I really don't want to endorse the postmodern as a slogan, and I don't think of myself as a postmodern thinker; I can understand why people are sick of this word. Yet fashion changes in theory are also significant symptoms, and here the drift towards the spatial in all kinds of registers does seem to me to mark an important shift in the world itself, which is to say, in the way capitalism functions and as a result of the way in which everyday life and culture are organized, not to speak of the realm of the aesthetic and so-called high art. That's why for me it was very important when I discovered this, that the other objective political economic face of postmodernity was globalization. I would want to insist that these two things are the same and that they are merely different registers of talking about the same thing. This may be a different way of expressing my dissatisfaction with the insufficiencies of the term *postmodern*.

**ARAVAMUDAN:** *Your recent book on science fiction,* Archaelogies of the Future, *perhaps addresses some of the questions that we've just raised about spatialization. We're intrigued by the notion of an archaeology of the future at a time when most cultural discourse tends to circulate between various forms of historicism and presentism. However, while neither of us is very conversant with the genre of science fiction, we nonetheless want to ask a few questions. One question regards the intriguing designation of Utopia as a subset of science fiction, which I think you take from Darko Suvin. We would like for you to expand on the implications of that in global terms. What we're especially thinking about is a relative absence of science fiction in many parts of the world that are now capitalistically advanced or advancing, such as India and China, for example. Do martial arts fantasies in China perform similar functions? However, you do seem to resist the collapse between science fiction and fantasy more generally. The counterexample would of course be Japan, which has had a very rich science fiction tradition. In film, there is no science fiction obsession in Bollywood, or even in alternative Indian cinema, to correspond with Hollywood's, although of course, intriguingly, Satyajit Ray wrote lots of science fiction, but he did not go about realizing these ideas filmically.*

**JAMESON:** I think that this is in general true. As far as I know there have been a few Korean science fiction movies. You could almost say that 2046 of Wong Kar-Wai is a partial break into this general area. As a Western tradition, science fiction has been built on pulp fiction and adventure stories all the way from Jules Verne to the 1920s and perhaps in the absence of that form of science fiction, the form as such would really have to be imported, it would have to be more of a jet-set postmodern influence rather than an organic development out of the national literature. The other thing to look at here is the role of the historical novel: I see that as a complementary form in which the thinking about time and about the past generated the practice of a whole new literary form just as the sense of the dynamics of emergent futures generated this form we call science fiction. This also has something to do with the rhythms of collective temporality, with the way history is experienced in the national situation, but it also very much posits its own generic conditions and its own purely literary and linguistic conditions as well. Now I think that the reason that Utopia is best seen in terms of science fiction, as Suvin suggested, is that Utopia is not a stable genre. It emerges and disappears at various places and various moments in time, even though there are a few generic constants that you can observe in these historically dispersed Utopias. But it is the genre of science fiction that marks a whole new formal attempt to think the otherness of the future. So when the questions that Utopia addresses come around again, as the result of political and social developments, and revolution—the timeliness of systemic change in the social order—becomes again visible, the form most readily available to think those possibilities of futurity is the science fictional one. There is a way in which, in modernity, science fiction henceforth serves as the most satisfactory vehicle for the expression of the Utopian impulse. But that is only one way of understanding Suvin's proposal, which has been quite revolutionary in science fiction studies. As for fantasy, yes, I think that has to be defined in a completely different generic way from science fiction. It's a much older kind of storytelling and, for me, much less interesting; although my idea would be that it also (but in a different way) reflects human powers and human production.

**ARAVAMUDAN:** *I'm still hesitant about the move to designate Utopia as a subset of science fiction. Does this suggest that Luddism has no Utopia component? What about Gandhi, Tolstoy, and Ruskin, or even twentieth-century peasant Utopianisms that demonize industrialism and technology per se? Or is Marxism inseparable from techno-Utopianism, seizing on the necessary manipulation of nature to better human ends rather than those of capital?*

**JAMESON:** Well, there are a number of science fiction works which posit precapitalist societies or Utopias, so that kind of regressive content (let's just say for descriptive purposes) is not at all inconsistent with the science fiction framework, and indeed I think it's a kind of powerful (and valuable) defamiliarization of the modern and the technological. I myself have a lot of personal sympathy for these so-called "regressive Utopias"—the pastoral ones—but it seems to me that the real political problem is not so much that they are historically regressive, but that it is unlikely given the present development of capitalism that it could be turned back to these conditions short of some kind of catastrophe. Revolutions have often come out of catastrophes, and there are also a lot of science fiction scenarios where the destruction of a high civilization gives way to a Utopian reconstruction of a kind of agrarian or pastoral society along the lines you mention, but I don't know that this can be a political program.

**ARAVAMUDAN:** *If "the desire called Utopia," as you put it in* Archaeologies of the Future, *involves an archaeology of traces from the future, this investment in catachronism (rather than anachronism) puts you in the same company as Derrida, whose notion of "democracy to come" (à-venir) is derived from the idea of weak messianicity in Benjamin. However, I also detect differences, in that you seem more taken with the various imaginations of the future of totality, whereas Derrida always seems to stop short of that. Does this difference reveal something significant?*

**JAMESON:** Well, I guess my reaction would begin with the word *weak*: it seems to me that it's hard to project any kind of powerful image of the future with an essentially weak—deliberately weak in the spirit of Vattimo—or gradualist development. I don't think that necessarily rules out the things that Derrida is talking about, though, because in order to achieve some sort of genuine radical democracy, all kinds of things would have to be changed in culture, as well as in the infrastructure and the organization of life. So his claim of weakness may not really be so gradualist as it seems. But my idea of the future as "disruption" presupposes the production of more powerful images of a way of life completely distinct from this one and that people can use thought experiments to begin to imagine radical alternatives to this one rather than some mere tinkering with the system. The other thing that Derrida has in mind probably has to do with the messianic traditions of communism and the ghosts of Stalin and of other "salvational" leaders. I think that the further analysis of populism is still on the agenda, but I find it difficult to think about these changes without a radical break, and that generally means a revolutionary and collective upheaval.

**ARAVAMUDAN:** *We also want to get at the question of Utopia and the future in a slightly different way, and I would like to quote a couple of sentences* *from your essay "The Future City" in response to Rem Koolhaas's wonderful essay "Junkspace":*

> *Writing . . . is the battering ram, the delirious repetition that hammers away at this sameness running through all the forms of our existence (space, parking, shopping, working, eating, building) and pummels them into admitting their own standardized identity with each other, beyond colour, beyond texture, the formless blandness that is no longer even the plastic, vinyl or rubber of yesteryear. The sentences are the boom of this repetitive insistence, the pounding on the hollowness of space itself; and their energy now foretells the rush and the fresh air, the euphoria of a re-lief, an orgasmic breaking through time and history again, into a concrete future.*

*Is criticism vicarious, or is it precisely a performance of Utopia as these lines seem to suggest?*

JAMESON: Yes, of course I was talking about Koolhaas's own style and this kind of powerful satiric impulse that he mobilizes, both denouncing the environment and also in some sense appropriating it insofar as he offers some new Utopian substitute for all of these things, rather than any kind of nostalgic return to beautiful buildings or the older architectural standards. So I suppose this could also describe the possible effects of literary Utopias, or at least the way in which they have to marshal the power to resist all of the habits and all of the spaces and institutions that we live with in our standard world. But this is really not a question I was able to solve in my book and remains for me an ambiguity or even an antinomy that, insofar as contemporary Utopias are not representational, they do not give us some brand-new space to think about but really involve an attempt to reinvent anew the very idea of Utopia. Fourier's work is, for example, a sort of a grab bag of essays and scenes and narratives and analyses, much of which is certainly discursive or non-narrative, but all of it marshaled as a way of constituting this battering ram that opens up the future.

KHANNA: *I also want to ask you something that comes from that Rem Koolhaas piece. You say in that piece that architecture seems to be the only aesthetic form remaining that favors analysis based on the auteur, and I'm wondering if you could speculate a little bit on why that may be. Do you think architecture retains the framework of the modern that somehow demands a more auteur-centered analysis more than other media, genre, or modes?*

*Is architecture fundamentally less splintered, or does it for some reason demand a kind of analysis that is less splintered despite what you said, for example, about the forms of pastiche and fragmentation that characterize postmodern architecture and film, for example? You seem to have favored yourself or at least been very interested in, a kind of auteur analysis of film. Can you say something about this interest in the auteur? Does it suggest potential revolutionary subjects that you don't want to give up on in postmodernism (or perhaps to give up to difference, or to desubjectivation?)*

**JAMESON:** That's a very interesting question, and I am not sure I have thought through it completely. I think that the attack on the auteur was not just an attack on the centered subject in terms of structuralist or psychoanalytic theory, but was also an attack on the dictator and the central political subject which was really never the working class, but more often Stalin or the other great revolutionary leaders. Now in my view it was the textualization of the arts that made a hierarchy of auteurs impossible and no longer conducive to a canon. You have one art show after another, and all of this disappears into the back rooms of the galleries. There are certainly more novels and books in the archives than anyone could read. What does stand out from that is the individual building, particularly when it is a megabuilding. Megastructures are meant to resist the city, yet the city is not recuperable in the same way, especially nowadays. But these megabuildings are, in a sense, meant to keep their autonomy. If you listen to auteurs like my friend Peter Eisenman, you will hear him say that buildings are just built to last thirty years nowadays, and they'll all disappear. I think this may be a little too modest on his part. A lot of them are shoddily made and fall to pieces in a few years, but I don't think that's the essence of the problem. I think the idea of the single great building which is the microcosm and the substitute for the city really still preserves the modernist notion of the political world and the single great work within which everything can be expressed. In that case it may be that which allows the greatest architects today to remain auteurs in spite of the disappearance of categories of style which were in the past instrumental in giving one an idea of the auteur and of the artist's specific personality and style. Yes, I guess I am still rather nostalgic for auteur criticism, still reluctant to see all of that disappear into anonymity and anonymous textuality or textualization. And that may be a feature of my experience in postmodernity, which is more negative and critical of the latter. It is certainly heartening to find some good auteurs in literature, if one can do that nowadays. There are probably not too many around. But in film this becomes for me a very big problem because I have become aware that really we do have a recrudescence of the auteur at least in terms of art cinema all over the world. I'll just mention Aleksander Sokurov for one, or Wong Kar-Wai himself, and these are people I think who are no longer characterized by the religious notions of modernism, by the kind of the aesthetic absolute found in Andrei Tarkovsky and other great high modernist filmmakers. Today the notion of autonomy of the work survives mostly in film, and there still seems to be a place for such filmmakers in the midst of the disappearance of those collective movements and new waves, those avant-gardes which I think are mostly gone from the scene of film all around the world. There remain these individual filmmakers whose work does really resemble an older modernist canon—not just Sokurov or Wong Kar-Wai, but also Victor Erice, Raul Ruiz, Abbas Kiarostami, Tsai Ming-liang, Bela Tarr, Kumar Shahani, Mani Kaul—and others whom I greatly admire but whose existence puzzles me. This may have something to do with the belated temporality of film with respect to that of literature; it may be due to the emergence of a world public in which there is still room for this kind of production alongside the commercial type. It is certainly commercially assisted by the film festivals, where globalization has made it possible for some of these more hermetic figures to continue to be financed.

**ARAVAMUDAN:** *Let me pick up on something you said earlier in response to my question about the auteur. I have a couple of questions following up on this response actually—about your notion of the subject, the other about architecture and critical regionalism. You say that the attack on the auteur, besides being a critique launched from structuralist and poststructuralist theory, was also an attack on the dictator, and not an attack on the working-class subject. I suppose I'm wondering why not—why, in a sense, there is a retention of the idea of a consolidated subject when it comes to potentially revolutionary people? Isn't that a reduction of a notion of difference to culture? Doesn't that reduce questions of difference always to the level of an ontic that in no way poses challenges to the ontological? Isn't that an avoidance of the really challenging questions about difference that may actually threaten the ontological frameworks we too often assume, and perhaps too often assume when it comes to conceptualizing the potentially revolutionary people? It seems to me that any future concept of Marxist internationalism would have to take on the idea of such radical alterity as posing fundamental* *questions about the structure of consciousness if it is not to reintroduce a class hierarchy into future Utopias.*

**JAMESON:** I think that people often tend to confuse questions of consciousness with purely cultural questions, or if you prefer—and this would revise your question a little bit—not to understand that cultural questions cut across all of these things, across matters of consciousness and the labor process and economic production. So in that sense those questions about the subject also end up touching on contemporary technology, information technology, and changes of that kind, and I think it's clear that what is at stake is some new kind of subject rather than the abolition of the subject or the death of the subject that the poststructuralists used to sometimes loosely talk about. But my problem with the slogan of difference is precisely the slippage I just referred to, namely, the tendency of this slogan to slip back into a purely cultural meaning as in multiculturalism or whatever and the difficulty, for me at least, of connecting it with an economic politics. As for consciousness, I think that in a way late capitalism does that for us already. There would not be this structural or poststructural sense of the death of the subject had the economic system not ended up abolishing its own individualism.

**ARAVAMUDAN:** *We're going to shift to a series of questions about religion. Your interest in allegory, fourfold medieval hermeneutics, and also the evocation of Dante's* selva oscura *at the Bonaventure Hotel has sparked a recent discussion in* PMLA *about your religious unconscious. Is there something to this? If so, would it be fair to characterize your religious unconscious and inclusive sensibility as that of a secularized Catholic (even though, of course, you weren't brought up Catholic)? Furthermore, is it perhaps time for you to write directly about religion, as it is arguably the greatest force in the world that is at least in some kind of opposition to the worship of Mammon today? I know that's an arguable statement, but nonetheless some people claim that it is. Do you have thoughts about the rise of political Islam, global fundamentalisms, and the gamut of religious revivals whether monotheistic, polytheistic, or spiritualistic?*

**JAMESON:** Well, my name is Scottish rather than Irish, even though I have Irish ancestors along with Germans. But really to be Catholic probably depends on your life with the church as an institution from an early age and your experience of the inner workings of the church hierarchy and the priesthood, the orders and the ritual. No, I think of myself rather in Max Weber's wonderful phrase as "religiously unmusical." I have no real experience of religion at all, and I remain an atheist if that means anything. But that's probably not a very interesting way of describing things either. I guess I should say rather that I have no religious temptations. As for the accusation that Marxism is really a religion, well, if somebody wants to come along and say that one's relationship to hope and the future and to a belief in political and social possibilities is an essentially religious one, they can do so, and I will agree that I do have an Absolute.

ARAVAMUDAN: *If I can interrupt, there's that famous moment, in, I think, Bertrand Russell's* History of Western Philosophy, *where he goes about saying the church is the Communist Party, the revolution is the second coming, Marx is Christ, Lenin is St. Paul, et cetera. He explores this whole series of analogies, but then of course an analogy is not a direct similarity in the way that people sometimes want it to be.*

JAMESON: The problem is that no existential sense of the religious accompanies any of that for me, and it is also the case that you can turn this argument around and argue that really the various religions are dim, obscure foreshadowings, and confused and figural anticipations of what eventually becomes secular history. So one could just as easily say that religion anticipates Marxism as to claim that Marxism is a religion. I don't mind admitting that it's connected to the Absolute. But I would say that my work is not really religious at all. Now I've heard Cornel West say that one of the great failures of American cultural studies is that they don't understand that American religion is also a part of American mass culture. I understand that, and I wish I were in a position to draw more theoretical conclusions. There is a certain dynamic of orthodoxy that one has to understand as part of group dynamics in general; it would require us to reflect on what a taboo is, what a prohibition is—these are ways in which the members of a group prove to themselves and to the leaders that they are really members of that group. That is, that they have to sacrifice certain things as a sign of affiliation. We must at least get away from this thought of the Other in which we imagine that inside the heads of believers something different is taking place than is going on in our heads, thereby hypostatizing or reifying belief as such, and alienating it in the literal sense of the word. We make it into something other—this incomprehensible thing that's going on in the head of a believer. But belief is not a psychic tonality of that kind that some people have and other people don't. I do think that the orthodox and dogmatic insistence on things is not a characteristic of belief, but is rather a characteristic of the way the group enforces its cohesion and its membership and excludes the nonmembers. These things are group dynamics rather than specifically religious ones, or dynamics connected to belief. Consciousness as such is really the same everywhere, and it never takes on special characteristics; it is rather the way you think about the self that's an object for consciousness. Now of course there are great religious movements one has to admire. Liberation theology was a very great thing, and I hope some of it at least has persisted. I have spoken to some of those people; I admire them very much. The militant church of the poor priests and the popular ministries can be extraordinary ways of mobilizing and transforming people and can generate extraordinary forms of political action. But religion for me is essentially *religio*, that is, the way in which the cohesion of the collectivity is first expressed. I tend to think that there aren't really any religious traditions as such because as a constructivist, I follow people like Hobsbawm in believing that the tradition is something that you make up in the present, so that even the so-called religious traditions are essentially postmodern products. Something like radical Islam came into being because of the weakness of the Left movements, many of which had been destroyed by the United States and its allies all over the Islamic world. It's a postmodern movement, and the sign was already visible in the extraordinarily creative ways in which the Ayatollah used modern media. Now, when we get to the United States and religion turns into so-called ethnic identity, then I think those are also not religious, but they are postmodern ways in which specific groups of people play at self-definition. If you're a secular Jew and then you decide to reendorse all of the traditional modes of Jewish religion, well that's a choice. The original ethnic groups when they came to this country had no choice. They were stereotyped without appeal, and that was a racial or ethnic confinement and oppression. But that's not the case of much of contemporary ethnic or identity politics.

ARAVAMUDAN: *I am very intrigued and largely convinced by your account of the contemporary religious revivals being various forms of what people call the neotraditional. They're entirely modern, but they pretend to be continuous with ancient things, which is not at all the case when you examine them. People have argued this about contemporary Islamic fundamentalism, Zionism, different forms of Christian fundamentalism, and the fascist Hindu right that in India is the product of modernity. But I would want to say a little bit more about religion as a political language, precisely because it's replacing the void that develops when the Left has been massacred in several of these places. On the one hand, by presenting itself as neotraditionalist, religion says that it's higher than or something different from politics, at least in the secular sense, and then often gets dismissed by secularists as a result of being outside the pale. Yet in many different ways it seems to be doing the work of undercover politics.*

**KHANNA:** *I would like to add one more thing. It seems to me that, yes, it is certainly the case that the Left was massacred in so many of these places, but it is also the case that in many places, for example in Algeria, you have the FIS (the Islamic Salvation Front) moving in exactly when a form of corruption is seen in the socialist government, when there are no social services being given, when the FIS has actually indeed occupied the place of the Left in terms of social services and in terms of welfare. So there is a kind of Left and Right categorization of religious groups breaking down. Are those terms any longer adequate to characterize the kinds of social movements associated with those sorts of religious groups?*

**JAMESON:** You can go back and say exactly the same things about nationalist movements which also soak up a lot of class passions and dynamics and appropriate them, allow them both to be expressed and to be diverted at one and the same time. That's the problem here. To what degree do they genuinely express class aspirations as in liberation theology? To what degree do they displace that and allow themselves to be used for something else? I think that one of these issues would have to do with social dichotomization, that is, the movement towards situations of conflict between two forces. The question turns to what is present in the way of vehicles for the expression of those conflicts. Sometimes we can use the word *confessional* rather than *religious* because I think that maybe clarifies the situation. In Northern Ireland, you've got this confessional thing in which class and other kinds of passions and national feelings are invested, but those are the vehicles that are available for that, and the other ones aren't around. When I talk about the mass destruction of communist parties in Iraq or in Indonesia and so forth, that's the effacement of one available vehicle for collective expression and agency, such that there is left only the other one, the religious one. The ambiguity of both religious movements such as the Iranian one and national movements all over the world is that the minute they absorb the collective class passions, those can be transferred and diverted to some other function which is generally restorative or conservative. I think that the radical Islamic thing is extremely ambiguous because after the end of the communist parties and before the formation of any real new worldwide movement of antiglobalization, they represented the only vehicle for anti-Americanism, for resistance to the West and to capitalism. But they are not anticapitalist. So it seems to me that when they finally do come to power, they don't know what to do with the world system, they don't have a strategy for opting out of that (leaving aside the question whether that would be possible anyway). But obviously that movement fills a political need in young people in the Middle East; it gives them a political passion and, as you say, also offers all kinds of social and educational services. Soon, in my view, the ultimate function of this politics was to offer a way of expressing and enacting an anticapitalist program, and to the degree that they don't do that, they get distorted and go in all kinds of other directions. I think that it was Partha Chatterjee who showed that the problem with modern nationalism is that it draws its strength from incorporating a kind of socialist dynamic; but then it can't go any further because it doesn't want to go beyond the bounds of the national program or project. That's still an excellent lesson when we're talking about Islam. Of course, in Iran it's also proof that there persisted a deeply passionate Iranian nationalism also expressing itself through their rather unique religion.

**KHANNA:** *To follow up on that, it also seems the case that it's exactly not in moments of shoring up national feelings through religion that this comes through, because also, of course, there are many religious and ethnic affiliations that seem to be about the breakdown of nations or indeed federations, so in the former Yugoslavia, the former USSR, et cetera, it seems to be that these new religious or ethnic affiliations seem to emerge particularly at the time of these kinds of breakdowns and in particularly violent ways, violent and genocidal. I suppose I'm wondering whether you think that in trying to understand this kind of violence that seems to accompany a breakdown in federation or in nation, part of what's going on is that there isn't, in a sense, any location to maintain force anymore. I'm trying to think about whether that distinction between force and violence in Benjamin is still useful in trying to understand the breakdown into forms of violence of this sort.*

**JAMESON:** In other words, that there's no legitimate source of order; but in a way, that's what's reflected here. The violence comes about, along with the religious revivals and all of the craziness of the new sects because there is no political vehicle for action. But I think one also has to be a little more sociological about this and understand that for many of the unemployed youth, violence becomes a way of life. People have said this about Northern Ireland; it's certainly the case in Afghanistan and maybe now in Iraq that the guerilla struggle is a way of life that you can't see beyond. I mean nothing is proposed which gives one a substitute for that kind of military action, and we shouldn't forget to what degree the military itself was like that in the past and offered both community and excitement to the people who chose to become a part of it. So one has to keep in mind the way in which all of these movements change by way of accretion, that is, that they begin for one purpose and then new functions are added to them; they win a kind of autonomy, they continue on the base of that autonomy which develops then yet another function, that of keeping itself going and perpetuating the situation. There has to be a temporal rhythmic analysis of the ways in which these movements develop because they don't necessarily preserve their original starting point but become institutions like any other. And I guess Benjamin's question about force versus violence is also a question about institutions. I would say that insofar as power and government have lost their legitimacy all over the world, these two things come to be indistinguishable. You look at police brutality in the United States and the attitudes of various citizens of American cities to police forces and you see that those are really not considered a legitimate force anymore, but very precisely, and rightly or wrongly, a kind of military occupation.

**ARAVAMUDAN:** *To stay on the same subject but shifting it slightly, I think towards the end of the* Postmodernism *book, you discuss the relationship between high technology, decadence, and fundamentalism. While you suggest certain kinds of high technology as being quasi-religious, you also see decadence as the otherness of capitalism, something that precedes it, but also that potentially comes after it, that it is constantly trying to prevent itself from falling into. What does this have to do, if anything, with the perception of the West as decadent and effete by current-day Islamic fundamentalisms? Or is that something different altogether?*

**JAMESON:** I am sorry I used the word *decadence* which I don't normally use and which certainly does have a very different flavor in its original homeland at the end of the nineteenth century. I simply meant that the habits of comfortable middle-class society, which really doesn't have to face the more agonizing economic problems with sustenance and work and services that other populations of the world face—that it's that picture of a smug and self-satisfied America which arouses both envy and resentment, and then offers a chance for Schadenfreude when horrible things happen to us. So that would be a geopolitical class feeling, I think, a class response to the global situation of haves and have-nots. Decadence, in American culture—I guess that's the kind of judgment one can't any longer make from the inside. I am sure that if we had the possibility of a different kind of culture, we would maybe be able to say that a lot of this luxury and consumerism is self-indulgence and we should be living in other ways. Gas guzzlers, suvs, consumerism in general—I would rather call such things collective addictions. You notice that when this "War on Terror" started, the one thing the president did not do was to demand sacrifices of the American people. He said they should go out and buy more things and keep shopping, to keep the economic machinery going. I don't know whether any war leader in history has ever said that to his home population; that's rather astonishing. So maybe that's what one can call decadent. But I don't think it's a very useful term.

**ARAVAMUDAN:** *What about high tech as a kind of quasi-religious thing?*

**JAMESON:** Well, before I used computers myself, I observed that everybody was really in what seemed to be a religious frenzy, trying to convert you to this wonderful thing and telling you all of its benefits and how they leapt out of bed in the morning and did their e-mail and how much they wrote as opposed to the older days; and then you have the transmission of this virus to the foreigners, especially the Eastern Europeans. I firmly believe that this envy of technology played its part in the Eastern European turn to capitalism. The passion for acquiring all of these new kinds of postmodern informational technologies was really delirious because what was involved was not just buying something additional like a new car. This process really amounted to consuming the postmodern itself; it is a symbolic appropriation of the most advanced equipment of the new stage of capitalism and of history. And so there was a symbolic consumption of information technology that I think really took place in a religious mode, just as Marx spoke of the religious structure of the commodity.

**ARAVAMUDAN:** *We're just finishing up on the religious, and this is a quick question, but I just wondered if you had a thought about the rise of terrorism and suicide bombing, because some people have tried to link that with religious extremism, while others have thought about it in terms of new forms of anarchism. As a suicide bomber, there is no alternative, because you just kill* *yourself without necessarily changing things. Here, a third possibility is military asymmetry: that you can't have a proper war, so the only way to impose violence is through breaking a network by way of attacks that are futile or suicidal from one perspective, but significant from another.*

**JAMESON:** The other thing—I think Michael Hardt has written on this—is the role of the body. There is a dialectic between the smart bombs and the airplanes that can't even see the populations on the ground and this mobilization of the body as such. It's certainly not the promise of this idiotic postmodern paradise with all of the *houris* [heavenly maidens] that is attracting these young people; it is very specifically a Sartrean existential choice. In general, this kind of weapon is part of an informational politics that you have to use because precisely you do not have an army that can match the one in the field. In these cases, however, it seems to me it's a little more than propaganda by the deed; it is the insistence on interrupting daily life whether it's in Israel or Iraq. I mean this sort of constant assurance that the colonizer is not going to be able to lead a peaceful existence. This is a kind of strategy that probably is connected to colonial occupation in the sense that you could never win a battle by doing this, but what you can do is to finally force the occupier to leave, and I think that's the aim, however realistic or unrealistic that may be.

**KHANNA:** *I want to ask you a question about allegory and its relation to Utopia, and also particularly, how it does and does not relate to Paul de Man's concept of allegory. And I suppose I want to ask you that question as a way of getting in a little bit on that relationship between the ethical and the political. In* Allegories of Reading, *Paul de Man says: "Allegories are always ethical, the term ethical designating the structural interference of two distinct value systems. . . . The ethical category is imperative (i.e., a category rather than value) to the extent that it is linguistic and not subjective. . . . The passage to an ethical tonality does not result from a transcendental imperative but is the referential (and therefore unreliable) version of a linguistic confusion. Ethics (or, one should say, ethicity) is a discursive mode among others."[2] In de Man, there seems to be an emphasis precisely on disjuncture in value systems and, more importantly, category systems—there's something of Lyotard's notion of the* différend *there as well, although that is perhaps more about disjuncture between sign systems and other such incommensurabilities. But I wonder whether, when you discuss the kinds of potential of allegory and the desire it seems to suggest, you want to side-step such notions of disjuncture. I'm* *interested in the chapter "Utopia and Its Antinomies" in* Archeologies of the Future *(and also, in a slightly different register in your work on Marc Angenot and literary history) about the way in which Utopian tradition from Thomas More onward absorbs, or as you put it, "interiorizes differences which generally remain implicit in literary history." So there are a few questions that emerge from this for me. One is the way in which your own reading practice is Utopian in the way it absorbs the kinds of disjunctures that de Man highlights. The second is how allegory and Utopia relate (is Utopia an allegory of the future)? And the third is what about this category of the ethical, or what de Man refers to as "ethicity" that is often related to the question of the singularity of the text, something lost in the sweep of an idea of tradition that absorbs argument within itself, into, as you put it, in a more Bakhtinian dialogue, rather than as a disjuncture. Is there a "discursive mode" of "ethicity" for you?*

**JAMESON:** I don't understand de Man in that sense. That's a very rich and suggestive passage, and I don't think that I am able to comment on it directly. I have always understood de Man—probably this is a very imperfect reading—I have always understood de Manian allegory as a way of designating the literary use of language as opposed to the ideological or communicational; a characterization of the way in which a text is reflexive and designates itself. He uses this structural idea in a very complicated and I think partly dialectical way. And I suppose my version of this would be the distinction between, let's say, science and ideology, or the way in which a text has something to do with the position of the subject. I follow Althusser in thinking science is a writing without a subject, while ideology is very much the positioning of the subject, and it involves opinions rather than knowledge: here also we have the difference between episteme and doxa played out on a linguistic or a literary level. But I would not, myself, approach these things in that way. I think the question of ethics is, for me, certainly a matter of ideology, but above all of the differentiation of good and evil, and here I very much go back to Sartre's ideas about the way in which evil secures the comfort and the good conscience of the self. Foucault, I think, develops this opposition later on, even though he never mentions Sartre. I would say that the ethical is always this kind of movement of bad faith, whereby you exteriorize something as the Other and label it as evil. So I think that whenever ethical categories are employed, we must suspect something else at work, and somehow deconstruct those categories in linguistic terms. And I certainly wouldn't commit myself to an ethics of literature or an ethics of language; I suppose the Sartrean category for that would be the much debated category of authenticity. But allegory is for me a rather different thing. And it has, I think, its relationship to Lévi-Strauss's *La pensée sauvage*. I think we have allegory when there is a problem of representation. Allegory is a solution to the representation of what is ultimately not representable, those being essentially totalities. And so obviously allegory is at home in the dynamics of theology or religious discourse because those posit nonrepresentable things. In many instances of political or social representation, it's also deployed in the sense that it's very difficult for any of us as individuals to grasp or to map the social dynamics as a whole. But one's problem in using the word *allegory* is that we've been trained for centuries to use this word to mean a one-on-one relationship—A stands for C and B stands for D—whereas I think it should be reserved for unique kinds of unrepeatable solutions either of a structural or a figural kind. Any time you try to deal with larger political entities like the collective or the nation, or the people, or even movements or groups, you confront the nonrepresentable; well then, we have to look and see how those things have been represented in order to identify the type of allegory that has been invented or mobilized to do that. We don't just function with various personifications. And this is another essential difference between my use of allegory and the traditional ones: the traditional concept always depended very heavily on the idea of personification. But in my opinion, this is what contemporary theories of allegory also seeks to avoid for the most part.

**ARAVAMUDAN:** *Just following from something you said towards the end of that answer. Can there really be politics without a logic of political representation? (I know there are a whole bunch of debates about this right now).*

**JAMESON:** Oh, I don't think so. I think you have to map out the situation—you have to invent the situation, so to speak. Meanwhile your perception of it and your description of it and your assessment of various forces at work—well, this is already representation and allegory. Our current political problem lies in the fact that globalization is obviously an even more complicated representational problem—so surely you don't get away from those problems anywhere in contemporary politics.

**ARAVAMUDAN:** *Well, I suppose then with recent questions that arise, with theories of the multitude and so on, I wonder whether there's a possible way that the mediating role of something like a party can be bypassed at some point.*

**JAMESON:** Surely all of those collective words—*the people, the multitude, the nation, the masses,* and so forth—these are all representations—so is general will—and I think all of them are attempts to model something that's not representable.

**ARAVAMUDAN:** *But wouldn't some argue that these are presentations rather than representations (*Vorstellungen *rather than* Darstellungen*)?*

**JAMESON:** I guess I don't acknowledge this distinction, which my notion of representation subsumes. But it does seem to me that representation is always implied—has to be implied—by these concepts, because you're differentiating, for example, the concept you're trying to produce of the multitude from that of the people, or the nation—or from social class, which we should also mention here. And such concepts are really narratives, representational pictures, so I don't see how one could avoid the problem. Now with the matter of the party—the party was supposed to be a mediation. That's a different matter. That gets us into representation in the other sense—political representation, *vertreten*—as in the parliamentary system. But it's hard to see how one could ever get away from a mediation of some kind, even if that's not the word people want to use anymore.

**KHANNA:** *I have a question for you about Marxist feminism (that follows up on an earlier one), and the question of sexual difference in the newer modes of production. In your essay "On Interpretation," which serves as the long introduction to* The Political Unconscious, *you comment on debates in Marxist feminism suggesting that the importance of "sexism and the patri-archal are to be grasped as the sedimentation and the survival of forms of alienation specific to the oldest mode of production of human history." Do you think there are ways in which new forms of sexual difference and new forms of the sexual division of labor emerge with new modes of production? Or is the question of sexual difference always in a time lag, whether future oriented (as in the formulation of affective labor by feminists in the 1970s that now has taken on wider circulation) or as a belated existence of multiple mo-ments of modes of production that look to an earlier moment?*

**JAMESON:** Yes. I'm convinced that there are all kinds of new and differ-entiated gender phenomena that emerge as society develops. I guess I think that on the one hand, some of the debates on gender or sexuality or sexism are Utopian in the sense in which they wish to map out, or experimentally to project what daily life in Utopia might be. But there's a tension between two kinds of Utopian politics here. On the one hand, it seems clear that many contemporary feminisms have been forms of a group consciousness in which a collectivity—a collectivity of sisterhood or whatever—affirms itself. That tends towards a more overt secession as seen in separatism and some forms of lesbian feminism. (This is a dualism that holds for all kinds of racial and ethnic politics.) The other kind of alternative would be absolute equality, gender-blindness, in which men and women would be equal in all kinds of ways and in which the aim of the political would be to get rid of these differences rather than emphasize them. Much of strategy and literature turns on this matter—whether it is the specificity of the group that's being emphasized or whether this is a kind of universal demand for equality. And I would assume that in the labor movement, for example, it would probably have to be the latter—the demand for equality; whence the tension between certain kinds of gender politics and class politics, which have sometimes seemed incompatible with each other. This is also connected with a different kind of representational or literary problem that you get in political literature. You can either insist on the oppression of the group or on its heroism. If you insist on the oppression, in a way you're insisting on the weakness of the group, and its failure to overcome its situation. If you insist on heroism, then you're projecting a kind of unreal set of political possibilities which don't really exist or don't exist yet. So it's very difficult to hold any balance between them. In that sense, there is a structural similarity between the feminist movement and a lot of other nonclass movements. I would say that a politics of the future would depend very much on the gender division of labor in a given society. I don't think there's any question but that late capitalism posits an equality of consumption. Whether it can achieve such market equality—which seems to me unrealistic—it nonetheless wishes to sell its products to as many different kinds of people as possible. This is a kind of niche marketing where each of the groups is addressed directly as specific kinds of consumers with specific needs, so in the postmodern situation there is both an equalizing effect of capitalism and then a reactivation of, let's say, secondary characteristics.

**KHANNA:** *Just a follow up to that, in thinking about the importance of Marxist feminism, I want to think about that category in relation to the global. It seems as if Marxist feminism always returns the question to the domestic, or frequently does, whether that's the national domestic or the domestic sphere. I think that this is partly because of the way in which in the heyday of Marx-*

*ist feminism in the 1970s it was very much a kind of domestic conversation that was going on. But of course, figures like Rosa Luxemburg and Alexandra Kollontai were in many ways far more attentive to the question of the international than many of their contemporaries were, and certainly more so than the later figures in the Marxist feminist tradition, with the exception of Spivak. There aren't many figures like her. So I am wondering if you see a future for an engagement with these early figures like Rosa Luxemburg? Does the argument of a text, for example, like* The Accumulation of Capital, *still hold for this moment of capitalism? Is it still a useful text to think about?*

**JAMESON:** Well, that was also the first text that insisted on the way in which the initial or primitive accumulation of capital was a third world event which depended on the colonization of the new world. In that respect her book remains an essential part of any kind of contemporary analysis of the situation. National feminism is, however, extremely dialectical, as we've seen recently where the Americans are going around the world boasting about how American women are equal and free and explaining to the embattled Iraqi or Iranian or Syrian women that we are therefore their spokespeople and their representatives. I think that the coordination of these different kinds of feminism gets very much entangled with geopolitics and with nationalism. What I would want to say is that any single-shot kind of politics—it's true of class as well—if it doesn't make its connections with the other thematics of a global politics, is going to emerge in that kind of one-dimensional way. If you look at race and gender and then class, you realize (even though it's a bad word) that a totalizing politics is the only solution. I know there are people who object to this word, but one can point out that Jesse Jackson's Rainbow Coalition, for example, was very much a totalizing operation in which Jackson never talked about women without talking about working-class women and about race; never talked about race without talking about class or gender; and that all of these things had to be done simultaneously. In the geopolitical situation, one would include this whole background of nationality and national divisions and national pride and national humiliation and so on as part of that, but certainly no one sees in any of those terms any immediately homogenous political movements that would involve in some coherent way all of these populations around the world. I think these are political movements that remain to be constructed. They are based on alliances and have all sorts of complicated representational dynamics. None of them can take anything—whether gender, race, or class—for granted. They are unique kinds of universalisms, and those things must also be understood in various situations and specific ways. As Žižek insists, the universal in Hegel is always the exception; there can never be a pure incarnation of the universal—it's always through its exceptions that you arrive at this universal, and that's true of politics as well.

**ARAVAMUDAN:** *How does the area of the biopolitical pose new challenges for Marxist approaches to society and political economy? What happens when the living but nonlaboring body becomes the Heideggerian "standing reserve" once externalized nature is depleted? Or is this development not qualitatively different from earlier Marxist accounts of the alienation of labor?*

**JAMESON:** I guess I would at first express hesitation of the kind I expressed about religion, namely, that if this whole new biopolitical thing is insisted on as a brand-new kind of politics in its own right, qualitatively and quantitatively different from a class politics or anything that went before it, then I must suspect it of being a diversion of some sort. Certainly any acknowledgment of the state of things in postmodernity/globalization, to use that as a single term with a slash, has to take into account the modified conditions of the body, the way it exists temporally—we mentioned that before: its mode of labor, the difference between current informational labor and the old-fashioned kinds, the form in which the crisis of the city exists. The ecology of biopolitics is that of the great transnational corporations, their control over drugs, their resistance to political regulation and to controls on pollution and things like that. One way or another you get back to the very structure of capitalism as such. But today maybe these natural disasters are more visible manifestations of this along with that monopoly on information and the media, which prevents us from getting back to these root causes. But biopolitics would include ecology; and there would be always a tactical question whether these causes, in particular ecology, are not better roads to political organization given the fact of all the recent floods and disasters, of global warming, of the degradation of the planet in general, and of nature, and the disappearance of the rain forest, et cetera—whether those are not political representations which mobilize the masses in ways that old-fashioned questions of labor don't. But I don't think you get away from class there. In the 1960s, when ecology became a political issue, you could see that it divided up between the politicals and the nonpoliticals. There were a lot of middle-class people who were very willing to do ecological politics, but no other kind. I don't think you can really get away from issues of class in that way, but surely the whole ecological thing and the biopoliti-cal issues are new and postmodern.

**ARAVAMUDAN:** *A quick follow-up on ecology: I guess the complexity of it as a politics is that it can be drawn into very right-wing kinds of formations of preservation or preventing other people's consumption to secure one's own, which is often how sometimes first world ecological movements are concerned with the sort of destruction of third world areas, which is a huge issue obvi-ously even for the peoples right there, but the question of subsistence and many of these other things make strong ecological third world movements quite difficult as opposed to say ecological movements within a more ad-vanced or developed society.*

**JAMESON:** And that happens in this country with the labor movement; that is to say, where an ecological movement wishes to control an area where a lot of jobs will be lost by this kind of control, then the working people re-sist these changes. But the other feature that has to be insisted on is that there really is no world government. The various treaties are all disguised ways in which the first world attempts to enforce its control of all potential raw materials—whether we're talking about patenting of native medicines and herbs or of the various regulations of prices and subsidies. It's very im-portant to understand that it's not just by treaties like Kyoto that one really resolves these problems, although certainly that treaty usefully highlighted the resistance of the center of the "free world" to ecological politics. For the moment, probably, it's alliances of countries who are threatened by ecologi-cal degradation which offer the first and most suggestive step. If one can imagine such alliances, they would depend very much on sources of capital; so this is why Venezuela is so threatening for the United States, since excep-tionally among non-Western parts of the world, they have a lot of money from oil, so they have a certain autonomy other countries lack.

**ARAVAMUDAN:** *Isn't there a rich irony about the recent rise of socialism in Latin America—the US's own backyard—just so soon after all the trium-phalism regarding the collapse of communism in Eastern Europe and China's embrace of capitalism?*

**JAMESON:** Well, I think that this is the moment at which what capitalism really means for these countries is becoming clear to them: especially in the framework of this obligatory developmentalist ideology where the sole function of these countries is to increase investment and profits. So they are now in a better position to understand the way in which free market policies prevent the reconstruction of some of these economies that were certainly damaged by some of their local dictatorships and fascisms, the way in which this unregulated market generates unemployment and presupposes a weakening or elimination of the social service systems. This is the way in which these populations come to a kind of antiglobalizing political consciousness today. And there is a desperate structural lag between the radical political parties themselves, which can only at best be social democratic and are really completely hamstrung by their political ideologies, and the demands of these newly conscious groups such as the landless, the unemployed, the new middle-class unemployed, and so forth.

**KHANNA:** *Shifting gears a little bit here, I have a question about world literature. I am interested in the way in which you understand the world in the formulation of world literature and world cinema or a global aesthetic or geopolitical aesthetic as well. If you're thinking world literature and world cinema, is the "world" in each of those categories the same? And also, another question related to that, why do you think it is that so many formulations of the category of world literature are currently coming from the political if not always the disciplinary Left? For example, Franco Moretti's work and Pascale Casanova's work, which has recently appeared in* New Left Review, *Gayatri Spivak's notion of "planetarity" developed specifically in relation to the notion of comparative literature and your own encyclopedic knowledge of global film and literature (and the way in which you developed ideas about the whole field of comparative literature in things like the Literature Program at Duke) have all contributed to changing the ways in which many of us understand comparison and literature in the world today. So I am curious to know why it is that these kinds of developments in notions of world literature and world cinema emerge from the Left?*

**JAMESON:** For one thing, the corporations and big business don't have as much of an investment in literature per se as they do in other kinds of fields, and so the Right in literature has been reduced to a kind of aestheticism and an art for art's sake defense of the canon, the great books, traditional literary and stylistic values, and so on, and really has very little interest in other parts of the world. But I think one should then think about language in this connection. I think one of the most alarming things for language itself is the spread of English as this universal lingua franca or world language; it does English and the production of literature in English very little good. Cinema overleaps this in a way because you can have subtitles. But this also is a block to world literature in the sense that world literature remains, if it is viable, profoundly anchored in local conditions and in the local language; and unless—as in India, for example—English is one of the local languages, we're dealing with translations that have to lose much of the tacit knowledge that was present in those texts. On the other hand, one can insist on students knowing a few foreign languages, but the non-European languages are very tough to acquire, and if anybody learns one of them, that's probably a specialized achievement in itself. So there is already a fundamental barrier here to the continuation of literature as a medium for these new international realities. That's why I think literature has been in crisis or has regressed to positions of regionalism, something which may not be quite the case so much with film, at least so far. I always like to refer to Goethe's idea of world literature: he didn't mean collecting all of the world classics, although that was also going on at that period, and the Shakuntala was being translated along with Shakespeare. There was an accumulation of great artistic products from what was actually being opened up by colonialism in the world at that time. Goethe's interest, however, was for contact between intellectuals as it was expressed in the great journals (*Revue des deux mondes*, the *Edinburgh Review*, etc.). It's that kind of transmission that Goethe means by world literature, something which suggests a first extrapolation to current globalized society: the one place where we can immediately appropriate these technologies lies precisely in transmission belts of that kind and contact between intellectuals, political and otherwise, and where we can create a network that hasn't yet come to being in the field of politics and political movements. Now this is, I think, one of the possibilities that we have for a new kind of world literature in this new system. The other proposal that I have is that we cannot have an immediate relationship as readers in one national situation with texts from other national situations. This seems to me a much more complicated and mediated process, in which we have to go through an understanding of the other national situation first in order to grasp the value and the positions of the works of that national situation insofar as they can be translated. Of course, translations don't have to be perfect. I like Walter Benjamin's idea that what a translation does is not render literally the meanings of the other text, if that were even possible or conceivable; but it gives you something of the foreignness of the other language and what it can do and something of the capacities as well as the strangeness of this other language. It gives you that through the deformation of your own national language. I like that very much, and it would seem to me to be the kind of opening on the other national realities that we need; that is, we have to know how different they are from our own. We're in a position, in the United States, of incredible parochialism: this is certainly one of the countries in the world the least interested in anything outside of itself, the least informed of what's going on, and with the least curiosity about the way other people live and the problems they face, as though we have all of that solved, and we're the final stage, the United States, in some Hegelian movement of world history towards its final apotheosis of freedom. So anything that is able to shake the American public out of this provincialism and parochialism and to give it some sense that other people have other priorities and other experiences and other needs and dilemmas and contradictions, that they face things that we don't even dream of here; this is, it seems to me, a very valuable aim for world literature.

**ARAVAMUDAN:** *Following from what you said, about world literature, it occurred to me that perhaps one could consider theory itself as a kind of minor genre of world literature. Following that observation, I wanted to ask you what you thought about the way books themselves still continue to be read nowadays and whether that is still happening in that same way? Do you have thoughts on the ways in which the old and the new media—radio, film, television, Internet—are reshaping the challenges for theory itself as a form of literature? And also the introduction of new vectors of novelty, speed, and obsolescence. University press editors say that most scholarly books, even the most successful ones, hardly sell at all after the first twelve months of publication, and as you know, there is considerable pressure to make books much shorter because society as a whole is suffering from ADHD (or attention deficit hyperactivity disorder)!*

**JAMESON:** Nothing escapes the universal process of commodification. And this fatally begins to happen in theory; to all theories brand names get attached. Spurious movements are invented even when they're not present. The writers' thoughts are thematized in various reified ways, and then theory gets both dramatized as a kind of supermarket of choices and of incompatibilities as well, and consumed in that way. We're in a society whose inner logic is that of commodification, and this is more and more the case in postmodernity where everything is tendentially commodified and where publishing is little by little subsumed by the great monopolies, and books and films are essentially only produced for the kinds of profit marketing has identified in advance. The bureaucrats of these big businesses make the decision about content or marketability of these former artworks and the autonomy of the old-fashioned publishers or even independent film makers. There will no doubt continue to be interesting novels and interesting films and interesting theory; but the price is ever greater, and it's very hard to see how one can reverse trends of that kind. But once you introduce the geopolitical dimension, everything changes—and films demonstrate one possible solution, in that other parts of the world begin to co-finance film production. While we don't have that in literature or theory yet, nonetheless it seems conceivable that things can be reopened in that way, via international networks. But the other thing that this crisis of theory means is Adorno's old disappearance of critical perspective and the evaporation of the negative. And I think that the replacement of critical thinking by the empirical, by the domination of positivism, the capitulation to everything that exists—which is more or less the market system nowadays—I think we must not underestimate this pull of the practical-empirical and the logic of the market. Certainly groups and networks can make a difference here, and one of the points of trying to construct or reconstruct a Left culture here or anywhere else is the gradual development of a counterweight or counterforce to the business culture and the profitability system.

**ARAVAMUDAN:** *To follow up the answer you just gave on theory, I was wondering whether you had thought about the figure of the intellectual in the way that some people still hang onto, whether it is Edward Said or the idea of the organic or the vernacular intellectual from Gramsci and so on? Now it seems to me more and more that the last bastion of the intellectual is the university, where there is some notion of academic freedom. Or are there still possibilities for this belief at a certain point anyway, when people felt very strongly about the kind of rise or the discovery of the organic intellectual?*

**JAMESON:** I hope there will still be a place for people like that, for future Chomskys, future radical intellectuals. I have never believed in the fashionable lament about the disappearance of free intellectuals and their cooptation by the university. The American university system was expanded in the 1960s and transformed into a very important social institution with many more people from all classes than at any time in its history. It thereby became a political forum and a place in which one's work should count politically both on the graduate and the undergraduate level. So I don't share the anti-intellectualism of some intellectuals who deplore that social transformation. On the other hand, I think what's far more sinister is the commercialization of the university: the way in which ever more segments of it are farmed out to big business and who often do the research of big business for free, so that the state support to universities tends to become a subsidy for these big businesses themselves, whether it's in pharmaceuticals or in agriculture or anything else. Our own privileged position comes from the fact that nobody is going to make much money out of the humanities, and therefore big business hasn't been very interested in taking us over and subsidizing us. The various proposals for teaching machines have not been terribly successful. High schools and grade schools—well, this is another matter, and I am sure that business is interested in this enormous textbook market. But the humanities are an underdeveloped part of the curriculum, and therefore we still have a little bit of freedom in that respect, because nobody really cares what we say. That's a positive as well as a negative.

**KHANNA:** *I have a question for you about music, actually. In some ways it relates to some of the things you just said, because there is of course an alternative politics to some forms of music, and also it is very clearly a huge business. I want to ask a question that goes in a slightly different direction from that, about your relation to music more generally. It is in some ways odd to me that you haven't written that much about it as far as I can tell, or perhaps I am wrong, in spite of your ongoing interest in Pound and Brecht—both of course have their hands in opera—and in Adorno, whose writings are so much about music, and you have written the foreword to Jacques Attali's* Noise, *where you seem particularly appreciative of the ways in which he understands music in terms of "the possibility of a superstructure to anticipate historical developments to foreshadow new social formations in a prophetic and annunciatory way." So I am wondering if you could say something about why you may be drawn to musical figures but not necessarily to analyzing music yourself?*

**JAMESON:** Music is clearly one of the most important components of American culture, and of postmodernity generally. People are listening to music all the time; it's a new spatial form they are surrounded with, and I wish I could write about that and music generally. But you would have to master current musical technology (a little like the nomenclature of wine tasting), and you would also have to have an incisive and sensory language to invoke the individuality of sounds and timbres, the way a great critic of poetry articulates the unspoken value of phrasing or an individual choice of words. It's a gift I admire but don't have.

**KHANNA:** *If I could just follow up for one second, I am interested, however, in why you are so drawn to figures who are musical (not necessarily the music itself). Do you think there's a kind of musicality to, I don't know, Adorno's prose, or the way in which he's invested in music actually gives him a different kind of vision of the work that you do comment on, or even with Pound's interest and his work on opera, or Brecht's?*

**JAMESON:** I admire Adorno's musical writings because I think these offer very useful and, how shall I say, abstracted forms of dialectical thinking. Music is so nonrepresentational that you can see the dialectic Adorno is working out in the things he writes about people like Schoenberg, in a way that you wouldn't if you had to deal with the content of a novel. I am more suspicious of the philosophical appeal to music as a metaphysical entity and a kind of nonconceptual nirvana—an aesthetic you can sometimes sense in the German tradition (indeed, I think that this valorization of music is in fact a German tradition).

**KHANNA:** *The last question: I would like to hear a little bit about why you think everyone is currently so interested in ends rather than in beginnings?*

**JAMESON:** But they shouldn't be. Remember Galeano's remark that things were too bad for us to have the luxury of pessimism. There are beginnings starting up all around us that have to be identified: the new antiglobalization (or alternate-worldist) movements from Seattle on, all kinds of exciting artistic developments within postmodernity (now that the break with modernism is accomplished and a thing of the past). Meanwhile the uneven development of the world is very propitious in that sense: however sterile the first world may have become, there are all kinds of other places in which interesting tendencies are starting up, despite universal commodification. It's a very exciting time.

NOTES

1. "Interview with Xudong Zhang," this volume.
2. Paul de Man, *Allegories of Reading* (New Haven: Yale University Press, 1979), 206.

# BIBLIOGRAPHY: FREDRIC JAMESON

## BOOKS

1961    *Sartre: The Origins of a Style* (Yale University Press).

"The Rhythm of Time," reprinted in *Sartre: A Collection of Critical Essays*, ed. Edith G. Kern, 106–20 (Prentice Hall, 1962).

"The Problem of Acts," reprinted in *Modern Drama: Essays in Criticism*, ed. T. Bogard and W. I. Oliver, 276–89 (Galaxy Books, 1965).

Translated into Japanese by Miyake Kunio et al. as *Sarutoru: Kaikisuru Yuibutsuron* (Ronsōsha, 1999).

1971    *Marxism and Form: Twentieth-Century Dialectical Theories of Literature* (Princeton University Press).

"Towards Dialectical Criticism," reprinted in *The Jameson Reader*, ed. Michael Hardt and Kathi Weeks, 340–58 (Blackwell, 2000).

Translated into Serbo-Croation as *Marksizam i forma: Dijalekticke teorije knjizevnosti XX veka*, trans. Disan Puhalo (Nolit, 1974).

Translated into Italian as *Marxismo e forma: Teorie Dialecttiche della letteraturea nel xx secolo*, trans. Renzo Piovesan (Liguori, 1975).

Partly translated into German as "Die ontologie des Noch-NichtSeins im ubergang zum allegorisch- symbolischen Antizipieren: Kunst als Organon kritisch-utopischer Philosophie," in ed. Burghart Schmidt, *Materialie n zu Ernst Blochs Prinzip Hoffnung*, 403–426 (Suhrkamp, 1978).

Translated into Japanese by Arakawa Ikuo as *Benshōhōteki Hihyō no Bōken: Marukusu Shugi to Keishiki* (Shōbunsha, 1980).

Translated into Korean by Yeo Hong-sang et al. as *Byeonjeungbeopjeok Munhak Ironui Cheongae* (Changjak kwa Pipyeongsa, 1984).

---

This bibliography was prepared by Darren Jorgensen with assistance from Koonyong Kim.

Translated into Portugese as *Marxismo e forma: teorias dialecticas da literatura no seculo XX*, trans. Iumna Maria Simon, Ismail Xavier and Fernando Oliboni (Editora HUCITEC, 1985).

1972    *The Prison-House of Language: A Critical Account of Structuralism and Russian Formalism* (Princeton University Press).

"Roland Barthes and Structuralism," reprinted in *The Jameson Reader*, ed. Michael Hardt and Kathi Weeks, 78–88 (Blackwell, 2000).

Translated into Serbo-Croatian as *U Tamnici Jezika: Kriticki prikaz Strukturalizma i roskog formalizma*, trans. Antun Soljan (Starnost, 1978).

Translated into Spanish as *La carcel del lenguaje: Perspectiva critica del estructuralismo y del formalismo ruso*, trans. Carlos de Manzano (Ariel, 1980).

Translated into Italian as *La Prigione del linguaggio. Interpretazione critico dello structturalismo e del formalismo russo*, trans. Giovanna Franci (Cappelli, 1982).

Translated into Japanese by Kawaguchi Kyōichi as *Gengo no Rōgoku: Kōzōshugi to Rosia Forumarizumu* (Hōseidaigaku Shuppankyoku, 1988).

Translated into Korean by Yun Jikwan as *Eoneoui Kaomok* (Kkachi Keulbang, 1990).

Translated into Chinese by Qian Jiaoru and Li Zixiu as *Yuyan de Laolong* (Baihuazhou Wenyi Chubanshe, 1995).

1979    *Fables of Aggression: Wyndham Lewis, the Modernist as Fascist* (University of California Press).

Partly reprinted as "Wyndham Lewis, the Modernist as Fascist," in *Twentieth-Century Literature*, 3, 1757–1761 (Chelsea House, 1986).

1981    *The Political Unconscious: Narrative as a Socially Symbolic Act* (Cornell University Press).

"Magical Narratives: On the Dialectical Use of Genre Criticism," reprinted in *Joseph Conrad*, ed. Elaine Jordan, 269–80 (MacMillan, 1996); in *Modern Genre Theory*, ed. David Duff, 167–92 (Longman, 2000); and in *Fantastic Literature: A Critical Reader*, ed. David Sandner, 180–221 (Praeger, 2004).

"On Interpretation: Literature as a Socially Symbolic Act," reprinted in *Twentieth-Century Literary Theory: A Reader*, ed. K.M. Newton (Macmillan, 1988), 181–86; in *The Political Unconscious* in *Marxist Literary Theory: A Reader*, ed., Terry Eagleton and Drew Milne (Blackwell, 1996), 351–74; and in *The Jameson Reader*, ed. Michael Hardt and Kathi Weeks, 33–60 (Blackwell, 2000).

"Romance and Reification: Plot Construction and Ideological Closure in 'Nostromo,'" reprinted in *Joseph Conrad*, ed. Elaine Jordan, 206–80 (St. Martins, 1996).

Translated into German as *Das politische Unbewusste. Literatur als Symbol sozialen Handelns*, trans. U. Bauer, G. Burger and B. Rohm (Reinbek, 1988).

Translated into Japanese by Ōhashi Yōichi as *Seijiteki Muishiki: Shakaiteki Shōchō-kōi toshite no Monogatari* (Heibonsha, 1989).

Translated into Italian as *L'inconscio politico: il testo narrativo come atto socialmente simbolico*, trans. Libero Sosi (Garzanti, 1990).

Translated into Chinese by Wang Fengzhen and Chen Yongguo as *Zhengzhi Wuyishi* (Zhongguo Shehui Kexue Chubanshe, 1999).

Translated into Korean by Lee Kyungdeok and Suh Kangmok as *Jeongchijeok Muuishik* (Min Um Sa, forthcoming).

1986   *Houxiandai Zhuyi yu Wenhua Lilun (Postmodernism and Cultural Theories: Lectures of Fredric R. Jameson at Beijing University)*, trans. into Chinese by Tang Xiaobing (Shanxi Shifan Daxue Chubanshe).

1988   *Nationalism, Colonialism, and Literature: Modernism and Imperialism* (Field Day Theatre Company).

Reprinted in *Nationalism, Colonialism, and Literature*, by Terry Eagleton, Fredric Jameson, and Edward W. Said, 43–66 (University of Minnesota Press, 1990).

Translated into Japanese by Masubuchi Masafumi, Andō Katsuo and Ōtomo Yoshikatsu as "Modanizumu to Teikokushugi" in *Minzokushugi. Syokuminchishugi to Bungaku* (Hōsei Daigaku Shuppankyoku, 1996), pages unknown.

Translated into German as "Moderne und Imperialismus," in *Hybride Kulturen: Beiträge zur anglo-amerikanischen Multikulturalismusde-batte*, ed. Elisabeth Bronfen and Benjamin Marius, 59–80 (Stauffenberg, 1997).

Reprinted in *The Modernist Papers*, 152–69 (Verso, 2007).

1988   *The Ideologies of Theory: Essays, 1971–1986* (University of Minnesota Press).

Vol. 1 *Situations of Theory*

Vol. 2 *The Syntax of History*

Translated into Japanese by Suzuki Akira, Shinozaki Minoru and Gotō Kazuhiko as *Nochini Umareru Mono e: Posutomodanizumu Hihan eno Michi 1971–1986* (Kinokuniya Shoten, 1993).

1990    *Late Marxism: Adorno; or, The Persistence of the Dialectic* (Verso).

Translated into Korean by Kim Yu Dong as *Hugi Mareukeuseujuui* (Hangilsa, 2000).

1990    *Signatures of the Visible* (Routledge).

Translated into Italian as *Firme del Visible: Hitchcock, Kubrick, Antonioni*, trans. Daniela Turco (Donzelli, 2003).

Translated into Korean by Nam Inyoung as *Boineungeosui Nalin* (Hannarae, 2003).

1991    *Postmodernism, or, The Cultural Logic of Late Capitalism* (Duke University Press).

Excerpts reprinted in *A Postmodern Reader*, ed. Joseph Natoli and Linda Hutcheon, 312–32 (State University of New York Press, 1993).

Excerpt published as "Postmodernism and the Market," published as *Mapping Ideology*, ed. Slavoj Žižek, 278–95 (Verso, 1994).

"Surrealism without the Unconscious," reprinted in *Transmission: Toward a Post-television Culture*, ed. Peter d'Agostino and David Tafler, 21–51 (Sage, 1994).

Excerpts reprinted in *From Modernism to Postmodernism: An Anthology*, ed. Lawrence E. Cahoone, 564–74 (Blackwell, 1996).

Excerpts reprinted as "The Westin Bonaventure Hotel," in *The Postmodern Presence: Readings on Postmodernism in American Culture and Society*, ed. Arthur Asa Berger, 103–11 (AltaMira Press, 1998).

Excerpts reprinted in *The Blackwell Reader in Contemporary Social Theory*, ed. Anthony Elliott, 338–50 (Blackwell, 1999).

Translated into Italian as *Il Posmoderno, o la logica culturale del tardo capitalismo*, trans. Stefano Velotti (Garzanti, 1989).

Partly translated into German as "Surrealismus ohne das Unbewusste," in *Philosophische Ansichten der Kultur der Moderne,* ed. A. Kuhlmann (Fischer Taschenbuch, 1994).

Translated into Spanish as *El posmodernismo o la Logica cultural del capitalismo avanzado*, trans. Jose Luis Pardo Torio (Studio, 1995).

Translated into Chinese by Zhang Xudong and Chen Qingqiao as *Wanqi Zibenzhuyi de Wenhua Luoji* (Sanlian Shudian, 1997).

Translated into Chinese by Wu Meizhen as *Houxiandai Zhuyi Huo Wanqi Zibenzhuyi de Wenhua Luoji* (Shibao Wenhua Chuban Gongsi, 1998).

Translated into Hebrew as *Grimberg-Hirsh Adi*, trans. Grimberg-Hirsh Adi (Libido Resling, 2002).

Translated into Korean by Lee Kyungdeok and Kim Koonyong as *Poseuteumodeonijeum ttoneun Hugi Jabonjuuiui Munhwa Nonri* (Bi Chulpansa, forthcoming).

1992    *The Geopolitical Aesthetic; or, Cinema and Space in the World System* (Indiana University Press and British Film Institute).

"Remapping Taipei," reprinted in *New Chinese Cinemas: Forms, Identities, Politics*, ed. Nick Browne et al., 117–50 (University of Cambridge Press, 1994).

"Totality as Conspiracy," reprinted in *The Jameson Reader*, ed. Michael Hardt and Kathi Weeks, 340–358 (Blackwell, 2000).

"'Art Naïf' and the Admixture of Worlds," reprinted in *Geopolitics of the Visible: Essays on Philippine Film Cultures*, ed. Rolando B. Tolentino, 25–65 (Ateneo de Manila University Press, 2000).

Translated into Spanish as *La estetica geopolitica cine y espacio en el sistema mundial*, trans. Noemi Sobregyues and David Cifuentes (Comunicacion cine, 1995).

1994    *Theory of Culture: Lectures at Rikkyo* (Rikkyo University Press).

1994    *The Seeds of Time* (Columbia University Press).

"The Constraints of Postmodernism" reprinted in *Rethinking Architecture: A Reader in Cultural Theory*, ed. Neal Leach, 247–54 (Routledge, 1997).

"The Antinomies of Postmodernity" reprinted in *The Cultural Turn: Selected Writings on the Postmodern, 1983–1998*, 50–72 (Verso, 1998); and in *The Jameson Reader*, ed. Michael Hardt and Kathi Weeks, 233–54 (Blackwell, 2000).

"Utopianism and Anti-Utopianism" reprinted in *The Jameson Reader*, ed. Michael Hardt and Kathi Weeks, 382–92 (Blackwell, 2000).

Translated into Chinese by Wang Fengzhen as *Shijan de Zhongzi* (Lijiang Chubanshe, 1997).

Translated into Japanese by Matsuura Shunsuke and Onoki Akie as *Jikan no Shushi: Posutomodan to Reisen-igo no Yūtopia* (Seidosha, 1998).

1998    *The Cultural Turn: Selected Writings on the Postmodern, 1983–1998* (Verso).

Translated into Chinese by Hu Yamin as *Wenhua Zhuanxiang* (Zhongguo Shehui Kexue Chubanshe, 2000).

Translated into Japanese by Aiba Atsushi, Kōno Shintarō and Shin Kunio as *Karuchuraru-tān* (Sakuhinsha 2006).

1998    *Brecht and Method* (Verso).

Translated into Chinese by Chen Yongguo as *Bulaixite yu Fangfa* (Shehui Kexue Chubanshe, 1998).

2000    *The Jameson Reader*, ed. Michael Hardt and Kathi Weeks (Blackwell).

2002    *A Singular Modernity: Essay on the Ontology of the Present* (Verso).

Translated into Italian as *Una Modernita Singolare: Saggio sull'ontologia del presenta*, trans. Carla Benedetti (Sasoni, 2003).

Translated into Chinese by Wang Fengzhen and Wang Liya as *Danyi de Xiandaixing* (Tianjing Renmin Chubanshe, 2004).

Translated into Japanese by Kuga Kazumi, Saitō Etsuko and Takizawa Masahiko as *Modan to iu fushigi: Genzai no Sonzairon ni tsuite no Shiron* (Kobushi Shobō 2005).

2004    *Selected Works of Fredric Jameson: Volume I–IV*, trans. into Chinese by Wang Fengzhen (Zhongguo Renmin Daxue Chubanshe).

2005    *Archaeologies of the Future: The Desire Called Utopia and Other Science Fictions* (Verso).

Translated into Korean by Lee Kyungdeok and Kim Koonyong as *Miraeui Kogohak* (Gil Chulpansa, forthcoming).

2007    *The Modernist Papers* (Verso).


ARTICLES, CHAPTERS, ESSAYS, INTERVIEWS

1967    "T. W. Adorno, or, Historical Tropes," *Salmagundi* 5: 3–42.

Revised as chapter 1 of *Marxism and Form*, 3–59 (1971).

Revision printed as "T. W. Adorno," in *The Jameson Reader*, ed. Michael Hardt and Kathi Weeks, 71–7 (Blackwell, 2000).

1968    "On Politics and Literature," *Salmagundi*, 7: 17–26.

1969    "Walter Benjamin, or, Nostalgia," *Salmagundi*, 10–11: 52–68.

Reprinted in *Marxism and Form*, 60–83 (Princeton University Press, 1971).

Reprinted in *The Legacy of the German Refugee Intellectuals*, ed. Robert Boyers, 52–68 (Schocken, 1972).

Reprinted in *The Salmagundi Reader*, ed. Robert Boyers and Peggy Boyers, 561–76 (Indiana University Press, 1983).

1969    "Introduction to T. W. Adorno," *Salgamundi*, 10–11: 140–43.

Reprinted in *The Legacy of the German Refugee Intellectuals*, ed. Robert Boyers, 141–43 (Schocken, 1972).

1969    Translation from German of T. W. Adorno, "Society," *Salmagundi* 10–11: 144–53.

Reprinted in *The Salmagundi Reader*, ed. Robert Boyers and Peggy Boyers, 49–57 (Indiana University Press, 1983).

1970    "The Case for Georg Lukács," *Salmagundi* 13: 3–35.

Reprinted in *Marxism and Form*, 160–205 (Princeton University Press, 1971).

1970    "On Raymond Chandler," *Southern Review* 6:2: 624–50.

Reprinted in *The Poetics of Murder: Detective Fiction and Literary Theory*, ed. Glenn W. Most and William W. Stowe, 122–48 (Harcourt Brace Jovanovich, 1983).

Reprinted in *The Critical Response to Raymond Chandler*, ed. J. K. Van Dover, 65–88 (Greenwood, 1995).

1970    "Seriality in Modern Literature," *Bucknell Review* 18:1: 63–80.

1971    "La Cousine Bette and Allegorical Realism," *PMLA* 86:2: 241–54.

1971    "Metacommentary," *PMLA* 86:1: 9–18.

Reprinted in *Contemporary Literary Criticism: Modernism through Post-structuralism*, ed. Robert Con Davis, 112–23 (Longman, 1986).

Reprinted in *The Ideologies of Theory 1*, 3–16 (University of Minnesota Press, 1988).

1972    "The Great American Hunter: Ideological Content in the Novel," *College English* 34:2: 180–97.

1972    Introduction to and translation of "The Rise of Hermeneutics," by W. Dilthey, *New Literary History* 3: 229–44.

1972    "Three Methods in Sartre's Literary Criticism," in *Modern French Criticism: From Proust and Valéry to Structuralism*, ed. John K. Simon, 193–227 (University of Chicago Press).

Reprinted in *Critical Essays on Jean-Paul Sartre*, ed. Robert Wilcocks, 97–119 (G. K. Hall, 1988).

1972    "Note from the Translator" and translation of "The Rise of Hermeneutics," by Wilhelm Dilthey, *New Literary History* 3:2: 229–44.

1972    "Herbert Marcuse," *Salmagundi* 20: 126–52.

1973    Review of *Literature and Society*, by Charles I. Glicksberg, *Comparative Literature* 25:3: 277–78.

1973    Review of *Paul Nizan: Committed Literature in a Conspiratorial World*, by W. D. Redfern, *French Review* 46:3: 631–2.

1973    "Generic Discontinuities in Science Fiction: Brian Aldiss' *Starship*," *Science Fiction Studies* 1:2: 57–68.

    Reprinted as "Generic Discontinuities in SF," in *Science-Fiction Studies: Selected Articles in Science Fiction, 1973–1975*, ed. R. D. Mullen and Darko Suvin, 28–39 (Gregg, 1976).

    Reprinted as "Generic Discontinuities in SF: Brian Aldiss' *Starship*," in *Archaeologies of the Future*, 254–66 (Verso, 2005).

1973    Introduction to *Marxist Esthetics*, by Henri Avron, trans. Helen R. Lane, vii–xxiv (Cornell University Press).

1973    "Wyndham Lewis as Futurist," *Hudson Review* 26:2: 295–329.

    Revised as chapters 1–4 of *Fables of Aggression*, 25–86 (University of California Press, 1979).

1973    Review of *Structures romanesques et vision sociale chez Guy de Maupassant*, by Charles Castella, *Modern Language Notes* 89:4: 753–58.

1974    "The Vanishing Mediator: Narrative Structure in Max Weber," *New German Critique* 1: 52–89.

    Reprinted in *Working Papers in Cultural Studies* 5 (1974): 111–49.

    Reprinted as "The Vanishing Mediator; or, Max Weber as Storyteller," in *The Ideologies of Theory* 2, 3–34 (University of Minnesota Press, 1988).

1974    "Benjamin as Historian; or, How to Write a Marxist Literary History: A Review Essay," *Minnesota Review* 2–3: 116–36.

1974    "Change, Science Fiction, and Marxism: Open or Closed Universes? In Retrospect," *Science Fiction Studies* 1:4: 272–6.

1974    "Demystifying Literary History," *New Literary History* 5:3: 605–12.

1974    Review of *On Realism*, by J. P. Stern, *Clio* 3:3: 346–52.

1974    Review of *Marxism and the Philosophy of Language*, by V. Voloshinov, *Style* 8:3: 535–43.

1974    "History and the Death Wish: *Zardoz* as Open Form," *Jump Cut* 3: 5–8.

1975    "After Armageddon: Character Systems in P. K. Dick's *Dr. Bloodmoney*," *Science Fiction Studies* 2:1: 31–42.

Reprinted in *Science-Fiction Studies: Selected Articles in Science Fiction, 1973–1975,* ed. R. D. Mullen and Darko Suvin, 187–98 (Gregg, 1976).

Reprinted in *On Philip K. Dick: Forty Articles from Science-Fiction Studies,* ed. R. D. Mullen et al., 26–32 (Terre Haute, 1992).

Reprinted as "After Armageddon: Character Systems in *Dr. Bloodmoney*," in *Archaeologies of the Future,* 349–62 (Verso, 2005).

1975    "Beyond the Cave: Modernism and the Modes of Production," *Bulletin of the Midwest Modern Language Association* 8:1: 1–20.

Reprinted in *The Horizon of Literature,* ed. Paul Hernadi, 157–82 (University of Nebraska Press, 1982).

Reprinted as "Beyond the Cave: Demystifying the Ideology of Modernism," in *The Ideologies of Theory* 2, 115–32 (University of Minnesota Press, 1988).

Reprinted in *Contemporary Marxist Literary Criticism,* ed. Francis Mulhern, 168–87 (Longman, 1992).

Reprinted in *The Jameson Reader,* ed. Michael Hardt and Kathi Weeks, 175–87 (Blackwell, 2000).

1975    "The Ideology of the Text," *Salmagundi,* 31–32: 204–46.

Revised and reprinted in *The Ideologies of Theory* 2, 17–71 (University of Minnesota Press, 1988).

1975    "L'inconscient politique," in *La lecture sociocritique du texte romanesque,* ed. Graham Falconer and Henri Mitterand, 39–48 (Hakkert).

1975    "Magical Narratives: Romance as Genre," *New Literary History* Autumn 7:1: 135–63.

Translated into Italian by Alessandro Gebbia as *Le narrazioni magiche: II "romance" come genere letterario* (Lerici, 1978).

Revised and reprinted as "Magical Narratives: On the Dialectical Use of Genre Criticism," in *The Political Unconscious,* 103–50, (Cornell, 1981).

1975    "Notes Toward a Marxist Cultural Politics," *Minnesota Review* 5: 35–39.

1975    "The Re-invention of Marx," *Times Literary Supplement,* 22 August, 942–43.

1975    "World Reduction in Le Guin: The Emergence of Utopian Narrative," *Science Fiction Studies* 2:3: 221–30.

Reprinted in *Science-Fiction Studies: Selected Articles on Science Fiction, 1973–1975*, ed. R. D. Mullen and Darko Suvin, 251–60 (Gregg, 1976).

Reprinted as "World-Reduction in Le Guin: The Emergence of Utopian Narrative" in *Ursula Le Guin's "The Left Hand of Darkness," (Modern Critical Interpretations)*, ed. Harold Bloom, 23–37 (Chelsea House, 1987).

Reprinted in *The Jameson Reader*, ed. Michael Hardt and Kathi Weeks, 368–81 (Blackwell, 2000).

Reprinted in *Archaeologies of the Future*, 267–80 (Verso, 2005).

1976    "Authentic *Ressentiment*: The 'Experimental' Novels of Gissing," *Nineteenth-Century Fiction* 31:2: 127–49.

Revised as "Authentic *Ressentiment*: Generic Discontinuities and Ideologemes in the 'Experimental' Novels of George Gissing," for chapter 4 of *The Political Unconscious*, 185–205 (Cornell, 1981).

1976    "Collective Art in the Age of Cultural Imperialism," *Alcheringa* 2:2: 108–11.

1976    "Criticism in History," in *Weapons of Criticism: Marxism in America and the Literary Tradition*, ed. Norman Rudich, 31–50 (Ramparts Press).

Revised and reprinted in *The Ideologies of Theory 1*, 119–36 (University of Minnesota Press, 1988).

1976    "Figural Relativism; or, The Poetics of Historiography," *Diacritics* 6:1: 2–9.

Reprinted in *The Ideologies of Theory 1*, 153–65 (University of Minnesota Press, 1988).

1976    "The Ideology of Form: Partial Systems in *La Vieille Fille*," *Substance* 15: 29–49.

1976    "Introduction/Prospectus: To Reconsider the Relationship of Marxism to Utopian Thought," *Minnesota Review* 6: 53–58.

Reprinted in *The Jameson Reader*, ed. Michael Hardt and Kathi Weeks, 361–67 (Blackwell, 2000).

1976    "Modernism and Its Repressed; or, Robbe-Grillet as Anti-colonialist," *Diacritics* 6:2: 7–14.

Reprinted in *The Ideologies of Theory 1*, 167–80 (University of Minnesota Press, 1988).

1976    "On Goffman's Frame Analysis," *Theory and Society* 3:1: 119–33.

1976    "Political Painting: New Perspectives on the Realism Controversy," *Praxis* 1:2: 225–30.

1976    "Science Fiction as Politics: Larry Niven," *New Republic*, 30 October, 34–38.

1976    "Battleground," *New York Review of Books*, 5 August, 45.

1977    "Class and Allegory in Contemporary Mass Culture: *Dog Day Afternoon* as a Political Film," *College English* 3:8: 843–59.

Reprinted in *Screen Education* 30 (1979): 75–92.

Reprinted with a few minor amendments in *Movies and Methods: An Anthology*, ed. Bill Nichols, 2: 715–33 (University of California Press, 1985).

Revised and reprinted in *Signatures of the Visible* (Routledge, 1990), 35–54.

Revised and reprinted in *Contemporary Film Theory*, ed. Antony Easthope, 95–107 (Longman, 1990).

Revised and reprinted in *The Jameson Reader*, ed. Michael Hardt and Kathi Weeks, 288–307 (Blackwell, 2000).

1977    "Ideology, Narrative Analysis, and Popular Culture," *Theory and Society* 4:4: 543–59.

1977    "On Jargon," *Minnesota Review* 9: 30–31.

Reprinted in *The Jameson Reader*, ed. Michael Hardt and Kathi Weeks, 117–8 (Blackwell, 2000).

1977    "Of Islands and Trenches: Neutralization and the Production of Utopian Discourse," *Diacritics* 7:2: 2–21.

Reprinted in *The Ideologies of Theory 2*, 75–101 (University of Minnesota Press, 1988).

1977    "Reflections in Conclusion," in *Aesthetics and Politics*, ed. and trans. Ronald Taylor, 196–213 (New Left Books).

Reprinted as "Reflections on the Brecht-Lukács Debate," in *The Ideologies of Theory 2*, 133–47 (University of Minnesota Press, 1988).

1977    "Imaginary and Symbolic in *La Rabouilleuse*," *Social Science Information* 16:1: 59–81.

Revised as "Realism and Desire: Balzac and the Problem of the Subject" for chapter 3 of *The Political Unconscious*, 151–84 (Cornell, 1981).

1978    "Imaginary and Symbolic in Lacan: Marxism, Psychoanalytic Criticism, and the Problem of the Subject," *Yale French Studies* 55–56: 338–95.

Reprinted in *Literature and Psychoanalysis: The Question of Reading Otherwise*, ed. Shoshana Felman, 338–95 (Johns Hopkins University Press, 1982).

Reprinted in *The Ideologies of Theory 1*, 75–113 (University of Minnesota Press, 1988).

Reprinted in *The Jameson Reader*, ed. Michael Hardt and Kathi Weeks, 89–113 (Blackwell, 2000).

1978     "The Symbolic Inference; or, Kenneth Burke and Ideological Analysis," *Critical Inquiry* 4:3: 507–23.

Reprinted in *Representing Kenneth Burke*, ed. Hayden White and Margaret Brose, 68–91 (Johns Hopkins University Press, 1982).

Reprinted in *The Ideologies of Theory 1*, 137–52 (University of Minnesota Press, 1988).

1978     "Ideology and Symbolic Action: Reply to Kenneth Burke," *Critical Inquiry* 5:2: 417–22.

1979     "But Their Cause Is Just: Capitalism, not Zionism, Is the Problem's Real Cause," *Seven Days* 3:11: 19–21.

Reprinted in *New Haven Advocate*, 31 October, 6.

1979     "Marxism and Historicism," *New Literary History* 11: 41–73.

Reprinted in *The Ideologies of Theory 2*, 148–77 (University of Minnesota Press, 1988).

1979     "Marxism and Teaching," *New Political Science* 2:3: 31–35.

1979     "Reification and Utopia in Mass Culture," *Social Text* 1: 130–48.

Reprinted in *Signatures of the Visible*, 9–34 (Routledge, 1990).

Reprinted in *The Jameson Reader*, ed. Michael Hardt and Kathi Weeks, 123–48 (Blackwell, 2000).

1979     "Towards a Libidinal Economy of Three Modern Painters," *Social Text* 1: 189–99.

Reprinted in *The Modernist Papers*, 255–68 (Verso, 2007).

1980     "Balzac et le problème du sujet," In *Le roman de Balzac: Recherches critiques, méthodes, lectures*, ed. Roland Le Huenen and Paul Perron, 65–76 (Didier).

Revised for chapter 3 of *The Political Unconscious*, 151–84 (Cornell, 1981).

1980     "SF Novel/SF Film," *Science Fiction Studies* 7:3: 319–22.

1981     "From Criticism to History," *New Literary History* 12:2: 367–76.

1981    "In the Destructive Element Immerse: Hans Jürgen Syberberg and Cultural Revolution," *October* 17: 99–118.

Reprinted in *Signatures of the Visible*, 63–81 (Routledge, 1990).

Reprinted in *Perspectives on German Cinema*, 508–25 (Prentice Hall, 1996).

1981    "Religion and Ideology: A Political Reading of *Paradise Lost*," in *1642: Literature and Power in the Seventeenth Century*, ed. Francis Barker, Peter Hulme, Margaret Iverson and Diana Loxley, 35–56 (Department of Literature, University of Essex).

Reprinted in *Literature, Politics, and Theory: Papers from the Essex Conference, 1976–84*, ed. F. Barker et al., 315–36 (Methuen, 1986).

Reprinted in *Paradise Lost: John Milton*, ed. William Zunder, 47–57 (St. Martins, 1999).

1981    "Sartre in Search of Flaubert," *New York Times Book Review*, 27 December, 5, 16, 18.

1981    "The Shining," *Social Text* 4: 114–25.

Reprinted as "Historicism in *The Shining*," in *Signatures of the Visible*, 82–98 (Routledge, 1990).

1981    "The Position of Marx's Theory of Ideology in Nineteenth-Century Thought," in *HU300: The Human Condition; Forms of Alienation in Modern Thought and Culture*, ed. Margaret Rose, unpaginated (course reader, School of Humanities, Open Campus Program, Deakin University, Waurn Ponds, Victoria, Australia).

1982    "*Ulysses* in History," *James Joyce and Modern Literature*, ed. W. J. McCormack and Alistair Stead, 126–41 (Routledge and Kegan Paul).

Reprinted in *James Joyce: A Collection of Critical Essays*, ed. Mary T. Reynolds, 145–58 (Prentice Hall, 1993).

Reprinted in *The Modernist Papers*, 137–51 (Verso, 2007).

1982    "On Aronson's Sartre," *Minnesota Review* 18: 116–27.

1982    "Futuristic Visions That Tell Us About Right Now," *In These Times*, 17 May, 5–11.

Reprinted as "Philip K. Dick: In Memoriam," *Archaeologies of the Future*, 345–8 (Verso, 2005).

1982    "On Diva," *Social Text* 6: 114–19.

Reprinted as "*Diva* and French Socialism," in *Signatures of the Visible*, 55–62 (Routledge, 1990).

1982    "Progress versus Utopia; or, Can We Imagine the Future?" *Science Fiction Studies* 9:2: 147–58.

Reprinted in *Archaeologies of the Future*, 281–95 (Verso, 2005).

1982    "Towards a New Awareness of Genre," *Science Fiction Studies* 9:3: 322–24.

1982    With Leonard Green, Jonathan Culler, and Richard Klein, "Interview: Fredric Jameson," *Diacritics* 12:3: 72–91.

1982    "Reading Hitchcock," *October* 23: 15–42.

Reprinted as "Allegorizing Hitchcock," in *Signatures of the Visible*, 99–127 (Routledge, 1990).

1982    With K. Ayyappa Paniker, "A Dialogue with Fredric Jameson," *Littcrit* 8:2: 5–26.

Reprinted in *Dialogues: Six Literary Interviews,* ed. K. Paniker, pages unknown (Postgraduate Department of English, Utkal University, Bhubaneswar, India, 1989).

1983    "Science versus Ideology," *Humanities in Society* 6:2–3: 283–302.

Reprinted in *The Modernist Papers,* 371–79 (Verso, 2007).

1983    "Euphorias of Substitution: Hubert Aquin and the Political Novel in Quebec," *Yale French Studies* 65: 214–23.

1983    "L'éclatement du récit et la clôture californienne," trans. Marcelle Mekiès, *Litterature* 49: 89–101.

1983    "On Balzac," *Boundary 2* 12:1: 227–34.

1983    "Postmodernism and Consumer Society," in *The Anti-aesthetic*, ed. Hal Foster (Bay), 111–25.

Reprinted in *Amerikastudien/American Studies* 29:1 (1984): 55–73.

Reprinted in *Postmodernism and Its Discontents: Theories, Practices,* ed. E. Ann Kaplan, 13–29 (Verso, 1988).

Reprinted in *Modernism/Postmodernism,* ed. Peter Brooker, 163–79 (Longman, 1992).

Reprinted in *Movies and Mass Culture*, ed. John Belton, 185–202 (Rutgers University Press, 1996).

Partly reprinted as "The Nostalgia Mode" in *Postmodern After-Images: A Reader in Film, Television, and Video,* ed. Peter Brooker and Will Brooker, 23–25 (Arnold, 1997).

Reprinted in *The Cultural Turn*, 1–20 (Verso, 1998).

Reprinted in *The Continental Aesthetics Reader*, ed. Clive Cazeaux, 282–94 (Routledge, 2000).

Reprinted in *Postmodern Debates*, ed. Simon Malpas, 22–36 (Palgrave, 2001).

1983   "Pleasure: A Political Issue," *Formations of Pleasure*, ed. T. Bennett et al., 1–14 (Routledge and Kegan Paul).

Reprinted in *The Ideologies of Theory 2*, 61–74 (University of Minnesota Press, 1988).

1983   "Morality versus Ethical Substance; or, Aristotelian Marxism in Alasdair MacIntyre," *Social Text* 8: 151–4.

Reprinted in *The Ideologies of Theory 1*, 181–5 (University of Minnesota Press, 1988).

1983   "The Ideological Analysis of Space," *Critical Exchange* 14: 1–15.

1983   Introduction to *The Historical Novel*, by György Lukács, trans. Hannah Mitchell and Stanley Mitchell, 1–8 (University of Nebraska Press, 1962).

1984   "Periodizing the Sixties," in *The Sixties without Apologies*, ed. Sayres et al., 178–209 (University of Minnesota Press).

Reprinted in *The Ideologies of Theory 2*, 178–208 (University of Minnesota Press, 1988).

1984   "Literary Innovation and Modes of Production," *Modern Chinese Literature* 1:1: 67–77.

1984   "Postmodernism, or, The Cultural Logic of Late Capitalism," *New Left Review* 16: 52–92.

Revised and reprinted in *Postmodernism*, 1–54 (Duke University Press, 1991).

Reprinted in *Storming the Reality Studio*, ed. L. McCaffery, 219–28 (Duke University Press, 1991).

Reprinted in *Rethinking Architecture: A Reader in Cultural Theory*, ed. Neal Leach, 238–246 (Routledge, 1997).

Reprinted in *Twentieth-Century Literary Theory: A Reader*, ed. K. M. Newton, 267–274 (St. Martin's, 1997).

Reprinted in *The Jameson Reader*, ed. Michael Hardt and Kathi Weeks, 188–232 (Blackwell, 2000).

Reprinted in *Media and Cultural Studies: Keywords*, ed. Meenakshi Gigi
Durham and Douglas M. Kellner, 482–519 (Blackwell, 2001).

1984    "The Politics of Theory—Ideological Positions in the Postmodernism Debate," *New German Critique* 33: 53–65.

Reprinted in *Interpretive Social Science: A Second Look*, ed. Paul Rabinow
and William M. Sullivan, 351–64 (University of California Press, 1987).

Reprinted in *The Ideologies of Theory* 2, 103–13 (University of Minnesota
Press, 1988).

Reprinted in *Modern Criticism and Theory: A Reader*, ed. David Lodge,
373–83 (Longman, 1988).

Reprinted in *Contemporary Critical Theory*, ed. Dan Latimer, 370–83
(Harcourt Brace Jovanovich, 1989).

Reprinted in *Contemporary Literary Criticism: Literary and Cultural
Studies*, ed. Robert Con Davis and Ronald Schleifer, 418–27 (Longman,
1989).

Revised for *Postmodernism* 55–66 (Duke University Press, 1991).

Translated into German by Karin Wurst as "Ideologische Positionen in der
Postmodernismus-Debatte," *Das Argument* 28:155 (1986): 18–28.

1984    "Wallace Stevens," *New Orleans Review* 11:1: 10–19.

Reprinted as "Exoticism and Structuralism in Wallace Stevens," in *The
Modernist Papers*, 207–22 (Verso, 2007).

1984    "Utopian and Fantasy Literature in East Germany—The Development of a
Genre of Fiction, 1945–1979," *Science Fiction Studies* 11:2: 194–9.

1984    Foreword to *The Postmodern Condition*, by Jean-François Lyotard, trans.
Geoffrey Bennington and Brian Massumi, vii–xxi (University of Minnesota
Press).

1984    Afterword to *Sartre: The Origins of a Style*, 2nd ed., 205–33 (Columbia University Press).

1984    "Flaubert's Libidinal Historicism: *Trois Contes*, Flaubert, and Postmodernism," in *Flaubert and Postmodernism*, ed. N. Schor  H. F. Majewski, 76–83
(University of Nebraska Press).

1984    "Rimbaud and the Spatial Text," in *Rewriting Literary History*, ed. Tak-Wai
Wong and M. A. Abbas, 66–88 (Hong Kong University Press).

1984    "An Overview," in *Rewriting Literary History*, ed. Tak-Wai Wong and
M. A. Abbas, 338–47 (Hong Kong University Press).

Reprinted in *The Modernist Papers,* 238–54 (Verso, 2007).

1984    Review of *Names,* by Don DeLillo, and of *Richard A.,* by Sol Yurick,
        *Minnesota Review* 22: 116–22.

1984    With Anders Stephanson and Cornel West, "A Very Partial Chronology,"
        *Social Text* 9–10: 210–15.

1985    Introduction to *Sartre After Sartre, Yale French Studies* 68: iii–xi.

1985    "Baudelaire as Modernist and Postmodernist: The Dissolution of the Refer-
        ent and the Artificial 'Sublime,'" in *Lyric Poetry: beyond New Criticism,* ed.
        C. Hosek and Patricia Parker, 247–63 (Cornell University Press).

        Reprinted in *The Modernist Papers,* 223–37 (Verso, 2007).

1985    "The Realist Floor Plan," in *On Signs,* ed. M. Blonsky, 373–83 (Johns Hop-
        kins University Press).

        Reprinted in *Narrative/Theory,* ed. David H. Richter, 313–23 (Longman,
        1996).

1985    "Architecture and the Critique of Ideology," in *Architecture, Criticism,
        Ideology,* ed. Joan Ockman, Deborah Berke, and Mary McLeod, 51–87
        (Princeton Architectural Press).

        Reprinted in *Ideologies of Theory 2,* 35–60 (University of Minnesota Press,
        1988).

        Reprinted as "Architecture and the Critique of Ideology," in *Architecture
        Theory since 1968,* ed. K. Michael Hays, 440–461 (MIT Press, 1998).

1985    Foreword to *Noise: The Political Economy of Music,* by Jacques Attali,
        vii–xiv (University of Minnesota Press).

1986    "An Introduction to Essays on Theories of the Text," *Texte: Revue de cri-
        tique et de théorie Littéraire* 5–6: 6–20.

1986    "Ideological Positions in the Postmodernism Debate," *Argument* 28: 18–28.

1986    "Four Ways of Looking at a Fairy Tale," in *The Fairy Tale: Politics, Desire,
        and Everyday Life* (exhibition, video program, and film program by Artists
        Space, October 30–November 26), 16–24.

1986    "Third World Literature in the Era of Multinational Capitalism," *Social
        Text* 15: 65–88.

        Revised as "World Literature in an Age of Multinational Capitalism," in *The
        Current Criticism: Essays on the Present and Future in Literary Theory,* ed.
        Clayton Koelb and Virgil Lokke, 139–58 (Purdue University Press, 1987).

        Reprinted in *Pretexts* 3:1-2 (1991): 82–104.

Reprinted in *The Jameson Reader*, ed. Michael Hardt and Kathi Weeks, 315–39 (Blackwell, 2000).

1986    "On Magic Realism in Film," *Critical Inquiry* 12:2: 301–25.

Reprinted in *Signatures of the Visible*, 128–52 (Routledge, 1990).

1986    "An Interview with F. R. Jameson by A. Stephanson on Postmodernism," *Flash Art* 131: 69–73.

Reprinted in *Universal Abandon*, ed. Andrew Ross, 3–30 (University of Minnesota Press, 1988).

Reprinted in *Postmodernism/Jameson/Critique*, ed. Douglas Kellner, 43–74 (Maisonneuve, 1989).

A longer version, "Regarding Postmodernism: A Conversation with Fredric Jameson," was reprinted in *Social Text* 17 (1987): 29–54 and 7 (1989): 3–30.

1986    "Hans Haacke and the Cultural Logic of Late Capitalism," in *Hans Haacke: Unfinished Business*, ed. Brian Wallis, 38–51 (New Museum of Contemporary Art, 1986–87).

1987    With Zheng Wanlong, Chen Jiangong, and Li Tuo, "Discussion: Contemporary Chinese Writing," *Polygraph* 1: 3–9.

1987    "Science-Fiction as a Spatial Genre: Generic Discontinuities and the Problem of Figuration in Vonda McIntyre's *The Exile Waiting*," *Science Fiction Studies* 14:1: 44–59.

Reprinted in *Archaeologies of the Future*, 296–313 (Verso, 2005).

1987    "Introduction to Borge" and "Interview with Thomas Borge," *New Left Review* 164: 51–64.

1987    "Reading without Interpretation: Postmodernism and the Video-Text," in *The Linguistics of Writing: Arguments between Language and Literature*, ed. N. Fabb et al., 199–223 (Manchester Press).

Reprinted with minor alterations as "Video: Surrealism without the Unconscious," in *Postmodernism*, 67–96 (Duke University Press, 1991).

Translated into French by V. Colonna, C. Liebow, and L. Allard as "La lecture sans l'interpretation: Le postmodernisme et le texte video," *Extrait de communications* 48 (1988): 105–20.

1987    "On *Habits of the Heart*," *South Atlantic Quarterly* 86:4: 545–65.

1987    "Interview: Andrea Ward Speaks with Fredric Jameson," *Impulse* 13:4: 8–9.

1987 "Shifting Contexts of Science-Fiction Theory," *Science-Fiction Studies* 14:2: 241–47.

1987 "Über einige Schwierigkeiten bei der Beschreibung des Krieges," *Weimarer Beiträge* 33:8: 1393–98.

1987 "The State of the Subject (III)," *Critical Quarterly* 29:4: 16–25.

1987 "Regarding Postmodernism: A Conversation with Fredric Jameson," *Social Text* 17: 29–54 (with Anders Stephanson).

1987 "A Brief Response," *Social Text* 17: 26–27.

1987 Foreword to *On Meaning: Selected Writings in Semiotic Theory*, by A. J. Greimas, trans. P. J. Perron and F. H. Collins, vi–xxii (University of Minnesota Press).

1988 "Cognitive Mapping," in *Marxism and the Interpretation of Culture*, ed. C. Nelson and L. Grossberg, 347–58 (University of Illinois Press).

   Reprinted in *Poetics/Politics: Radical Aesthetics for the Classroom*, ed. Armitava Kumar, 155–71 (St. Martins, 1999).

   Reprinted in *The Jameson Reader*, ed. Michael Hardt and Kathi Weeks, 277–87 (Blackwell, 2000).

1988 "*History and Class Consciousness* as an 'Unfinished Project,'" *Rethinking Marxism* 1:1: 49–72.

1988 "Postmodernism and Utopia," in *Utopia Post Utopia: Configurations of Nature and Culture in Recent Sculpture and Photography*, exhibition catalogue, Institute of Contemporary Art, Boston, January 29-March 27, 11–32 (MIT Press).

   Revised as "Space: Utopianism after the End of Utopia," in *Postmodernism*, 154–80 (Duke University Press, 1991).

1988 "Interview with Fredric Jameson," by Jay Murphy, *Left Curve* 12: 4–11.

1988 "On Negt and Kluge," *October* 46: 151–77.

   Reprinted in *The Phantom Public Sphere*, ed. Bruce Robbins for the Social Text Collective, 42–74 (University of Minnesota Press, 1993).

1988 "Should Rivers and Forests Enjoy the Protection of the Law? Are We Obliged to Protect Our Twenty-second–century Descendants from the Contamination of Today's Nuclear Trash?" Symposium held by Christopher Stone, *Literature and Culture*. Contributors: Stanley Fish, Fredric Jameson (sound disc). Research Triangle Park, NC, National Humanities Center.

1988    "The Brick and the Balloon: Architecture, Idealism, and Land Speculation,"
        in *Anyhow*, ed. Cynthia C. Davidson, 106–121 (Anyone Corporation).

        Reprinted in *The Cultural Turn*, 162–89 (Verso, 1998).

1989    "Nostalgia for the Present," *South Atlantic Quarterly* 88:2: 517–37.

        Revised in *Postmodernism*, 279–96 (Duke University Press, 1991).

        Reprinted in *Classical Hollywood Narrative: The Paradigm Wars*, ed. Jane
        Gaines, 253–74 (Duke University Press, 1992).

        Reprinted in *Postmodern After-Images: A Reader in Film, Television, and
        Video*, ed. Peter Brooker and Will Brooker, 25–35 (Arnold, 1997).

        Reprinted in *Literary Theories: A Reader and Guide*, ed. Julian Wolfreys,
        395–409 (New York University Press, 1999).

1989    "The Space of Science Fiction: Narrative in A. E. Van Vogt," *Polygraph* 2–3:
        52–65.

        Reprinted in *Archaeologies of the Future*, 314–27 (Verso, 2005).

1989    "Afterword: Marxism and Postmodernism," in *Postmodernism/Jameson/
        Critique*, ed. Douglas Kellner, 369–87 (Maisonneuve).

        Reprinted in *New Left Review* 176 (1989): 31–45.

1989    Foreword to *Caliban and Other Essays*, by Roberto Fernandez Retamar,
        vii–xii (University of Minnesota Press).

1989    *Modernity and Postmodernism* (sound cassette, ca. 60 minutes).

1989    "Marxism and Postmodernism," *New Left Review* 176: 31–46.

        Reprinted in *Postmodernism/Jameson/Critique*, ed. Douglas Kellner, 369–87
        (Maisonneuve, 1989).

        Reprinted as excerpt entitled "A Third Stage of Capitalism," *Frontier*,
        Feb. 10, 1990: 22, 26.

        Reprinted in *"The Cultural Turn,"* 33–48 (Verso, 1998).

1989    "Modernity after Postmodernism," *Sociocriticism* 5:2: 23–41.

1990    With Roland Boer, "A Conversation with Fredric Jameson," Ideological
        Criticism of Biblical Texts Consultation of the Society of Biblical Literature,
        17 November, Society of Biblical Literature Annual Meeting, New Orleans
        (personal tape).

1990    "Dialectics and Utopia," plenary address at the American Academy of
        Religion/Society of Biblical Literature Annual Meeting, New Orleans, 17–20
        November (tape).

1990 "Spatial Equivalents: Postmodern Architecture and the World System," *The States of "Theory": History, Art, and Critical Discourse*, ed. David Carroll, 125–48 (Columbia University Press).

Revised as "Architecture: Spatial Equivalents in the World System," in *Postmodernism* (Duke University Press, 1991), 97–129.

1990 "Critical Agendas," *Science-Fiction Studies* 17:1: 93–102.

1990 "A Third Stage of Capitalism," *Frontier* Feb. 10: 8–9.

1990 "Commentary: Reappropriating Greek Sacrifice," *Journal of Modern Greek Studies* 8:1: 135–39.

1990 "Postmodernism and the Market," in *The Retreat of the Intellectuals: Socialist Register 1990*, ed. Ralph Miliband, Leo Panitch, and John Saville, 95–110 (Merlin).

Revised and reprinted as "Economics: Postmodernism and the Market," in *Postmodernism* 260–78 (Duke University Press, 1991).

Reprinted in *Mapping Ideology*, ed. Slavoj Žižek, 278–95 (Verso, 1994).

1990 With Sabry Hafez, "On Contemporary Marxist Theory: An Interview with Fredric Jameson," *Alif* 10: 114–31.

1990 "Theory in a New Situation," *Voprosy literatury* 6: 86–9.

Printed in Russian only.

1990 "Clinging to the Wreckage: a conversation with Stuart Hall," *Marxism Today*, September 1990, 28–31.

1990 "Envelopes and Enclaves: The Space of Post-civil Society," Interview with Michael Speaks. *Assemblage* 17: 30–37.

1991 "On Literary and Cultural Import-Substitution in the Third World: The Case of the Testimonio," *Margins* 1: 11–34.

Translated into Spanish by Ana Maria del Rio and John Beverley as "De la sustitución de importaciones literarias y culturales en el tercer mundo: El caso del testimonio," *Revista de critica literaria latinoamercana* 36 (1992): 121–33.

1991 "Spätmarxismus: Adorno in der Postmoderne," *Argument* 188: 565–75.

1991 "Sōseki and Western Modernism," *Boundary* 2 18:3: 123–41.

Reprinted in *The Modernist Papers*, 294–310 (Verso, 2007).

1991 "Thoughts on the Late War," *Social Text* 28: 142–46.

1991   With Horacio Machín, "Conversacion con Fredric Jameson," *Neuvo texto critico* 4.1: 4–18.

1991   "Conversations on the New World Order," in *After the Fall: The Failure of Communism and the Future of Socialism*, ed. Robin Blackburn, 255–68 (Verso).

1991   "Demographies of the Anonymous," in *Anyone,* ed. Cynthia C. Davidson, 46–61 (Rizzoli).

1992   Introduction to *Eugénie Grandet*, by Honoré de Balzac, v–xxv (Everyman's Library).

1992   "Spatial Systems in *North by Northwest*," in *Everything You Always Wanted to Know about Lacan (But Were Afraid to Ask Hitchcock)*, ed. Slavoj Žižek, 47–72 (Verso).

1992   "Geopolitical Aesthetics," *Polygraph* 5: 78–83.

Revised as "Introduction: Beyond Landscape" to *The Geopolitical Aesthetic*, 1–8 (Indiana University Press, 1992).

1992   "Benjamin's Readings," *Diacritics*, 22.3–4: 19–34.

1992   "Response," in "Final Panel of Respondents," in *Screening Europe: Image and Identity in Contemporary European Cinema*, ed. Duncan Petrie, 86–90 (British Film Institute).

1992   "Allegories of Anywhere," in *Anywhere,* ed. Cynthia Davidson, 172–7 (Rizzoli).

1992   "The Film-Makers Panel: Introduction; Reply," in *Screening Europe: Image and Identity in Contemporary European Cinema*, ed. Duncan Petrie, 93–4; 86–90 (British Film Institute).

1992   "A Conversation with Fredric Jameson," *Semeia* 59: 227–37.

1993   "The Synoptic Chandler," *Shades of Noir: A Reader*, ed. Joan Copjec, 33–56 (Verso).

1993   "On Cultural Studies," *Social Text* 34: 17–52.

Reprinted in *The Identity in Question*, ed. John Rajchman, 251–95 (Routledge, 1995).

Reprinted in *A Cultural Studies Reader: History, Theory, Practice*, ed. Jessica Munns and Gita Rajan, 613–45 (Longman, 1996).

1993   "In the Mirror of Alternate Modernities: Introduction to Kōjin Karatani, *The Origins of Japanese Literature*," *South Atlantic Quarterly* 92:2: 295–310.

Reprinted as "Foreword: In the Mirror of Alternate Modernities," in *Origins of Japanese Literature*, by Kōjin Karatani, ed. and trans. Brett de Bary (Duke University Press).

Reprinted in *The Modernist Papers*, 281–93 (Verso, 2007).

1993  "Americans Abroad: Exogamy and Letters in Late Capitalism," in *Critical Theory, Cultural Politics, and Latin American Narrative*, ed. Steven M. Bell, Albert H. Le May, and Leonard Orr, 35–60 (University of Notre Dame Press).

1993  "Actually Existing Marxism," *Polygraph* 6–7: 170–95.

Rewritten and expanded for *Marxism beyond Marxism*, ed. Saree Makdisi, Cesare Casarino, and Rebecca E. Karl, 14–54 (Routledge, 1996).

Reprinted as "Five Theses on Actually Existing Marxism," *Monthly Review* 47:11 (1996): 1–10.

Reprinted as "Five Theses on Actually Existing Marxism," in *In Defense of History: Marxism and the Postmodern Agenda*, ed. Ellen Wood and John Foster, 175–183 (Monthly Review Press, 1997).

Reprinted as "Five Theses on Actually Existing Marxism," in *The Jameson Reader*, 164–71 (Blackwell, 2000).

Translated into German by Jürgen Pelzer as "Fünf Thesen zum real existierenden Marxismus," *Argument* 38:2 (1996): 175–81.

1993  Foreword to *Politics, Ideology, and Literary Discourse in Modern China: Theoretical Interventions and Cultural Critique*, ed. Liu Kang and Xiaobing Tang, 1–7 (Duke University Press).

1993  Introduction to *South Atlantic Quarterly* 92:3: 417–22.

1994  "Céline and Innocence," *South Atlantic Quarterly* 93:2: 311–19.

Reprinted in *The Modernist Papers*, 45–51 (Verso, 2007).

1994  "Culture, Technology and Politics in the Postmodern Conditions," *Ichiko Intercultural* 6: 96–107.

1994  "Ontology and Utopia," *L'Esprit créateur*, 34:4: 46–64.

1994  "Exit Sartre," *London Review of Books*, 7 July, 13–14.

1994  "Representations of Subjectivity," *Social Discourse*, 6:1–2: 47–60.

1994  "Tadao Ando and the Enclosure of Modernism," *ANY* 1:6: 28–33.

1994  "Remapping Taipei," in *New Chinese Cinemas: Forms, Identities, Politics*, ed. Nick Browne et al., 117–50 (Cambridge University Press).

1994    "Art, Post–modernity, and the Periphery in Latin America: A Conversation in Bogotá," *Art Nexus* 14: 76–80.

1994    "Marxist Literary Criticism Today: The Case of Goethe's *Faust*," *Literary Studies*, 5:13: 7–24.

1994    "The Uses of Apocalypse," in *Anyway*, ed. Cynthia Davidson, 32–41 (Anyone Corporation).

1995    "Is Space Political?" in *Anyplace*, ed. Cynthia Davidson, 192–205 (Anyone Corporation).

Reprinted in *Rethinking Architecture: A Reader in Cultural Theory*, ed. Neal Leach, 255–70 (Routledge, 1997).

1995    "Marx's Purloined Letter," *New Left Review* 209: 86–120.

Reprinted in *Ghostly Demarcations: A Symposium on Jacques Derrida's Specters of Marx*, ed. Michael Sprinker, 26–67 (Verso, 1999).

1995    "The Sartrean Origin," *Sartre Studies International* 1:1–2: 7–8.

1995    "An Unfinished Project," *London Review of Books*, 3 August, 8–9.

Reprinted in *London Review of Books: An Anthology*, ed. Jane Hindle, 88–97 (Verso, 1996).

1995    "Radicalizing Radical Shakespeare: The Permanent Revolution in Shakespeare Studies," in *Materialist Shakespeare: A History*, ed. Ivo Kamps, 320–28 (Verso).

1995    "The New Forms of Capital: *Catholic Agitator* Interviews Fredric Jameson on Postmodern Capitalism and the Colonization of the Unconscious," *Catholic Agitator* 25:3: 4–6.

1996    "South Korea as Social Space," Interview with Paik Nak-chung in *Global/Local: Cultural Production and the Transnational Imaginary*, ed. Rob Wilson and Wimal Dissanayake, 348–71 (Duke University Press).

1996    "Prussian Blues," *London Review of Books*, 17 October, 2, 6–7.

Reprinted as "Ramblings in Old Berlin," *South Atlantic Quarterly* 96:4 (1997): 715–27.

1996    "Space Wars," *London Review of Books*, 4 April, 14–15.

1996    "Après the Avant Garde," *London Review of Books*, 12 December, 5–7.

1996    "XXL: Rem Koolhaas's Great Big *Buildings*roman," *Village Voice*, May, 17–19.

1996    With David Harvey and Masao Miyoshi, "Who's Green? Of Recycling . . . and the Recycling of Progressive Politics," *Borderlands* 41: 28–32.

1996 "Longevity as Class Struggle," in *Immortal Engines: Life Extension and Immortality in Science Fiction and Fantasy*, ed. George Slusser et al., 24–42 (University of Georgia Press).

Reprinted in *Archaeologies of the Future*, 328–44 (Verso, 2005).

1996 "On the Sexual Production of Western Subjectivity: Or, Saint Augustine as a Social Democrat," in *Gaze and Voice as Love Objects*, ed. Renata Salecl and Slavoj Žižek, 154–78 (Duke University Press).

1996 "City Theory in Jacobs and Heidegger," in *Anywise*, ed. Cynthia Davidson, 32–39 (MIT Press).

1997 "Marxism and Dualism in Deleuze," *South Atlantic Quarterly* 96:3: 393–416.

Reprinted in *A Deleuzian Century?* ed. Ian Buchanan, 13–36 (Duke University Press, 1999).

1997 "Theo Angelopoulus: The Past as History, the Future as Form," in *The Last Modernist: The Films of Theo Angelopoulos*, ed. Andrew Horton, 78–95 (Greenwood).

1997 "Culture and Finance Capital," *Critical Inquiry* 24:1: 246–65.

Reprinted in *The Cultural Turn*, 136–69 (Verso, 1998).

Reprinted in *The Jameson Reader*, 255–74 (Blackwell, 2000).

1997 "Ramblings in Old Berlin," *South Atlantic Quarterly* 96:4: 715–27.

1997 Interview with Fredric Jameson, in *Lukács after Communism: Interviews with Contemporary Intellectuals*, ed. and int. Eva L. Corredor, 75–94 (Duke University Press).

1997 "Absent Totality," in *Anybody*, ed. Cynthia C. Davidson, 122–31 (Anyone Corporation).

1998 "The Brick and the Balloon: Architecture, Idealism, and Land Speculation," *New Left Review* 228: 25–46.

Reprinted in *The Cultural Turn*, 162–90 (Verso, 1998).

1998 "Notes on Globalization as a Philosophical Issue," in *The Cultures of Globalization*, ed. Fredric Jameson and Masao Miyoshi, 54–77 (Duke University Press).

Translated into Chinese by Ma Ding as "Dui Zuowei Mingti de Quanqiuhua de Sikao," in *Quanqiu Hua de Wenhua*, 54–80 (Nanjing Daxue Chubanshe, 2002).

1998    With Zhang Xudong, "Marxism and the Historicity of Theory: An Interview with Fredric Jameson," *New Literary History* 29:3: 353–83.

Reprinted in *The Jameson Reader*, 149–63 (Blackwell, 2000).

1998    "Persistencies of the Dialectic: Three Sites," *Science and Society* 62:3: 358–372.

1998    Review of Robert Fitch, *The Assassination of New York*, *ANY Magazine* 22: 50–51.

1999    "Time and the Concept of Modernity," in *Anytime*, ed. Cynthia C. Davidson, 208–16 (Anyone Corporation).

1999    "History Lessons," in *Architecture and Revolution: Contemporary Perspectives on Central and Eastern Europe*, ed. Neil Leach, 69–80 (Routledge).

1999    "The Theoretical Hesitation: Benjamin's Sociological Predecessor," *Critical Inquiry* 25:2: 267–88.

Reprinted in *Rethinking the Frankfurt School: Alternative Legacies of Cultural Critique*, eds Jeffrey T. Nealon and Caren Irr, 11–30 (State University of New York Press, 2002).

2000    "Globalization and Political Strategy," *New Left Review* II (4): 49–68.

2000    "On the Matrix," *Centre Pompidou*.

2000    "'Art Naïf' and the Admixture of Worlds," in *Geopolitics of the Visible: Essays on Philippine Film Cultures*, ed. Rolando B. Tolentino, 25–65 (Ateneo de Manila University Press).

2001    "The Imaginary of Globalization," in *Collective Imagination: Limits and Beyond*, ed. Enrique Larreta and Candido Mendes, 21–52 (UNESCO).

2001    "On Neal Bell, *Monster*," *South Atlantic Quarterly* 99:2–3: 371–75.

2001    Introduction to *Lenin and Philosophy and other essays*, by Louis Althusser, vii–xiv, (Monthly Review Press).

2001    Review of *A Defense of History and Class Consciousness: Tailism and the Dialectic* by Georg Lukács, *Radical Philosophy* 110: 36–39.

2001    "The Iconographies of Cyberspace," *Polygraph* 13: 121–27.

2001    "Europe and Its Others," in *Unpacking Europe*, ed. Salah Hassan and Iftihar Dadi, 294–303 (NAi).

2001    "'If I Find One Good City, I Will Spare the Man': Realism and Utopia in Kim Stanley Robinson's *Mars* Trilogy," in *Learning from Other Worlds:*

*Estrangement, Cognition, and the Politics of Science Fiction and Utopia*, ed. Patrick Parrinder, 208–32 (Duke University Press).

Reprinted in *Archaeologies of the Future*, 393–416 (Verso, 2005).

2001    Et al., "11 September: Some LRB Writers Reflect on the Reasons and Consequences," *London Review of Books*, 4 October 4, 23.

2002    "The Dialectics of Disaster," *South Atlantic Quarterly* 101:2: 297–304.

Reprinted in *Dissent from the Homeland*, ed. Stanley Hauerwas and Frank Lentricchia, 55–62 (Duke University Press, 2003).

2002    "The Story of a Year: Continuities and Discontinuities in Marc Angenot's 1889," *Peripheries of Nineteenth-Century French Studies: Views from the Edge*, ed. Timothy Raser, 29–56 (University of Delaware Press).

2002    "Radical Fantasy," *Historical Materialism* 10:4: 273–80.

Revised and reprinted in *Archaeologies of the Future*, 57–71 (Verso, 2005).

2003    Foreword to *Philosophy and Revolution: From Kant to Marx*, by Stathis Kouvelakis, trans. G. M. Goshgarian, xi–xiv (Verso).

2003    "The End of Temporality," *Critical Inquiry* 29:4: 695–718.

2003    "Future City," *New Left Review* 21: 65–79.

2003    "Fear and Loathing in Globalization," *New Left Review* 23: 105–14.

Reprinted as "Fear and Loathing in Globalization," in *Archaeologies of the Future*, 384–92 (Verso, 2005).

2003    "Morus: The Generic Window," *New Literary History* 34:3: 431–51.

Reprinted in *Archaeologies of the Future*, 22–41 (Verso, 2005).

2003    "The Experiments of Time: Realism and the Providential," in *Il romanzo*, vol. 4, ed. Franco Moretti, 183–213 (Einaudi).

2003    "Pseudo-Couples," review of *Somersault*, by Kenzaburo Oē, *London Review of Books*, 20 November, 21–23.

2003    "Aronoff and Ideology," in Peter Eisenman, *Blurred Zones: Investigations of the Interstitial; Eisenman Architects, 1988–1998*, 60–68 (Monacelli).

2004    "Storia e elegia in Sokurov," in *Alessandr Sokurov: Eclissi di cinema*, ed. Stefano Francia di Celle, Enrico Ghezzi, and Alexei Jankowski, 127–33 (Twenty-first Toronto Film Festival, 2003).

Translated as "History and Elegy in Sokurov," *Critical Inquiry* 33:1 (2006): 1–12.

2004    "Thoughts on Balkan Cinema," in *Alphabet City: Subtitles*, ed. Ian Balfour and Atom Egoyan, 231–57 (MIT Press).

2004    Foreword to *Critique of Dialectical Reason, Volume 1: Theory of Practical Ensembles*, by Jean-Paul Sartre, ed. Jonathan Rée, trans. Alan Sheridan-Smith, xiii–xxxiii (Verso).

2004    "*Dekalog* as *Decameron*," in *Fredric Jameson: A Critical Reader*, ed. Sean Homer and Douglas Kellner, 210–22 (Palgrave Macmillan).

2004    "Symptoms of Theory or Symptoms for Theory?" *Critical Inquiry* 30:2: 403–8.

2004    "Politics of Utopia," *New Left Review* 25: 33–56.

2004    "Marc Angenot, Literary History, and the Study of Culture in the Nineteenth Century," *Yale Journal of Criticism*, 17:2: 233–53.

2005    "Rousseau and Contradiction," *South Atlantic Quarterly* 104:4: 693–706.

2005    "Notes on the Nomos," *South Atlantic Quarterly* 104:2: 199–204.

2005    "Lolita: 50 Years Later," *Playboy*, December, 160, 162.

2005    "Foreword: A Monument to Radical Instants" in *The Aesthetics of Resistance*, by Peter Weiss, trans. Joachim Neugroschel, vii–xlix (Duke University Press).

        Reprinted in *The Modernist Papers*, 380–419 (Verso, 2007).

2006    "First Impressions," review of *The Parallax View*, by Slavoj Žižek, *London Review of Books*, 17 September, 7–8.

2006    "Lacan and the Dialectic: A Fragment," in *Lacan: The Silent Partners*, ed. Slavoj Žižek, 365–97 (Verso).

2006    Foreword to *Critique of Dialectical Reason, Volume Two*, trans. Quintin Hoare, ix–xxiii (Verso).

2006    "Live Jameson," Interview with Ian Buchanan, in Ian Buchanan, *Fredric Jameson: Live Theory*, 120–32 (Continuum).

2007    "Perfected by the Tea Masters," review of *Japan-ness in Architecture*, by Arata Isozaki, *London Review of Books*, 5 April, 21–23.

2007    "Lenin and Revisionism," in *Lenin Reloaded: Toward a Politics of Truth*, ed. Sebastian Budgen, et al., 59–73 (Duke University Press).

# Interviewers

**MONA ABOUSENNA** is Professor at Ain Shams University in Cairo and the author of books on Brecht and on nationalism.

**ABBAS AL-TONSI** is the author of numerous works on Arabic linguistics and on ideology and narrative form.

**SRINIVAS ARAVAMUDAN** is Professor of English and Director of the John Hope Franklin Humanities Institute at Duke University. He specializes in eighteenth-century literature and postcolonial studies and is the author of *Tropicopolitans: Colonialism and Agency, 1688–1804* (which won the outstanding first book prize of the Modern Language Association in 2000) and *Guru English: South Asian Religion in a Cosmopolitan Language.*

**JONATHAN CULLER** is Class of 1916 Professor of English and Comparative Literature at Cornell University and a former editor of *Diacritics.* His books on contemporary theory include *Structuralist Poetics, On Deconstruction, Literary Theory: A Very Short Introduction,* and, most recently, *The Literary in Theory.*

**SARA DANIUS** is Associate Professor in the Department of Literature at Uppsala University and teaches aesthetics at Soedertoern University College. She has been a Fellow at the Wissenschaftskolleg in Berlin and a visiting professor at the University of Michigan. She is the author of *The Senses of Modernism: Technology, Perception, and Aesthetics* and *The Prose of the World: Flaubert and the Art of Making Things Visible.*

**LEONARD GREEN** has taught in the English Department at Cornell University and the University of Rochester. He is a practicing artist who lives in New York City.

**SABRY HAFEZ** is Professor of Modern Arabic and Comparative Studies at the School of Oriental and African Studies of the University of London. He is the author of numerous books and articles on Arabic literature and narrative theory.

**STUART HALL,** for many years the central figure of the Birmingham Center for Cultural Studies and co-editor of the journal *New Times,* retired from the Open University in 1997. He is the author of many books and articles, including *The Hard Road to Renewal, Resistance Through Rituals, The Formation of Modernity, Questions of Cultural Identity,* and *Cultural Representations and Signifying Practices.*

**STEFAN JONSSON** is a writer, scholar, and senior literary critic at *Dagens Nyheter,* Sweden's leading newspaper. A graduate of the Program in Literature at Duke University, he has been a Fellow at the Getty Research Institute in Los Angeles and a visiting professor at the University of Michigan. His new book, *A Brief History of the Masses: Three revolutions, 1789, 1889, 1989,* is forthcoming from Columbia University Press.

**RANJANA KHANNA** is Margaret Taylor Smith Director of Women's Studies and Associate Professor in the English Department, the Literature Program, and Women's Studies at Duke University. She is the author of *Dark Continents: Psychoanalysis and Colonialism* and *Algeria Cuts: Women and Representation 1830 to the Present.*

**RICHARD KLEIN** is Professor of French at Cornell University and a former editor of *Diacritics.* In addition to articles on criticism and critical theory, he is the author of the books *Cigarettes Are Sublime, Eat Fat,* and *Jewellery Talks.*

**HORACIO MACHIN** is a visiting professor at Angelino State University, Texas. He is the author of several essays in the area of Latin American culture, cultural studies, and intellectual change, and the co-editor of the book *Marcha y America Latina.* His forthcoming volume is titled *Intellectuals: Cultural Interpreters in the River Plate Region.*

**PAIK NAK-CHUNG** taught in the English Department of Seoul National University from 1963 until his retirement in 2003, except for a period of five years after being expelled in 1974 for demanding a democratic constitution. He remains active as a literary critic and editor of the South Korean literary and intellectual quarterly journal *Changbi* (which he founded in 1966). Since 2005 he has also served as the South Korean Chair of the All-Korean Committee for Implementation of the June 15 Joint Declaration (at the first summit meeting of the two Koreas in 2000).

**MICHAEL SPEAKS** is a writer, educator, and design strategy consultant. He has published and lectured internationally on contemporary art, architecture, urban design, and scenario planning. Former Director of the Graduate Program and founding Director of the Metropolitan Research and Design Post Graduate Program at the Southern California Institute of Architecture in Los Angeles, he has also taught in the graphic design department at the Yale School of Art, and in the architecture programs at Harvard University, Columbia University, the University of Michigan, the Berlage Institute, UCLA, TU Delft and Art Center College of Design. He is founding editor of the cultural journal *Polygraph* and former editor at *ANY* in New York, and is currently a contributing editor for *Architectural Record.* He heads the Los Angeles-based design strategy consultancy Design Stories.

**ANDERS STEPHANSON** is Professor of History at Columbia University where he teaches, among other things, the history of U.S. foreign relations. He has been wishing for some time to write a Minima Moralia on that subject matter.

**XUDONG ZHANG** is Professor of Chinese and Comparative Literature and Chair of the Department of East Asian Studies at New York University. He is the author of *Chinese Modernism in the Era of Reforms; Postsocialism and Cultural Politics: The Last Decade of China's Twentieth Century;* and, in Chinese, *Traces of Criticism and Cultural Identity in the Age of Globalization: A Historical Rethinking of Western Discourses of Universalism.* He is the Chinese translator of Walter Benjamin's *Charles Baudelaire* and *Illuminations,* and the editor and translator of Fredric Jameson's *The Cultural Logic of Late Capitalism.*

# INDEX

Nietzsche, Friedrich, 70, 147
Nostalgia, 60

Ontology, 28
Opinion, 4–5

Paik, Nam June, 29, 47, 69
Pedagogy, 12
Perestroika, 101. *See also* Soviet
Pérez Galdós, Benito, 83
Periodization, vii, 19, 82. *See also*
  Postmodernism
Philosophy, 1
Plebianization, 114
Political action, 36, 118; and feminism,
  42, 231–32
Political unconscious, 43
Positivism, 144.
Postmodernism, vii, 44, 64, 77, 113,
  212–14; and architecture, 53; and
  the depthlessness of the image,
  45–6, 61; and globalization, 8, 85,
  160; homoepathic response to, 59;
  and hyperspace, 48; and mass
  media, 68; and modernism, 44,
  49, 169; and periodization, vii; and
  philosophy, 146; and standardization, 117
Pound, Ezra, 4
Proust, Marcel, 55, 69
Public intellectuals, 4. *See also* Opinion

Radical tradition, 14, 21, 150, 198. *See
  also* Sixties, Thirties
Rauschenberg, Robert, 65–66, 69
Realism, 82–83
Reification, 35–36, 59
Religion, 223
Representation, 36, 141, 230
Resistance, 53
Revolutionary movements, 33
Rohe, Mies van der, 64

Rosler, Martha, 167
Rushdie, Salman, 201

Sartre, Jean-Paul, 1, 28, 47, 80, 95, 143,
  150, 153, 176, 206, 228
Schiller, Friedrich, 56, 80
Schizophrenic subject, 63
Scott, Walter, 87
Simon, Paul, 161, 167
Sixties, 14, 28, 39, 45, 60
Socialist culture, 57
Society of the spectacle, 15, 19, 165. *See
  also* Postmodernism
Sontag, Susan, x, 140
Soviet: communism, 174, 185; intellec-
  tuals, 75; model, 139; perestroika, 101;
  socialist realism, 83; society, 51
Space, 56–57, 123–24, 158, 212
Stages theory, 90
Stroheim, Erich von, 83
Subject, 27; schizophrenic, 63
Suvin, Darko, 215
Synchronicity of the nonsynchronous,
  87, 95

Tafuri, Manfredo, 56, 64, 132
Tangai, Kenzo, 124
Technology, 226
Temporality, 47, 125, 158, 212
Text, x, 12
Theory, 71, 145, 189; as brand, 21, 146,
  172; as language, 1–2; as literature,
  2; and philosophy, 1, 172; resistance
  to, 174
Third world, 57–59; literature, 83, 97,
  111–12, 159–60
Thirties, 14, 39
Tokyo, 124, 125–28
Tolstoy, Leo, 82
Totalization, 29, 33, 69, 84, 105, 142,
  157, 232
Transcoding, 132, 173, 184

FREDRIC JAMESON is William A. Lane Jr. Professor of
Comparative Literature at Duke University. His two most
recent books are *Archaeologies of the Future* (2005) and *The
Modernist Papers* (2007). He is Director of the Institute for
Critical Theory at Duke University, and the series editor
of Duke University Press's Post-Contemporary Interven-
tions. He is also the co-editor, with Masao Miyoshi, of *The
Cultures of Globalization* (1998).

IAN BUCHANAN is Professor of Critical and Cultural
Theory at Cardiff University. He is the author of *Fredric
Jameson: Live Theory* (2006); *Deleuzism: A Metacommen-
tary* (2000); *Michel de Certeau: Cultural Theorist* (2000).
He is the editor, with Caren Irr, of *On Jameson: From Post-
modernism to Globalization* (2005).

Library of Congress Cataloging-in-Publication Data
Jameson, Fredric.
Jameson on Jameson: conversations on cultural Marxism /
Fredric Jameson; edited by Ian Buchanan.
p. cm.
Includes bibliographical references and index.
ISBN-13: 978-0-8223-4087-4 (cloth : alk. paper)
ISBN-13: 978-0-8223-4109-3 (pbk. : alk. paper)
1. Marxian school of sociology. 2. Dialectical materialism.
3. Civilization, Modern—Philosophy. 4. Jameson, Fredric.
I. Buchanan, Ian. II. Title.
HM471.J35 2007
301.01—dc22
2007018002